Forests of Lilliput

FORESTS OF LILLIPUT

Line Drawings
by Stanley Wyatt

he Realm of Mosses and Lichens

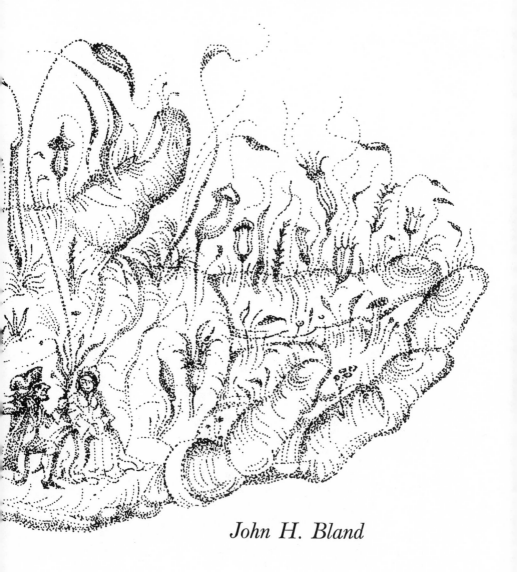

John H. Bland

PRENTICE-HALL, INC.   Englewood Cliffs, New Jersey

Forests of Lilliput: The Realm of Mosses and Lichens
by John H. Bland
© 1971 by John H. Bland
All rights reserved. No part of this book may be
reproduced in any form or by any means, except for
the inclusion of brief quotations in a review, without
permission in writing from the publisher.
ISBN 0-13-326868-3
Library of Congress Catalog Card Number: 70-143811
Printed in the United States of America   T
Prentice-Hall International, Inc., London
Prentice-Hall of Australia, Pty. Ltd., Sydney
Prentice-Hall of Canada, Ltd., Toronto
Prentice-Hall of India Private Ltd., New Delhi
Prentice-Hall of Japan, Inc., Tokyo

10 9 8 7 6 5 4 3 2

Design by Janet Anderson

To Libits, for what it may mean to her

Preface

IDENTIFICATION of mosses and lichens by families is a relatively simple matter. There is a widespread notion, however, that to master a thing, all that is needed to do is to name it. In my opinion, the fallacy that makes naming an end in itself is one of the things that is wrong with education today. It is to go beyond mere naming and to deal with mosses and lichens as objects of interest both in themselves and as a part of the scheme of nature, that this book has been prepared.

My object is to present mosses and lichens in such a simple, easily understood way that you can recognize most of them without botanical training or use of a microscope. Their common names—as well as their scientific names—are emphasized. The many aspects—historical, scientific, romantic and practical—of this small bit of the everyday out-of-doors are brought out. My hope is to present them freshly, to show their unsung, unnoticed role in the economy of nature, their ubiquitous occurrence, occasional role in the rise and fall of industry—indeed, rise and fall of a civilization—and to engender a deep respect for nature's way of doing business. In mosses and lichens, strength is mingled with humility, gentleness and charm, with elemental essence, reflecting the gladness of wind, sun and rain. They hide earth's scars. To know them is to feel a nearness to the texture of nature, a love of the lovely, and a sadness, too, as with an old Welsh poet: "Oh Lord, thou wert a little unkind to make these dales and vales so beautiful and the days of the shepherd so few."

Introduction

IF you are trained in botany, horticulture, wildlife management, or any other pure or applied biological science, it is much too easy to assume that everyone else has at least some understanding of living organisms, plant and animal. The whole web of their interdependence is so complex as to be awesome, yet in total concept so logical that anyone and everyone should be able to comprehend it. The problem is that not everyone does; otherwise, we human beings would not have reached the state of environmental danger in which we find ourselves today.

Until recently, man has been only a minor factor in the total picture of plants, animals, water, soil, and air. In the very beginning, his environment contained so many hostile elements that he not only developed an attitude of being on guard, but took pride in overcoming and subduing the natural world. We cannot blame him for giving more attention and effort to the hostile elements than to the helpful ones: indeed, many of the latter were so unspectacular that he hardly knew they existed. Why should he have to realize that the carbon dioxide he exhaled was used by plants which then returned the oxygen he needed; that with the help of sunlight, plants could combine this same carbon dioxide with water to manufacture the starches and sugars which satisfied his hunger; that the cover of forest absorbed the rains, cooled the soil, and provided a rich habitat which he could enjoy with relative ease and comfort? There was so much of everything, everywhere. Why should he have to think about it?

And yet here we are, approaching the dawn of the twenty-first century, and suddenly we are aware that our inborn attitudes of overcoming and using the natural world are now the very things which endanger us. Man is not the superior animal he thought he was—at least not so superior as to consume and destroy the earth's other organisms without concern for the eventual effect upon himself. He does not exist alone; his is only one factor in the total web. Only by recognizing this fact and applying it intelligently can he survive.

It is extremely appropriate, then, that this book should appear now. In these fundamental plants which few men realize even exist, we see a glimpse of the total, marvelously constructed system. Algae and fungi, growing interdependently as lichens and mosses are the stepping-stones—in reality, cornerstones—to all life. I can think of no better introduction to an understanding of our place in the total scheme of our environment than this extremely timely book.

Carlton B. Lees

Acknowledgments

SINCE it has taken me twenty years to do this book, I owe obligations to many who in the aggregate, ever so gradually, taught me how to do it. My long-standing fascination with mosses and lichens was first aroused by Professor Millard Markle of Earlham College, who as a teacher and scientist had the rare ability to convey his own sense of hidden marvels within and behind the commonplace. To him, and to the pioneering examples of A. J. Grout and Albert Schneider, I owe an especial debt.

Professor Carroll Dodge read and reread the entire manuscript, making many needed changes in the text and identifying or adding the correct names for lichen illustrations. I am grateful and fortunate to have had this distinguished lichenologist—both as critic and teacher—review the manuscript.

My deep appreciation goes to Mrs. T. Carter Harrison whose literary advice and salesladyship brought it to publication.

Miss Amy Clampitt imposed literary felicity in awkward sections of the manuscript, for which I am grateful.

Mr. Wing Woon, Department of Photography, University of Vermont College of Medicine, took many of the pictures and taught me the joy of moss and lichen photography.

My wife, Elizabeth, read and reread the manuscript in its many forms, offering a happy mixture of gentle and tough criticism and never ceased believing it must one day be published.

John H. Bland

xi

Contents

	Preface	vii
	Introduction by Carlton B. Lees	ix
	Acknowledgments	xi
I	A Whole New World	1
II	Lichens: Six of One, Half Dozen of the Other	10
III	Lichen Anatomy and Reproduction	26
IV	About the Bryophytes	38
V	At Work in Nature's Economy: The Challenge of Dry Land	55
VI	Quaking Bogs, Peat Mosses and Liverworts	75
VII	"Wretched Food in Barbarous Countries"	88
VIII	Botany and Medicine	104
IX	The Great Lichen Industries	119
X	Miniaturized Gardening	129
	Key to Common Lichens by Growth and Structure	142
	Key to the Mosses by Habitat	165
	Reading List	197
	Glossary	200
	Index	203

A Whole New World

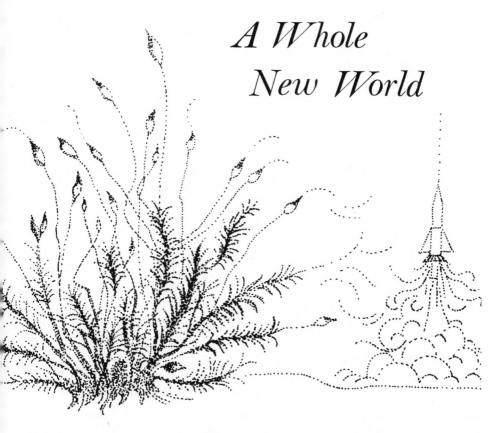

Lichens and mosses—how of these? Meek creatures, the first mercy of the earth, veiling with hushed softness its dustless rocks; creatures full of pity, covering with strange and tender honor the scarred disgrace of time, laying fingers on the trembling stones to teach them rest. How is one to tell of the rounded bosses of furred and beaming green, the starred divisions of rubied bloom, fine filmed, as if the Rock Spirits could spin porphyry as we do glass.

Yet as in one sense the humblest, in another they are the most honored of the earth children. Unfading as motionless, the worm frets them not, and the autumn wastes not. Strong in loveliness, they neither blanch in heat nor pine in frost. To them, slow fingered, constant-hearted, is entrusted the weaving of the dark,

*eternal tapestries of the hills. Sharing the stillness of the unimpas-
sioned rock, they also share its endurance; and while the winds of
departing spring scatter the white hawthorn blossoms like drifted
snow, and summer dims on the parched meadow, the drooping of
its cowslip gold—far above among the mountains, the silver
lichen spots rest, star-like, on the stone; and the gathering orange
stain upon the edge of yonder peak reflects the sunset of a thousand
years.*

—John Ruskin

In the summer of 1954 Mars was comparatively near to
Earth—only 35,120,000 miles away. Many astronomers took
this opportunity for a new study, among them Dr. E. C. Slipher
of Lowell Observatory, who directed the National Geographic
Society's expedition.

Dr. Slipher and his colleagues spent six months in South
Africa photographing Mars on film dyed in blue, yellow-green
and red. Each color brought out different aspects of the
Martian scene. In the summer of 1955 Dr. Slipher made the
important announcement in *National Geographic* magazine that
the photographs had revealed a hitherto unobserved marking
almost as large as Texas, an area of approximately 200,000
square miles. He calls this "the greatest change observed in the
geography of the planet since its surface was first mapped 125
years ago."

The late Percival Lowell, founder of the Observatory, had
advanced the theory that the hypothetical "canals" of Mars are
great irrigation ditches dug by intelligent beings to bring the
water of the melting polar ice caps to the arid equatorial
regions.

Though Percival Lowell's "canals" (first discovered by Giovanni V. Schiaparelli in 1877) have been regarded by skeptics
as optical illusions, enough photographs have been made to
convince Dr. Slipher that the "canals," actually gross, irregular
surface features, are real. But are the canals in fact irrigating
ditches, dug by intelligent beings, as Percival Lowell believed?
Dr. Slipher does not believe this. But other, more generally
accepted markings on Mars include vast green areas which turn

russet brown as autumn and winter approach, and green again in spring and summer. There is a connection between the melting of the polar caps and the changing of the russet brown areas to green.

Dr. Slipher's newly discovered area is also green, which to him and other astronomers implies the existence of vegetation: "On Mars we behold a world in a sad state of decrepitude still able to support a struggling form of vegetation, but nearing the end of its planetary life." This opinion is now shared by most astonomers, who grant his contention that the green areas "bear eloquent testimony that Mars is not a dead world."

But what *kind* of vegetation exists there? There is no oxygen on Mars. After examining the recent findings of the Mariner spacecraft, scientists doubt if even water vapor, an essential to life, is present on Mars. The Polar caps may be carbon dioxide—dry ice! No super telescope or camera is needed to visualize the botanical monstrosity that would be able to grow on a planet of frightful desolation, almost airless, with no rivers, lakes or oceans and a daily temperature fluctuation of from 85° F. to 95° below zero.

But lack of oxygen does not necessarily rule out life. Certain primitive plants can generate their own oxygen; so may it be on other planets. And one such botanic "monstrosity"—a group of them in fact—already exists on earth. Lichens growing on our planet could survive such extremes. They are the toughest plants that grow.

Lichens are notably inconspicuous—hiding in plain sight— but found nearly everywhere in nature once you are aware of them. Thriving on neglect, they are far more competent to hold their own in the struggle for existence than most higher plants. They grow on Main Street as well as in the most forbidding environments on earth, even flourishing on rocks just below the level of eternal snow on mountain tops. Many lichens favor alpine and arctic country where they thrive on barren, windswept rocks. At low temperatures they become metabolically and chemically inert, resisting cold due to gradual dehydration by wind. New lichen growths are found under the snow all winter. They were seen by Dr. Charles Houston in 1953 at an altitude of 18,000 feet on K_2 in the Korakoram range of the Himalayas.* Rocky outcrops near the North and South poles bear lichens; conversely, lichens do well on desert rocks too hot to touch.

In an experiment on temperature adaptation in lichens, plants were dried in air and then in a dessicator. They were exposed to a temperature of 268° centigrade for one to seven hours. On return to room temperature, the plants resumed normal metabolism.

Lichens are more than perennial. Theoretically at least, many are immortal and, are aptly described as "time stains." Explorers noted that lichens seen on a cairn thirty years before had not spread to adjacent rock surfaces. A few lichen colonies are estimated to be over 2,000 years old—older than the oldest redwood trees. As expected, they grow very slowly, appropriate to their longevity and poverty of habitat.

More provocative even than that are the test results published in 1959, by William Sinton, also of the Lowell Observatory, that show the presence of large organic molecules on Mars by specific infrared spectroscopic tests. Spectroscopic bands observed are most probably produced by large organic molecules. Such molecules are seemingly produced in localized regions in relatively short periods of time. Growth of vegetation certainly is the most logical explanation of the appearance of organic molecules. At first the band observed seemed an enigma for it had not been found in any terrestrial plants. Similar bands have been shown, however, in the examination of a common lichen called Physcia, and now an indentical band in the alga, Cladophora. Evidence points to the presence on Mars of unidentified organic molecules as well as some complex sugar molecules; these molecules may well represent carbohydrates stored as food in lichens or algae or both.

Any person with the slightest interest in nature has seen and wondered about the more obvious lichens and mosses. What are they doing growing on damp earth, bare rock or dead trees? Why are the "murmuring pines and the hemlocks bearded with moss"? How can a bare rock cliff serve plant

---

*Houston, Charles S., and Bates, Robert H., *K₂, The Savage Mountain*, McGraw-Hill Book Company, Inc., 1954.

needs as the lichen covers the naked stone with delicate mantles of shades of green, gray or yellow? Exquisite branching lobes of the Boulder Lichen are natural artistry. Lovely vermilion fruiting cushions of the Cladonia are a crimson of purest shade; goblets of another Cladonia are perfect fairy cups. Lichens grow in spectacular abundance and beauty in the tropics; cement facings and brick buildings along city streets bear lichens even in such hostile circumstances. What is nature up to?

Mosses too can be found any month of the year, indicating that, as a group, their growth is not limited by high or low temperatures. They tolerate extremes of heat and cold; some flourish in arctic wastes, others prefer a habitat near hot springs (*Archidium alternifolium*). In tropical rain forests, woody plants thrive while moss vegetation sharply declines, but mosses flourish in alpine and arctic and subarctic regions where higher plants fail to gain a foothold and fade out. Mosses grow in the

A particularly showy group of *Cladonia cristatella*. The puffy masses at the end of the stalks are a bright red, accounting for the lichen's common names of Scarlet Crested Lichen and British Soldier

gloom of caves and in the intense glare of exposed mountain crags. Regardless of their aquatic ancestry, many species survive prolonged drought.

The common mosses shrivel in bright sun, and though dry and crumbling in the heat, they spring to bright green, vigorous life in the rain and shade. One can watch the leaves of the Hairy Cap Moss roll up tight and retain moisture, only to unroll in the rain.

Certain other mosses—*Orthotrichum*—grow on tree trunks and manifest great tolerance for water. Others are at home in the perpetual dankness of northern bogs, and still others are among the first plants to appear in burnt-over areas. One recluse among the mosses is found only in the darkness of holes and caverns, and has evolved its own luminescence.

As one becomes intimately familiar with these plants, he gains a deeper appreciation of their ecological value, their sophisticated structure and even of their economic importance.

Broom Moss, *Dicranum scoparium,* grows up to four inches in height. As the illustration shows, its leaves all grow in the same direction, as if blown by the wind

Since mosses and lichens are the first plants to appear in territory unfavorable to other plants, they may have been among the first to make their way from sea to land. In some distant geologic time they may have reigned supreme in the plant world. While lavishly spreading their chaste embroideries over rocks and trees, these beautiful, humble plants are engaged in mighty tasks, covering alpine and arctic wastes, clothing desert rocks and bare cliffs and serving as pioneers who carry life where it could not otherwise be. Their mechanical retention and storage of soil particles is of tremendous importance in building up and maintaining the layer of vegetation without which animal life could not exist. Their tasks are enormously out of proportion to their size.

These often unplant-like plants have aroused man's curiosity throughout history. Some wonderfully absurd opinions have cropped up as to their origin and uses, and various species have assumed the limelight for brief periods in the history of mankind. Now identification of lichens and mosses is a simple accomplishment, requiring only a smattering of botanical knowledge.

To understand the nature of mosses and lichens, one must first know how they relate to the rest of the plant kingdom. We may begin, then, by asking: What is a plant?

The answer to this question is less simple than one might suppose. Out of approximately 350,000 species that have been described by botanists to date, about 175,000 are flowering plants—those which have leaves, stems, roots, flowers, fruits and seeds. Many other members of the plant kingdom, however, lack some or even all of these structures.

The common origin of all these diverse forms is a matter of speculation. It is generally believed that the earliest living cells formed themselves eons ago in the warm saltwater of primeval seas, out of the random combination of carbon, hydrogen, oxygen and various mineral salts—including potassium, phosphorus, sodium, calcium and sulfur—through many transitional stages, into the complex molecules that are the basis of living matter, or protoplasm. These first living cells were strange borderline beings, not quite animal, not quite plant. It is doubtful whether they originally possessed chlorophyll; but after millions of years certain of these earliest living things did evolve the ability to draw carbon dioxide from the air and the sea and to transform it, with the aid of sunlight, into the organic material necessary for growth. As a by-product, oxygen was liberated into an atmosphere hitherto poor in that element. When this took place the first true plants had come into being.

Meanwhile—it is believed—there had begun to evolve another group of organisms, which were without chlorophyll but which survived by feeding upon plant life. Thus arose the first animals. From that remote day animals have remained dependent upon plants, either directly or indirectly, for life and growth. The uses and cultivation of food plants are intimately bound up in the history of the human race. In addition plant products and derivatives continue to be essential, in greater or lesser degree, for clothing, shelter, fuel, transportation and the maintenance of our health and well-being.

In all probability bacteria or similar organisms were in existence during Pre-Cambrian times; in fact there are electron microscopic pictures of fossil bacteria, evolved over two billion years ago. Pre-Cambrian Gunflint chert, a geological sediment found in southern Ontario, had in it well-preserved rod-shaped and coccoid bacteria demonstrated in the electron microscope; it is the oldest known structurally preserved evidence of life.* Biological systems surely evolved long before Gunflint time. Such bacteria were among the earliest forms of living organisms. It has been suggested that modern chlorophyll of all green plants is a derivative of a bacteriochlorophyll, a photosynthetic pigment known to be present in certain purple and brown bacteria.

Thus the beginnings of life, the origin of the mechanism of photosynthesis—and their effects on the history of the earth—may be closely related to the origin and evolution of bacteria. The electron microscope provides a powerful new tool to the methods of micropaleontology, allowing direct vision of truly

---

*Schopf, J. W., Barghoorn, E. S., Maser, M. D., and Gordon, R. O. "Electron Microscopy of Fossil Bacteria Two Billion Years Old," *Science*. 149, 1365-1376, Sept., 1965.

ancient life. Indeed bacteria have such an essential role in the disintegration of organic and inorganic substances that it is impossible to comprehend how the balance of nature could have been maintained without them.

It was from bacteria—or at least from organisms which must have been quite similar—that the rest of the vegetable kingdom, the "higher plants," evolved.

Lichens: Six of One,
Half Dozen of the Other

THE naming and classification of living things is a continuing
process, one that is still under review and subject to future
revision. One system of classification places all known plants
within four groups of phyla: Thallophyta, Bryophyta, Pter-
idophyta and Spermatophyta.

The thallophytes (from the Greek word *thallos,* "young
shoot," and *phyton,* "plant") include species varying in size from
a single cell to a length of 200 feet or more—reached by the
giant kelp of the Pacific Ocean. Organic remains in the rocks,
however, provide conclusive evidence that thallophytes were in
existence ages before the initial appearance of the higher
plants. In fact approximately three-fourths of known geologic
time had elapsed before any of the higher plants appeared.

Whatever their size, thallophytes share a lack of differentiation; they lack distinct structures such as stems, leaves and roots. Some consist of filaments and others of flat plates, or mats of cells. The algae (singular, alga) which belong to this group, sometimes consist of a single cell, sometimes of single or branching filaments which are multicellular. For example, the tiny plants that compose the green scum often found on the surface of a pond are species of algae which rival bacteria in their claim to antiquity, having exerted considerable influence on the history of life on earth since Pre-Cambrian times. They are thought to be responsible for the formation of extensive deposits of limestone and petroleum. The blue-green algae are probably the oldest. Other algae live in the soil, where they are so numerous that one gram of earth may contain as many as a million individual plants. Still others live attached to the claws of lobsters and crayfish, or on the backs of turtles. They do well along lake shores and brooks, on cold, foggy coasts, even between the extremes of high and low tide. They are pioneers in the scheme of plant succession, in which they form a permanent stage. Some aquatic algae are capable of locomotion, a trait that generally serves to distinguish plants from animals.

All algae contain chlorophyll, the green pigment that enables plants to synthesize their own food; but in some the green is masked by other pigments. Certain algae, for example, manage to exist in the snow, tingeing arctic and alpine snowfields with pink.

Algae show great variation in color—brown, orange, red, yellow, green, blue-green, yellow-green or purple—and in their modes of reproduction. In form they may be disc-shaped, globular, thread-like, leaf-like, sheet-like or paddle-shaped. They may be branched or unbranched, attached, or free-floating. Among the most conspicuous algae are those commonly known as seaweeds.

In contrast to the algae, another major group of thallophytes do without chlorophyll but still qualify as plants. These are the fungi (from the Latin word for "mushroom"), which include not only the familiar mushrooms and toadstools of fields and woods, but the molds that form on decaying bread or fruit, or that impart the distinctive flavor of certain cheeses; the mildews, rusts and smuts that may infect field and garden crops; the yeast used in making bread; and the organisms responsible for such skin diseases as ringworm and athlete's foot.

Fungi often consist of either a loose web or a compact mass of filaments called *hyphae*. The hyphae about the base of a toadstool is the parent plant, a simple fine network of white threads called a *mycelium*. Since they lack chlorophyll, they cannot manufacture their own food but must obtain organic molecules already elaborated by other organisms, either living or dead. Thus all are either parasites or saprophytes.

Fungi as a group are quite old; well-preserved mycelium and spores have been found in the fossilized tissues of very ancient higher plants. In the long geologic past fungi played the same role in nature as they do at present, preventing the endless accumulation of dead vegetable matter. Some have acted as parasites preying upon living plants. Many blanks in the plant fossil record are a consequence of the destructive activity of the fungi.

The lichens' unusual tenacity in the most forbidding environment suggests that they must possess a distinctively different biological make-up than other plants; and indeed, they do. In these fascinating composite plants certain one- or few-celled algae associate with filamentous fungi to form the lichen.

Fungi die when the food supply is gone, but, as lichens, freed from dependence on decaying organic matter, they survive rigorous environmental pressures on bare rock. Lichen growth rates are far below those of isolated fungi which, in lichens, come into equilibrium with that of the algae. Lichens developed tough, gelatinous tissue, and thick gelatinized cell walls, allowing water storage in prolonged drought.

Small fungi on decaying wood or tree bark may resemble lichens. A certain test in such forms is to examine the plant microscopically and see if there are algal cells tangled in a weft of fungal threads. Growths protruding through the outer crust of tree bark, pushing between torn edges, are usually fungi; those resting on the bark—with or without penetrating—are lichens. Growing parts of a lichen (thallus) are on the surface of bark or soil; growing parts of a fungus (mycelium) are concealed below the surface—only the fruits are visible. Fungi grow in the tissues of the host, rarely growing on rocks as lichens commonly do.

Fungi, when in a lichen, live in a stable biological equilibrium with algae, incorporating the algal cells into the lichen's structure. Algal cells are arranged and confined in a definite layer; fungal tissue forms a tough outer *cortex* and a loosely woven pith or inner core. The fungus directs the growth of the lichen, determining whether the plant encrusts itself so it cannot be removed without breaking up; forms mats, small shields or ribbons lightly attached to the substrate; or forms branchings and fringes attached at only one point.

The algal host suffers no harm, and, in fact, obtains decided advantages—i.e., protection against mechanical injury, excessive sunlight and drying, and a supply of inorganic substances necessary for growth. In turn, the alga growing in the tissue of the fungus diverts some of the food it manufactures to provide nutrition for the fungus.

Common, often inconspicuous, lichens grow in spreading encrustations, horizontal leafy or ruffled expansions, upright

The Easter Lichen, *Stereocaulon paschale*

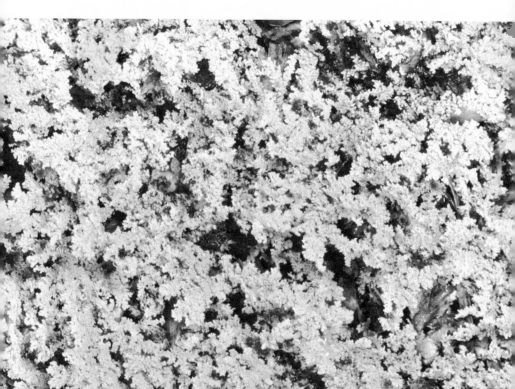

stalk or strap-shaped fronds, in pendulous filaments or hanging streamers. Their size varies from a few millimeters to thirty feet in length. They have neither true leaves, nor stems nor roots. (Some branching lichens hang in fringes of gray, ghostly drapery from the time-worn evergreens of the Northeast. The branchings of these lichens are hollow tube-like structures, not at all like true stems.) Most others flourish on tree trunks, decaying wood, rock or soil. Their vegetative body, or thallus, is extremely long-lived. They are of varying color—white, yellow, brown, gray and black—and are the subdued splashes of color one sees in woods or old pastures. Rosettes of branched structure growing on trees and rocks are likely to be Parmelia and Evernia. Rock Tripe (*Umbilicaria*) will be found on rock faces or high granite summits. A bright, orange, papery lichen (*Xanthoria*) is very common on trees or rocks.

Some grow as simple, dry, crust-like plants, crumbling at a touch. Any greenish-gray, pale gray, olive green, brown or orange growths observed will probably be lichens. Gray-green lichen covering fence rails and dry logs with fine granules and flakes is probably Cladonia, Psora or Biatora. A discolored area on a rock or tree bears inspection: A chalky or mealy-looking coating on vertical rock cliffs or spreading to moss-covered trees is a lichen whose sterile encrustations never branch or reach a higher stage of development. Encrustations of various tints are lichens which either do not fruit or happen not to be fruiting at the moment. If one does find "fruits" on the plant—in flattened, colored discs, lumpy, bright-colored knobs or tiny tubs—it is certainly a lichen. Certain types grow with tiny cups or horn-of-plenty-like formations whose rims are encrusted with minute brown- and red-colored cushions.

The lichen plant body is called the *thallus,* a composite structure which appears under the microscope as a dense, intricately branching network of characteristic white or translucent filaments and elongated, segmented cells. Some bear orange or yellow pigment: This is the mycelium of the fungal partner; the green, chlorophyll-bearing algal cells are entangled and embedded within it. The cell walls of the fungus are characteristically thick and gelatinized, a mechanism for holding water and retarding evaporation. But where the fungal hyphae are entwined in close contact with the algae in the thallus, their cell walls are very thin, allowing exchange of metabolic material and water between the two plants. In this partnership, chlorophyll-bearing algae manufacture sugar from carbon dioxide and water, using the energy of sunlight— through the process of photosynthesis. The fungus in turn is able to collect and retain large quantities of water—a task the algae carry on less efficiently, if at all, in an independent existence.

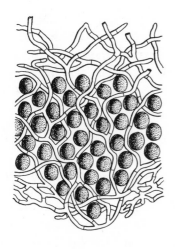

Fungal tissue and algae in the thallus of *Lecanora* (from Albert Schneider's *General Lichenology*, Binghampton, 1897)

In the opinion of most botanists, however, the benefits are not entirely equal, and to some degree the fungus may be regarded as parasitic upon the alga. Fungi normally obtain their food through *haustoria,* modified extensions of their hyphae, specialized absorptive organs which often penetrate the cells of the plant or animal the fungus parasitizes. Fungal haustoria occur in many lichens, and the relationship between

Umbilicaria pustulata

Parmelia perlata

Fungal haustoria enclosing algal cells, as seen in the lichens *Umbilicaria pustulata* and *Parmelia perlata (from Schneider)*

the lichen alga and the fungus depends on the degree of evolutionary advancement of the fungus. In primitive lichens the fungal filaments actually penetrate into the cytoplasm of the algal cells and are more parasitic than those of leafy or branching lichens. In higher forms the parasitism is gentle and subtle; the fungal filaments seem only to clasp the surface of the algal cells. Only the fungal cells in direct contact with algal cells are able to assimilate products of photosynthesis; the other fungal parts of the plant are "skeletal," serving to support and protect.

It is not clear how fungi of lichens lacking haustoria obtain their food from algae; the nutrient substances probably diffuse out of the algae and into fungal cells where digestive enzymes promote absorption and consumption. In any lichen, however, when the two component parts of a lichen are artificially separated, the alga can exist independently; the fungus, on the other hand, cannot.

As to the time when the first lichen was formed, no one can say. Since lichens do not fossilize, the geological record tells little of how and when they evolved. But algae antedate fungi; thus the composite lichens must have begun their existence ages later than the first algae and fungi. This indirect evidence suggests that lichens are not ancient, but a relatively recent evolutionary product descending from the fungus group of Ascomycetes. (This fact provides one possible argument against lichens' growing on Mars: If Mars' lichens are anything like Earth's, their algae and fungi would have to have evolved independently over a period of millions of years. Algae require at least some moisture; fungi require a warm, moist environment and an abundance of organic matter to survive, and these conditions are known not to prevail on Mars today. We do not know what the Martian environment might have provided in eons past.)

Actually, lichen evolution is in many respects problematical and still being debated. Professor A. H. Church, a prominent lichenologist, thought there was little difference between the Dog Tooth Lichen and some fossil seaweeds—except that the lichen had lost assimilating cells which were replaced in function by intrusive green or blue-green cells of algae. Annie L.

Smith, in her book, *Lichens,* interestingly refers to these algae as "skinned seaweeds." Professor Church traces the theoretical development of lichen fungus from seaweeds, proposing that after migrating from the sea, lack of nitrogen kept the plant impoverished, and failure to obtain water kept it small and restricted to short seasonal growth periods.

O. V. Darbishire, an English scientist, objecting to this theory, preferred to think of lichens as land plants, descended from simple fungi that adapted to parasitic and saprophytic land living. He based his assumption on the air spaces or pores in the thalli of lichens, which to him represented a long line of land ancestors, no matter how simple. The first lichen fungi probably started on land, but their exact origin still remains an unsolved riddle.

Lichens can be classified into three types: crustose (flaky or crusty), foliose (papery or leafy) and fruticose (stalked or branching), named in order of their degree of specialization and development. In terms of evolution the earliest forms were the crusty types, followed by the leafy and branching varieties.

Crustose lichens are minute, inconspicuous, the most primitive and the least showy. One species that readily attracts attention is the Rosy Crust Lichen (*Baeomyces roseus*). After a

Rosy Crust Lichen, *Baeomyces roseus,* an earth-dweller

rain one notices a rosy tint on bare stretches of rocky ground, which on investigation is seen to be caused by a carpet of the lichens. The Manna Lichen, or "Earth Bread," is another crustose lichen (*Lecanora esculenta*). Some advanced crustose species are transitional between crustose and foliose; others have lobed margins which can be detached only in small fragments. The thallus frequently cracks into little islands called areolae, which are blue, green, yellow or gray. They are often spread in a black basal layer, the hypothallus, made up of black nonlichenized hyphae which often project beyond the edge of the main thallus, showing a black border at the thallus' edge.

Foliose lichens are the most conspicuous and are usually recognized as lichens; they are familiar as dainty, lace-like or ruffled mats of any color (seldom bright green) growing on rocks and trees. They have spreading, leaf-like expansions of one or many lobes, more or less adherent to their substrate, but less firmly moored than the crusty type.

Pseudocyphelaria crocata, one of the leafy (or foliose) lichens
(N.Y. State Museum and Science Service)

Foliose lichens are characterized by two growth forms, one being leaf-like, lobed at the edge, and attached to the substrate by the many *rhizines* (tiny root-like strands extending downward from the underside of the thallus, often penetrating the substrate); the other grow as a circular thallus, attached to the bark, rock or soil substrate at a central point, appropriately called umbilicate.

Shield Lichens (*Parmelia perlata*), which cover trees and rocks everywhere, Rock Tripe (*Umbilicaria vellea*), which conspicuously clothe rocks and walls, and *Anaptychia speciosa, Peltigera canina* and *Cetraria juniperina* are all characteristic of foliose types. The uninitiated may regard these as fungi.

The third, most specialized type of lichen is the fruticose, stalked, or branching lichen with less of a thallus and frequently having vertical, erect growth. Branching lichens grow from a basal point on the substrate (upright or pendulous, depending on where they grow) in elongated cylindrical or strap-shaped stalks or branches.

Puffed Shield Lichen, *Parmelia physodes,* foliose species that becomes arboreal, and *Ramalina calicaris,* a fruticose lichen

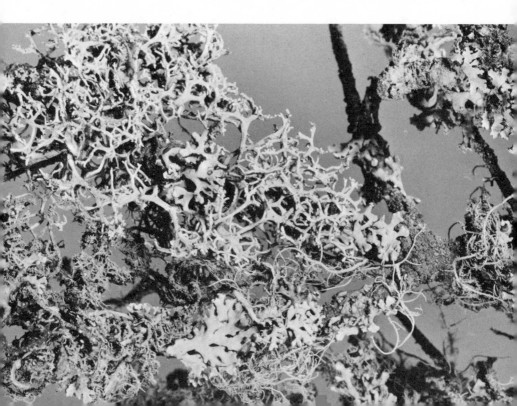

Shield Lichen *Parmelia rudecta,* here growing on tree bark, is a foliose form

Frayed Lichen, *Cladonia degenerans,* easily the least photogenic of the fruticose group

The poet speaking of "the wiry moss that whitens all the hill," in fact, referred to the elaborately branched Reindeer Lichen (*Cladonia rangiferina*). "Coral Fungus" is a name given to a common branching lichen with bright red, cushion-like fruits (*Cladonia cristatella*). The Ladder Lichen (*Cladonia verticillata*) is a good example of a fruticose lichen. The Cladonia have a basal crustose thallus and an upright stalk, the podetium, opening into a cup-like structure, the scyphus from which butterflies might sip a drop of dew. Goblets and sod flakes—the crustose part of Cladonia—spreading over the ground some times give a misty, cobwebby appearance, as though the spiders of the world held a year-long convention there. The accompanying illustration shows a large cluster of the Spoon Lichen, a Goblet Lichen type with small goblets growing out of larger ones.

Such branching lichens vary widely, from long pendulous, thread-like strands of *Usnea trichodea* or *florida* (Old Man's Beard)—a common tree lichen which Longfellow referred to when he wrote "Bearded with moss and in garments green"—to the stiff, short, flat ribbon-like lobes of Evernia. Intermediate types form a spectrum.

Growth of the branching lichens occurs only at the tips. The growth is upward at the tip and the plant dies away at its base, much like sphagnum or peat mosses. The reproductive bodies are borne on the tips of the branches or the edge of the scyphi.

In crustose lichens, algae are distributed uniformly through the lichen tissues. Sometimes the lichen is only a thin structureless mixture of fungal hyphae and algae.

The structure of papery and stalked lichens, however, is more differentiated: Algal cells are confined to a definite layer close to the outer surface of the plant. Here, the fungal tissue differentiates into a tough outer cortex, a mass of variously developed cells. Just under the cortex is the algal layer, or *gonidial zone*. The algal cells are dispersed in a continuous layer or scattered clumps through a tight tangle of fungal filaments, some attached to the algae.

Beneath the algal layer is the pith layer (medulla), loosely-woven, fibrous, or cotton-like, probably an area of storage and release of many chemical substances. In most leafy lichens,

Close-up of a frond of Reindeer Lichen, *Cladonia rangiferina*

Ladder Lichen, *Cladonia verticillata,* forms a bewildering laby-
rinth of spikes and antler-shaped branches

Spoon Lichen, *Cladonia gracilis*

Mealy Goblet Lichen, *Cladonia chlorophaea,* and Smooth Goblet Lichen, *Cladonia conista.* A few strands of British Soldier, *Cladonia cristatella,* appear at the top of the picture

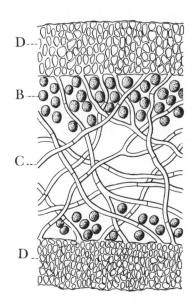

Cross section of the thallus of *Cetraria juniperina,* a foliose lichen. (B) refers to the algal layer, or gonidial zone, (C) to the medulla, or pith layer, (D) to the protective cortex *(from Schneider)*

A close-up of *Usnea florida,* Old Man's Beard *(N.Y. State Museum and Science Service)*

there is a second lower cortex usually of darker color and covered with rhizines, beneath the pith layer. In branching lichens, the pith is the central core of the branchings, and in some species, the pith lines a central hollow of the branches.

The forms of individual lichens vary widely. What may appear to be veins in some species are ribs to provide support and strength for spreading parts. What seem to be roots are, in fact, the rhizines, the fine, hair-like blackish-brown cords of hyphae extending from the under side of the thallus to the substrate, anchoring the lichen. It is thanks to these rhizines that the more primitive lichens rank among the most tenacious members of the entire vegetable kingdom, almost becoming a part of their environment. Some crustose lichens such as Lecidea grow in the upper layers of crystals of sandstone and limestone, sending their hyphae as deep as six to eight millimeters into the upper layers of rock crystals—all of which assures that the plant cannot be budged unless the mountain goes first.

Lichen Anatomy and Reproduction

ALL lichen algae exist independently in nature, but "lichenized" fungi have not been found independent of their algal partners. Probably this is because a fungus, when part of a lichen thallus, changes greatly, into a form characterized by gelatinous tissues, a firm hard cortex and fine branching threads. The umbilical anchor, too, is produced by the fungus, holding the lichen to twig, rock or earth. The algal form and structure is not so radically altered by the association. Since the algae cannot tolerate swings of hydration and dehydration, somewhere in its evolutionary development the fungus had to "learn" to absorb and hold large amounts of water, effectively resisting alternate wetting and drying. As a result, lichens can survive years of drought and resist dessication with little injury. The gelatinous substance of the lichen surface forms an outer "skin" in dry spells, checking evaporation, and the thickened upper cortex of some foliose lichens prevents loss of water.

Nevertheless, water is still essential to the lichen's metabolism. Their water content varies from 2 to 10 percent of dry weight on dry days, to over 300 percent on rainy days. Respiration occurs two to three times faster when the lichen is wet.

Gas exchange (oxygen, carbon dioxide and water vapor) usually takes place through the *cyphellae*—tiny, round-shaped bodies scattered over the lower surface, usually having a definite rim. If they are only holes through which hyphae emerge, they are called *pseudocyphellae.* Cyphellae are aerating organs; true breathing pores occur rarely in lichens, but small holes and tiny vents in the thallus allow movement of air into the internal tissues. Lichens can even absorb vapor directly from the atmosphere and survive with exceedingly low water content, another explanation for their drought-resisting power.

When placed in a moist atmosphere, in fact, lichens, dry for years, become as gray-green and lovely as ever. They have no special organs for water conduction but absorb water over their entire surface. The moisture is not drawn up as sap through any system of tubes, but is rather sopped up by capillary attraction through the tissues, in the manner of a sponge. Fungi (mushrooms) and algae (seaweed) take up water in the same manner. Certain gelatinous lichens have a great power of imbibing water, swelling up enormously in damp surroundings, becoming water reservoirs. Some become water-logged when placed in damp surroundings. One genus *(Collema),* when thoroughly wet, weighs thirty-five times more than when dry!

Crusty lichens absorb more water, weight for weight, than leafy forms, and foliose, rock-growing lichens are the most water retentive.

An interesting experiment is to put a mass of dry, brittle, cracking Reindeer Lichen in water, and see it expand into a beautiful fresh plant. It absorbs half its weight in water in ten minutes. On sunny mountain slopes, Reindeer Lichen spreads lavishly over the ground in a soft carpet of gray. It is crisp and crumbling when dry but resilient and sponge-like when wet.

One appreciates the lichen's absorptive powers by comparing the wet forest trail with a dry one. After a drenching shower dead logs and tree stumps are brightly decorated with the beautiful frosty green, coral-like Cladonia. The red tips suggest fairy candles. The lovely brown fruits are in striking contrast to the frosty green branches.

The foliose lichen, Rock Tripe lies flat on the rock when wet. Its upper surface is a leathery, brownish-green shield, held to the rock at the center of its under surface by a strong, cord-like attachment. It may grow as large as a man's hand, even up to one foot in diameter. The under surface is soot-black. As the air about the plant becomes dry, the edges begin to curl, bringing the black under surface to the light. If the dry atmosphere persists, the edges roll up in an irregular fashion. With each change in the humidity of the air, the Rock Tripe curls and uncurls. At one time its brownish-green upper surface is exposed, at another its black under surface, as it writhes and twists in response to humidity.

Lichen metabolism increases, of course, with moisture. Assimilation of carbon dioxide by lichens depends upon the

Smooth Rock Tripe, *Umbilicaria mammulata,* in moistened condition

water content of their tissues, maximum being attained at saturation. About one-fourth of available light can pass through the layers of lichen tissue when wet; only about one-tenth when the thallus is dry.

Since every lichen is a two-part organism, individual lichens display different characteristics, depending on the behavior of the various fungal and algal cells in their makeup. Although the fungus component dominates, certain lichens display their dual nature in such matters as reproduction. The fungus produces its own spores in sacs (*asci;* singular, *ascus*). Special arrangements of the spore sacs as "fruits" are distinctive, aiding in identification.

A few tropical lichens have as their fungus component the mushroom or bracket fungi group (Basidiomycetes), but the fungal component in most lichens belongs to one of the sac fungi (Ascomycetes), so named because of their club-shaped ascus or sac where they form reproductive spores. The spores play the same reproductive role in lichens as they do in the Ascomycetes existing independently.

For some reason the fungus does not "realize" that it and its fungal descendants cannot survive without algae. The fungus produces spores continuously as long as it is in the lichen (strangely, when separated and isolated in pure culture, it ceases to do so). The characteristic fruiting body appears on the surface of the thallus and is called an *apothecium.*

Lichen apothecia resemble fruiting bodies of the corresponding nonlichen species of Ascomycetes fungi. They are distinctive, aiding in identification of lichen species. Apothecia are open, dish-shaped, sometimes cup- or urn-shaped, or lumpy modifications. They may be closed, spherical bodies embedded in the substance of the lichen, and may be black, brown or brightly colored. When closed, the fruiting bodies are called perithecia.

The perithecia of some Cladonia species are bright red tips or knobs, in rich color contrast to frosty green branching. Their cups' edges may be adorned with a ring of bright red-brown tips, suggesting a fairy cornucopia. Occasionally goblets grow from rims of goblets below. Some resemble branchings of coral from which the name Cladonia (branching) is derived.

Thecia (apothecia perithecia) may be in several locations: at the ends of branches in branching lichens, distributed over the upper surface in leafy ones, and at the edges or periphery in lacy, embroidery-like species. In open apothecia, the upper and outer layer is the spore layer, completely exposed. Under the spore layer is the fruit base or *hypothecium*. In an open apothecium the hypothecium is pie-plate- or pancake-shaped. Its edge shows outside the spore layer forming the true rim of the fruit. This may or may not be surrounded by an outer rim, a raised part of the lichen thallus, not structurally a part of the apothecium. The outer rim contains algal cells but is colored like the lichen. The true rim contains no algal cells and is the

Cross section of an apothecium of *Umbilicaria pustulata* showing the characteristic urn-shaped silhouette *(from Schneider)*

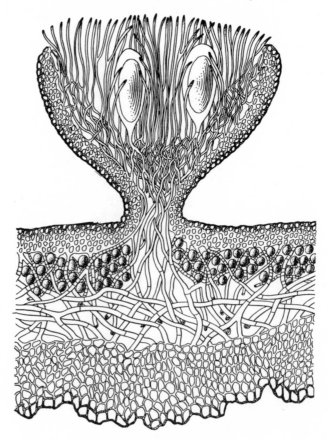

same color as the apothecium. Rarely, if ever, are the lichen and its apothecium colored alike.

When examined microscopically, the spore layer is seen to consist of spore sacs or asci. These have the appearance of inverted test tubes in a palisade-like growth of parallel arranged fungal threads. The spore sacs do not mature their spores simultaneously. One spore sac with spores in early stages may stand beside another with fully developed spores. The accompanying, much-enlarged drawings show spores, spore sacs, and fungal supporting structures, the paraphyses.

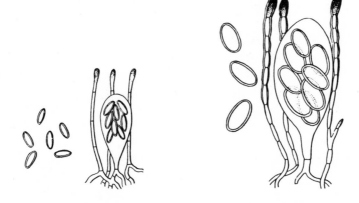

The spores and club-shaped spore sacs of *Cetraria juniperina* and *Parmelia perlata (from Schneider)*

Bits of apothecia first soaked in water and cut in thin sections with a razor blade or merely crushed, will disclose the spores, ranging through various sizes and shapes, depending on the species. This requires magnification, is easily done and requires no special skill. Spores may be arranged in the sac end-to-end like beads, or be irregularly situated.

Various spores are elliptical, needle-shaped, potato-shaped or otherwise curved or spiral. Each consists of a single cell or two or more cells, in which case the partitions between the cells are readily seen. In an individual spore, cells can be observed in varying stages of division.

As spores reach maturity they may be tinted brown, purplish or black, though they will be colorless or have a faint greenish tinge up until that point. When the spores are ripe, they are squeezed out through the perforated summit of the spore sac; there may be from one to a hundred in a spore sac, the usual number being eight.

Just inside the wall of the closed perithecium and beneath and around the spore cavity lies a layer similar to the hypothecium. In closed thecia (perithecia) the spore cavity is enclosed within a wall, opening at the summit by a pore for the escape of the spores. The spores discharge through the narrow orifice, oozing out in a droplet of gluey slime.

Amazingly, all these complicated and often beautiful structures are wholly useless as far as lichen reproduction is concerned. Apothecia, perithecia and their respective spores come from the fungal component alone. If the spores are to "reproduce" new lichen plants, they must make contact with free-living algae of the appropriate species. This has never been observed or proved, and moreover, algae of the proper species are scarce outside of lichens.

Just beneath their surfaces most lichens also produce peculiar flask-shaped bodies whose function is unknown, called *spermagonia.* On the lichen surface they appear as dark dots or granules; under the microscope they are observed as tiny cavities and openings through a pore on the surface of the thallus.

Spermagonia produce large numbers of spore-like bodies, rod-shaped and much smaller than spores, spermatia. Modern lichenologists sometimes use the term microconidia to describe them. The spermagonia are true fungal structures, but do not occur in pure cultures of the fungus separate from the lichen. In Cladonia the spermagonia are conical or ovoid black structures opening by a pore, at the tips of the branches or along the margins of the cups. In Cetraria they are found at the tips of short spines along the margins of the lobes as in the Iceland Moss (*Cetraria islandica*).

In most lichens spermagonia are matched by microscopic female reproductive structures found in the medulla in two parts—a coil in the medulla and a structure called a trichogyne extending from this coil to the upper cortex. There are similar structures in independent fungi. Some lichenologists have proposed that the apothecia develop as a sexual process following extrusion of spermatia from the spermagonium which then is carried by air currents or insects and attaches to the trichogyne; its nucleus migrates downward to the coil pairing with the female nucleus in the coil. The apothecium and spores allegedly develop then from this sexual union. For many species, however, this process has not been confirmed by actual scientific observation.

Many lichens have propagation methods other than spores, however. A small fragment broken off a lichen thallus, provided it contains algal cells, grows into a new and complete lichen in favorable circumstances. Simple mechanical fragmentation of the thallus and dispersal by wind, rain and the feet of animals serves for propagation of countless individuals, particularly brittle dry lichens. It is probably the main means of propagation. Many lichens also depend on the unique *soredia* which they develop on their surfaces. Soredia are tiny, powdery, mealy bodies on the surface of thalli, made up of a few algal cells caught up in a weft of gelatinized fungal hyphae. On branching lichens, such as Cladonia, they appear as gray or white granules on the podetia or surface of the sod flakes—the crustose part of Cladonia. Soredia, on dispersal, grow into new lichens precisely like the parent individual. Soredia can also be gray, pale blue, green or yellow. Those of the Sulphur Dust Lichen give the colorful appearance of powered sulphur, hence the lichen's common name.

Soredia originate in the gonidial (algal) layer and emerge through a crack or pore into the upper cortex. About 30 percent of all lichens have soredia. If they erupt in conspicuous powdery clumps, they are called *soralia,* really the same as soredia but more constant in form and position on the thallus.

Many lichens also produce *isidia,* containing algae and all the necessary tissues of the fungus. These are small coral-like outgrowths on the surface of the thallus, having a few algal cells caught up in a few fungal strands, differing from soredia and soralia in having a cortex. Isidia really are lichens in miniature. They suggest tiny cones on a narrow stalk, and are occasionally branched. Isidia may form over the whole surface of the thallus or may be restricted to the margins. At a microscopic level they consist of extensions and protuberances of cortical, gonidial, and medullary tissues as finger-like, cylindrical outgrowths. When dry, they break off easily and propagate rapidly.

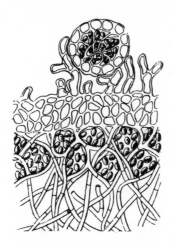

Cross section of an isidium on the Dog Tooth Lichen, *Peltigera canina (from Schneider)*

The algal components of lichens are called gonidia, and until 1867 when Schwendener proved that their microscopic green cells were ordinary green and blue-green algae, lichenologists thought the green bodies emerged somehow from the tips of the fungal hyphae. Some algae grow as independent plants in nature as well as being "incorporated" as a lichen. In the unnatural environment of lichen tissues algae become stunted and change in other ways, often making identification difficult. The most common alga found in lichens is a green one called Trebouxia (Phylum chlorophyta). Cystococcus, one of three algae seen as crumbly greenness on the shaded side of tree trunks, is another that gave up its singular existence. As many as thirty different algae have been identified in lichen thalli.

Algal cells in the lichen thallus have two anatomical arrangements. When the algae are in a definite, layered zone just below the surface of the thallus and above the medulla, the thallus is called *heteromerous;* this is the most common arrangement. If the algae are scattered through the medulla, a core of the thallus, the structure is *homoiomerous,* or not layered.

Occasionally filamentous algae are incorporated in lichens and the lichen then takes its external form from the alga instead of the fungus, as is usual. A filamentous blue-green alga (Nostoc) is a common algal member of lichens, in which threads of the fungus weave through the algal chain. In dry times the lichen shrinks to a papery crust; with dew or rain its algal sheaths swell and the plant becomes pulpy and gelatinous.

The lichen thallus would be plain white in color if it were not for the algal layer. Lichens having green algae are generally mineral gray or gray-green in color. When the thallus is wet, the previously dry and opaque fungal hyphae absorb water and become translucent, and the algal color is more apparent. Black or brown lichens which develop a gelatinous surface when wet contain one of the blue-green algae of the phylum cyanophyta, such as Stigonema or Gloeocapsa. Very few lichens have the bright green color of mosses or other chlorophyll-bearing plants—one exception being *Peltigera aphthosa,* one of the Dog Tooth lichens.

More than one species of alga can exist within the same lichen. *Cephalodia* are wart-like tubercles or swellings sometimes found on the surface of the thallus. They are abnormal growths, usually light brown in color, made of the normal lichen fungal hyphae, but with different algal components than the rest of the lichen. Their forms vary—orbicular, tiny flat lobes or branching structures, they probably serve the function of moisture retention in a small way.

Since the fungus and alga forming the lichen evolved in nature, it is reasonable to expect that the same lichen (fungus and alga) could be produced if the two are appropriately brought together. However, despite numerous efforts, lichens have not been successfully synthesized until very recently.

Ninety years ago when the true nature of lichens was discovered, Gaston Bonnier, a French botanist, claimed to have achieved many true lichen syntheses. He described synthetic cultures of fungus and alga brought together; five days after germination, a clasping filament of the fungus had laid hold of the alga and symbiotic growth had begun; fifty days later a small lichen thallus was formed, complete with fruits. However, Bonnier's experiments contain inconsistencies and unexplained points. Others were unable to reproduce his results using sophisticated methods, ensuring a pure culture of both fungus and alga.

Both the algal and fungal components of lichens have been separately cultured in the laboratory. The lichenized algae, when separated in pure culture from the fungus, grow well on nutrient media in total darkness, retaining their chlorophyll and green color. This is strange and unexplained behavior, unlike any other known chlorophyll-bearing green plants! They can grow as saprophytes, obtaining organic substances from the environment (culture medium) without photosynthesis, at least in the usual sense.

The fungal member is rarely found free in nature. When cultured artificially from spores in the laboratory, it behaves strangely indeed. Its slow growth rate is the only resemblance to its behavior in a lichen. It does not grow in the form of the lichen thallus at all, but in shapeless mounds of dense white to brownish thread-like fungus tissue. No fruiting bodies or spores appear. A slow growth proceeds until the growth medium is dry or used up and the plant dies.

Not until 1966 did Dr. Vernon Ahmadjian finally succeed in artificially reestablishing the separated alga and fungus of *Cladonia cristatella,* a triumph and milestone in lichenological research.*

In a previous attempt at lichen synthesis, Dr. Ahmadjian showed that one condition necessary for fungus and alga union in a lichen is starvation. Fungal spores and algal cells were cultured separately from the same lichen and placed together again on nutrient growth medium, including some sugar; the fungal spores germinated to form many branching colorless filaments and the alga developed normally, reproducing freely. The filaments showed no tendency to seek out the algae or become associated with adjacent algal cells. They grew over one another, showing only intimate mingling. However, if all organic nutrients, particularly sugar, are excluded from the growth media, or after the nutrient media is exhausted, the

---

*Ahmadjian, V. "Artificial Reestablishment of the Lichen *Cladonia cristatella,*" *Science,* 151: 199–201, Jan., 1966.

fungus changes in appearance, showing straggling thin segments, and short side branches appear that contact walls of algal cells. These connections become more frequent with time, and take on more the appearance of the fungus in the lichen. After several weeks a close weft of fungal filaments has numerous connections with algal cells; there is some evidence of differentiation into lichen tissue. Dr. I. MacKenzie Lamb, Director of the Farlow Herbarium, suggests that further progress in lichen synthesis depends on whether the complex environmental circumstances the lichen experiences in nature can be simulated. Surfaces on which lichens grow must be arranged as well as alternating cold and warmth, wetting and drying; and time is a necessary ingredient in such an experiment, perhaps forty or fifty years. "No crash programs can be initiated in lichen synthesis."

About the Bryophytes

Somewhat more advanced than the lichens are the bryophytes, to which—as their name (from the Greek word *bryon,* "moss") suggests—the mosses belong. Typically they are small and green, made up of tiny, leafy stems, and usually no more (often less) than an inch in height.

But any description of mosses should begin with a mention of certain plants that are not mosses at all. One of these is the so-called "Spanish Moss" that hangs in long gray streamers from trees in the South. This is not a moss but a bromeliad, a flowering plant closely related to the pineapple. "Reindeer Moss," so-called, is one of several gray-green, fruticose lichens, as we have already seen. The "Irish Moss" often collected along the Atlantic Coast for use as food is, in fact, one of the algae (although some mosses may become salt-tolerant, none grow in seawater). The "moss campion," which grows extensively in the mountains of the West, has foliage which bears a strong resemblance to that of a true moss, although it is in reality a flowering plant. So is the "moss phlox" of rock garden fame. The club-mosses are pteridophytes and are botanically closer to the ferns than to the true mosses; one member of the group is called the Staghorn Moss because of its antler-shaped fruiting structures.

Criteria for identification of a moss are fairly simple: Any small green plant (lacking green leaves, lichens are easily distinguished from mosses and liverworts) having leafy stems without flowers and growing in such proximity as to form velvety cushions, is probably a moss.

Mosses may be scattered singly, but more often grow crowded together. They may grow in clusters or cushions and suggest a tiny fern forest or a grove of Lilliputian trees. They may be only one-sixteenth of an inch in height, though most mosses range from a larger fraction of an inch to a few inches tall. One may be completely confident that the plant is a moss if it has a slender bristle-like stalk or seta that seems to be a continuation of the stem and bears at its upper end a spore case or capsule.

All mosses are able to synthesize their own food. They differ from more highly developed plants, however, in that they lack a vascular system—the veins or conducting tubes that carry water, minerals and foodstuffs up through the roots and into the leaves, stems and other structures.

Liverworts, inconspicuous plants of damp, shady places, growing on rocks, soil, the roots of trees and decaying wood, are often found as shiny, bright green, somewhat fleshy plants, growing flat or extended like a ribbon in a moist habitat. Liverworts are rarely more than an inch high and do not generally spread over large areas as many mosses do. All liverworts have a distinct upper and lower surface; they almost never grow erect, but lie flat, anchoring themselves by means of rhizoids, the root-like processes found in all bryophytes. The common name "liverwort" comes from the pattern of grooves that often divides its surface into block-like or hexagonal sections, giving the plant a liver-like appearance. Some liverworts have the appearance of a bright green papery lichen; but this need cause no confusion since true lichens are only rarely bright green. Liverwort plants are separately male and female. At certain seasons each bears stalks capped by umbrella-like structures, that form sperms in the male plants, egg cells in the female. The sperms escape and fertilize the eggs, which remain in place and develop into sporophytes. Each sporophyte gives rise to many spores, which when released and dispersed develop into the familiar liverwort plants.

The most popular theory on the origin of mosses and liverworts holds that they arose from algae: Green algae gradually changed their habitat from an aquatic to a terrestrial one. If, indeed, they derived from an algal ancestor, then primitive bryophytes required an abundant water supply—and

Short Pogonatum Moss, *Pogonatum brevicaule,* in close-up, showing the distinctive spore cases and setae

Mnium Moss, showing the distinctively swan-necked spore case and setae

modern ones still do, at least to carry on reproduction. Moss ancestry is certainly very ancient. Plant evolutionists generally regard mosses and liverworts as among the first plants to compose a land flora, but whether they were the *first* land plants is open to question. Unlike some of the more highly developed bryophytes, the liverworts and hornworts have never ventured far from the water out of which their ancestors emerged. Some idea of what early nonvascular land plants may have been like can be seen by examining a common thallose liverwort such as *Riccia frostii,* among the most primitive of all bryophytes.

Unfortunately there is little testimony remaining in the rocks to prove the ancestry of the mosses and liverworts. The first known land plants are called the Psilophytales, vascular plants (more advanced than mosses and liverworts by the very reason of being vascular) whose fossil record is traceable back 376 million years. Psilophyte fossils were found on the Gaspé Peninsula and in New England rocks where they once formed dense forests. Their fossil remains show that they possessed stems and primitive leaves, but presumably no roots or flowers. However, some fossil remains of mosses have been found and studied—generally the leafy plants and a few spores, difficult to identify. The majority have been found in rocks of the Pennsylvania Period (Upper Carboniferous), laid down about 250 million years ago. (Some botanists believe that mosses and liverworts enjoyed their greatest prosperity during the Devonian and Silurian periods, 376 to 400 million years ago.)

These fossil bryophytes are less advanced than primitive Psilophytales, as well as being much smaller in size and different in appearance. A large group of botanists now believe that bryophytes are not derived directly from algal ancestors, but rather from forms derived from algae that led in one line to Bryophytes and in another line to the Psilophytales.

In any case, mosses have undergone little change since ancient times; fossil mosses are similar to modern forms of mosses and liverworts. An Andreaea and a Sphagnum fossil found in Peruvian and brown coal mines in Germany differ little from their present-day counterparts.

To date, some 23,000 species have been described by botanists. Mosses themselves (Musci) have been further divided into three subclasses: Sphagnobrya, Andreaeobrya and Eubrya. It is to this final subclass that the greatest number of species has been assigned.

In general, however, differing habits of growth serve to separate mosses into two large groups. Those belonging to a large group known as acrocarpous mosses (from the Greek words *akros*, "highest," and *karpos*, "fruit") have typically erect-growing stems, branched only slightly or not at all, with the seta and spore-bearing capsule at the tip of the stem. Mosses of this group often form a deep, thick growth. Tufts may develop as a new annual growth anywhere from six inches to several feet in diameter added to that of the preceding year.

Mosses belonging to the second group, described as pleuro-carpous (from *pleura*, "rib" or "side"), have a stem that is generally prostrate or creeping and freely branching, with the spore case borne on the side of the stem. Such mosses usually form thin, flat, tangled mats. Each year the stems and branches of the new growth spread and intertangle with the old. Sometimes the primary stem may be creeping, with erect, somewhat branched secondary stems, and the mats thus formed may become so tangled that separating individual plants becomes next to impossible. Sometimes two or more kinds of moss may become intertangled to a degree that identification becomes difficult. These, of course, are not good specimens for study.

For anyone setting out to look for specimens along a woodland road or trail or in an open place, the first moss to be met will almost certainly be one of the common Hairy Caps of the genus *Polytrichum* (Greek, "many hairs"). The Hairy Cap mosses were the first to receive a common name, from the long hairs that grow from the cap over the capsule and form the "hairy cap." Although there are variations in size and shape, all the mosses are essentially alike in structure and function. Thus, since the Hairy Caps are all of sufficient size that their principal parts can be readily identified, it is logical to begin with them in a study of the anatomy and life history of mosses.

An examination of a single moss plant under a hand lens will reveal its simple structure. The stem, as in all mosses, is primitive, lacking the vascular bundles by which liquids are carried upward in the stems of higher plants. There is almost no differentiation among the cells, except that those on the outside may have somewhat thicker walls so as to function as a primitive sort of bark. (An imperfect conducting system is, however, found in a few species of moss.) Similarly, mosses have no true roots. The branched, filamentous structures known as rhizoids (from the Greek word, *rhiza*, "root") are simple hair-like tubes or mere chains of cells, whose only function is that of anchorage. There is no evidence that they serve to absorb water or minerals from the soil as do the roots of higher plants.

Throughout the plant kingdom leaves are so arranged as to permit the greatest amount of exposure to the light. The Hairy Cap mosses are no exception. Their long, slender leaves are placed on the stem in a spiral sequence or "story." In some Hairy Cap species, every eighth leaf will be found to lie directly above the first in the sequence; in others, there are thirteen leaves to a "story."

Awned Hairy Cap, *Polytrichum piliferum*

The long, narrow leaf of the Hairy Cap is one of the most highly developed among mosses. As a general rule the moss leaf has a thickness of only one cell layer, except along a thickened midrib and sometimes around the margin. (Many species, however, have only a partial midrib or lack it entirely.) In a few species the midrib may extend beyond the tip into a bristle-like structure; others may have a double midrib.

The shape of a leaf may be lance-like and sharply pointed, or oval and paddle-like. In some species the margins may be toothed or serrated; they may be flat or rolled one way or the other, to an extent that varies with the environmental humidity. A thickened margin is found only in leaves of relatively large size. The thickened epidermis and the stomata, or breathing pores, found in the leaves of higher plants are entirely lacking in those of mosses.

Large-Leafed Mnium, *Mnium punctatum* and *elatum,* has leaf cells so large that they can be readily seen with a hand lens— sometimes even with the naked eye. But the leaves themselves are extremely thin and shrivel strikingly as the plant dries

The Hairy Cap leaf, however, is several layers thick, with a relatively broad midrib. Since the delicate cell walls of their upper surfaces permit water and gases to pass through them, such leaves are capable in a very primitive way of conducting water, as higher plants do. When the sun shines on them, a bank of fresh, green plants rapidly shrinks, turning brown and crisp, as though dead.

Mosses spread their leaves to catch all possible moisture in the cup-like bases of their leaves, at the leaf angle. Lower-leaf cells are very thin-walled, particularly designed for maximum absorption. Mosses can be divided into three groups on the basis of how much water they require:

A.   True aquatic mosses such as the Fountain Moss live in water.

B.   True terrestrial mosses such as Grimmia require very little water.

C.   Mixed types—a large variety of mosses—need only a moderate water supply.

The aquatic and the terrestrial mosses are the two extremes, while the great bulk of the bryophytes falls somewhere in-between. The Hairy Cap is also part of this latter category.

Leaves of higher plants have a waxy or cuticular covering, a moisture-conserving adaptation which is lacking in the moss leaf. Water is lost very quickly from the moss leaf, but the absence of waterproofing permits the leaf to absorb even the least available amount of moisture—as provided by evening or morning dew or an occasional short rainstorm—quite rapidly. With the arrival of rain or dew the greenness reappears, as though new life had been magically injected. No illustration can do justice to the spectacular, seemingly immediate, appearance of fresh green plants in what seemed to be a bed of brown lifeless Hairy Caps.

The mechanism behind this phenomenon, however, can be easily observed. When the sun shines on them, the plants do not actually wither and die; instead, the edges of the leaves roll inward and tighten against the stem, so that their horny tips and thick, brown under-surfaces are exposed to the sun. The leaves are only one cell layer in thickness except those on dry rocks and ledges, where a double layer of extremely thick-walled cells prevents evaporation. But the cell walls of the under-surface, unlike those above, are impervious to moisture, and thus guard against undue loss of water by evaporation.

Mosses and liverworts reproduce by means of spores: one-celled particles of living matter with a firm protective covering, which develop inside a lidded spore case. But the spores of bryophytes are only superficially similar to the spores produced by fungi and lichens. For one thing the spore cases seen dangling on tiny brown "lampposts" above a bed of moss do not grow directly out of the parent moss plant, as do the fruiting bodies of fungi and lichens. Rather, these structures are the

Single plants of Common Hairy Cap Moss, *Polytrichum commune,* in various degrees of hydration. Note how the various years' growth becomes increasingly apparent as the leaves absorb moisture

end result of sophisticated sexual reproduction, a union of male and female components.

To explain this odd arrangement, we have to go back to the mosses' probable ancestors, the algae, where sexual reproduction, with a mobile, swimming gamete attracted to another, sedentary gamete, is a common thing.

The use of hard-walled, quick-germinating spores is an ideal way of dispersing plants on land, and the mosses, as well as other forms, had to *invent* spores to meet the challenge of the dry environment. But like the fungi in lichens which still "remember"—and continue to practice—their original forms of reproduction, the mosses still rely on water to carry the sperms to the egg cells, and are thus aquatic in this crucial part of their life cycle.

Each moss and liverwort lives out its existence passing from one into a second strikingly different form. The only applicable—but still not accurate—analogy is that of a butterfly, which exists both as a winged "adult" and as a caterpillar, one form alternating with another in endless succession. In the case of the bryophytes, however, it's as if the caterpillar mated and laid eggs that hatched into butterflies—and that the butterflies then gave off spores that developed into caterpillars, i.e., alternating forms.

To be more specific and scientific, the leafy moss plant itself (or "caterpillar")—the stem, leaves and tiny root-like projections known as rhizoids—makes up what is known as the *gametophyte* (gamete-producing plant) generation. The short-lived "butterfly"—the spore capsule itself, with the long, bristle-like stalk (known as the seta) on which it is borne, and the tiny structure (the "foot") by which the seta is attached to the stem, are known collectively as the *sporophyte* (spore-producing plant) generation.

To illustrate this remarkable duality, one may as well start with the more familiar gametophyte generation—the moss plant itself—which differentiates into male and female individuals. As the gametophyte plant develops, it produces a cluster of *bracts,* also known as perichaetal leaves (from the Greek *peri-,* "all round," and *chaeto-,* "hair," the latter a reference to the bristle-like seta). Plants bearing these at the apex of the stem are described as acrocarpous; those bearing them on small lateral branches are described as pleurocarpous. The bracts together with the organs they enclose—the antheridia and archegonia—are known respectively as the male and female receptacles.

In the common Hairy Cap Moss the male and female organs are on separate plants. The species is thus said to be dioicous (Greek, "two households"). Mosses in which both male and female parts are found on the same plant are said to be monoicous ("one household"). Because of their flower-like appearance, the male receptacles of the common Hairy Cap are often miscalled "moss flowers."

In a healthy bed of Hairy Cap Moss will be several that do not produce spore cases, but instead bear a rosette of stiff, highly modified leaves known as bracts. These plants are the male gametophytes. A single one may consist of what appears to be a series of rosettes divided by sections of the stem, each section growing out of the one below. Each section and its terminal rosette is the result of a year's growth; thus, taken together, they show the age of the plant. Among the bracts of the rosette there develops an organ known as the *antheridium* in which the male gametes or germ cells are produced. This is a globe-like, somewhat elongated and swollen sac, supported by a slender stalk and covered by a sterile jacket.

The corresponding female gametes are produced on other individuals in an organ known as the *archegonium*. Within the elongated central cavity of the archegonium is a large egg cell, together with a variable number of what are known as neck canal cells. When the archegonium reaches its full development, these cells break up, filling the cavity with a mucilaginous substance which draws in the moisture of dew or rain, causing the jacket to expand until it ruptures at the tip of the neck.

Meanwhile the small cubical cells within the antheridium have undergone a development of their own, each ultimately producing two motile sperms with whip-like tails. Once these are mature, moisture in the environment causes the sterile jacket to rupture at the tip, permitting the sperms to escape. Propelled by their whip-like tails, they swim through the surrounding dew or raindrops, irresistibly drawn by the mucilaginous substances exuded from the archegonium. Many sperms may enter the neck of a single archegonium, but only one—whichever first reaches the egg—is needed to bring about fertilization. It is from the union of sperm and egg, or male and female gamete, that the sporophyte generation, consisting of seta and spore case, will develop and grow, resting in and obtaining nourishment from the female plant.

The fertilized egg is known as the zygote or zygospore. Its nucleus consists of the fusion of the nuclei of the two gametes. This cell divides (first the nucleus divides and then the cell is partitioned between the new nuclei by a membrane through the middle) to form two new cells, and these in turn divide and redivide. Each cell thus produced contains within its nucleus the set of chromosomes of the female parent, brought to it by the egg, and the set found in the male parent, brought to it by the sperm. In contradistinction from the gametes and the gametophyte itself, which are described as haploid (from the Greek word *haploos,* "single" or "simple") and which contain one set of chromosomes, the zygote is described as diploid (Greek, *diploos,* "double"), and contains two sets. The sporophyte formed by the zygote is consequently diploid. But the cells that form the spores it produces undergo reduction division so that the spores themselves are haploid, and the gametophytes that develop from them are therefore haploid, and give rise to the haploid gametes.

The infant sporophyte begins its development as the diploid zygote divides to form first two cells, then four, eight and so on as each new cell divides in its turn. It absorbs food from the leafy gametophyte through the organ called the "foot," which will later be visible as the base by which the seta appears to be attached to the stem of the gametophyte. Since, aside from the carbon dioxide absorbed through the stomata of the spore capsule, the sporophyte is entirely dependent upon the gametophyte for nutrition throughout its existence, it may be considered in effect a parasite upon the gametophyte generation. Just as in the higher mammals there is no organic connection between the placenta and the uterus in which the infant develops, so there is none between the gametophyte and sporophyte generations of the humble moss. Thus, for all the increased complexity in other aspects of evolutionary development, the essential mechanism of reproduction has undergone remarkably little change.

Observation of fertilization in the plant is difficult; about the best one can hope for is to observe the rapidly elongating, lance-like sporophyte while it is still in the process of development.

The spore cases of each species of moss are distinctive and serve to differentiate one species from another.

In Hairy Cap mosses, the spore case is a thin-walled cylindrical box with four or six sharp perpendicular edges that give it a prismatic appearance. It sits atop a long, bristle-like seta, which functions principally to raise the spore case to a height that will enable the widest possible distribution of spores. Close observation of a bed of moss will show the fascinating way in which the setae twist and turn in response to changes in the environment so as to bring the developing spore case into the optimum position for obtaining light and water. In the Hairy Cap the seta and spore case together suggest a tiny Turkish pipe. The Ditrichum, or Forked Moss, illustrates graceful, long, frequently twisted and tortuous, slender setae with an asymmetrical hairy cap and a typical spore case.

The last stage of the sporophyte generation is the development within the spore case of what are known as spore mother cells. The first stage of a new gametophyte generation may be said to take place as the mother cells begin producing, in groups of four, the small cells known as tetrads or tetraspores (from the Greek prefix *tetra-*, "four"). As they mature, these break apart into tiny one-celled bodies containing chlorophyll. In dioecous plants such as the Hairy Cap Moss, it would appear that two of the spores in each tetrad contain one Y chromosome each and will produce male plants, whereas the two others contain only X chromosomes and will produce female plants.

Before the developing spores reach maturity the spore case is covered with a light brown, conical, hairy cap or hood, known as the veil or calyptra (Greek, "covering for the head"), the part from which the common and scientific names of the Hairy Cap Moss are taken. This veil is actually the upper part of the archegonium, torn off at its base and carried upward as the seta lengthens and the spore case develops. This covering falls off naturally when the spores are ripe; or it may easily be lifted off with forceps to reveal the operculum, a tightly closed circular lid, suggesting a miniature tam-o'-shanter or pixie cap. Variations in the shape of the operculum are another way of distinguishing between species. In the development of the spore case, one or two rows of cells become modified in such a way as to form a zone of separation. When these cells become distended with moisture, they are displaced as a ring so that the outer layer of cells in the upper part of the spore case takes the form of the operculum.

The careful dissection of a mature spore case reveals a thick-walled, protective outer layer of cells. Within this hull or rind are, first, a few layers of thinner-walled supporting cells; then a layer of loose tissue with spaces between the cells. Tiny stomata, or breathing pores in the outer wall—the number of which varies with the species—admit the air, from which the plant draws carbon dioxide. This constitutes the only nutrition taken directly by the sporophyte.

Inside the spore case is a mechanism that can be examined under a hand lens when the operculum is removed. Bordering the rim of the spore case are anywhere from four to sixty-four blunt teeth, known collectively as the peristome (Greek, "around the mouth"). The number varies from one species to another, but is always a multiple of four.

Spores depend upon wind and air currents for their distribution. Thus, they must be carefully protected from moisture, which would cause them to aggregate and fall to the ground as soon as they were released. If they should germinate prematurely or in adverse circumstances, they would decay. Thus it is an advantage for the spores to be released a few at a time, rather than all at once. In Hairy Cap mosses, each of the teeth (numbering from thirty-two to sixty-four) is attached by its central tip to a thin membranous disc or diaphragm which forms a sort of natural saltshaker. In dry weather the teeth tend to shrink and curve inward at the same time as the disc also shrinks, leaving a ring of small openings between the teeth. It is through these spaces that spores can be released whenever a current of air moves the spore case from its upright position.

The seta on which it is carried is exceedingly elastic and springy in dry weather; bent to one side and then released, it springs back with the resilience of a steel wire, scattering a small cloud of spores. In wet weather, unfavorable to the distribution of spores, the seta loses its elasticity. At the same time, the teeth and the membranous disc expand, effectively closing the spore case to either the escape of spores or the entry of so much as a drop of moisture.

Some mosses have pendant, partly inclined or horizontal spore cases. In these, other mechanisms prevent the spores from being liberated prematurely. For example, the spore case may have two rows of teeth: The inner row, acts as a sieve, while the outer one protects the spores from moisture by the hygroscopic device already described. The spore cases of both Bugs on a Stick and the Powder Gun Moss all point with their caps toward the source of light. The position of the spore case and the flattening of its upper surface are adaptations for the absorption of light. When anything touches the upper surface of a mature capsule, e.g., a drop of rain or the feet of a large insect, the spores are ejected in miniature puffs to a height of two inches, as though fired from a gun. This effect may be observed if a mature spore case is tapped gently with a stick. The nozzle-like mouth is aimed upward in order to fire the spores to the greatest possible height. The wind aids in dispersing the spores; so may a passing animal, to whose fur they may cling and thus be carried to a spot favorable for germination.

Released spores are minute, one-celled, dust-like particles of living matter, brown, yellowish or greenish in color, each containing chlorophyll and capable of producing a new individual. Their outer surface seems to be water-resistant to a certain degree, so that a spore requires a good deal of soaking before it begins to germinate.

A spore that has been carried by the wind to moist earth or some other favorable spot soon becomes swollen with moisture. It bursts its shell and puts forth a slender, many-celled thread, which rapidly elongates and puts forth branches. This phase of the life history of a moss or liverwort is known as the *protonema.* The chlorophyll it contains gives the moss a bright green color.

As it spreads in a fine green web over wood, stone or soil, it bears a close resemblance to certain species of algae. (It is interesting to note that in the ferns or pteridophytes, whose evolutionary development has carried them a step beyond the bryophytes, the germinating spore likewise produces a flat plate of green cells, the prothallium, which is remarkably similar to the protonema and to the growth habit of the thallose liverworts in their adult stage.) Underneath, some of the cells which are brown or colorless and lack chlorophyll, elongate and penetrate downward, seeking the darkness of the substrate. These form the filamentous rhizoids which act not as true roots, but merely for anchorage.

Soon, as a result of continued cell divisions in the protonema, one or several buds appear, each of which sends forth a young leafy shoot. With the appearance of the first leafy plants, the protonema usually disappears. (As their descriptive name suggests, thallose liverworts such as *Ricciocarpus natans* have never developed beyond the ribbon-like or thallus stage that follows upon the germination of the spore. Riccia grows as a simple prostrate thallus, with only a few of the specialized structures—namely spores and rhizoids—not possessed by its aquatic ancestors, the algae.) In some mosses, such as those of the genus *Pogonatum,* the protonema may persist and continue to function in the same way as the leaves. After becoming fully mature, these extensions of the protonema are ready to produce male and female gametes and begin the cycle all over again.

Sexual reproduction gives mosses the advantage (which lichens do not have, incidentally) of being able to mix genetic materials, so that the next generation will not be a strict carbon copy of the preceding one. Even so, it has not led to as bewildering a variety of characteristics as sexual reproduction and interbreeding have brought about in some other forms of life. Certain mosses make it impossible for the plants to fertilize themselves, so that germ cells must come from a nearby colony. In these species the male and female parts are borne in the same cluster—the antheridia only during the first year, the archegonia during the second. Such mosses are described as "polyoicous." (In still others, described as "polygamous," the antheridia and archegonia are found, variously distributed, on the same leafy gametophyte.)

Like their algal ancestors, however, mosses often take advantage of asexual reproduction. Mosses are notable for their powers of regeneration, and any part of either the gametophyte or the sporophyte, under suitable conditions, can develop into an entire new plant. In fact, some mosses may not produce spores at all. In a dry season they become brittle, and are easily broken into small pieces that can be carried by the wind to a new location. Since the cells of mosses are undifferentiated—without a strictly predestined function—a cell from almost any part of the plant may produce a protonema under favorable circumstances.

In addition, some mosses regularly produce structures for asexual reproduction. These are small buds, usually—though not necessarily—found on the stem. After being shed, or occasionally even before, they form protonema and develop into plants. In other mosses, and particularly in the liverworts, asexual bodies called *gemmae* (Latin, "buds") are produced. These are single cells or aggregates of cells so highly specific in form that they often are a means of identification. In some mosses sexual reproduction has been abandoned, and the species is propagated entirely in this vegetative manner, even though the plants continue to bear male and female parts! This development has been notable in dioicous species, whose male and female parts may be widely separated and in which the sperm and egg may never meet for lack of the liquid medium which alone makes fertilization possible.

These interesting, diminutive and ancient plants contribute to the balance of nature out of all proportion to their size—and are quite able to maintain and extend their important place in the natural economy.

At Work in Nature's Economy: The Challenge of Dry Land

ALTHOUGH there is argument about whether the bryophytes were the first land plants, there is no doubt that lichens, along with mosses, are today's botanical pioneers in conditions unfavorable to more complex plants. Few lichens are found where other vegetation is richest, flourishing lush and rank; the pioneer work of soil-making lichens is not needed. But where there is no plant cover—for example, when a mountain side has been denuded by floods, frost or wind—all trees and shrubs are carried away with the superficial soil. Nothing remains to tempt other plants to grow on the forbidding rocky base. Then the opening wedge on the uncompromising rock is usually driven by the lichens, carried by the wind, as tiny fragments of plants from some parent growing in a valley far away. They cover the

55

bare cliffs with delicate mats of light green, gray and yellow. They need no soil; the hard rock meets their needs. All green plants do similar work, but not under such seemingly hopeless and primitive conditions.

Linnaeus, in the late eighteenth century, described a succession of plants as follows:

> *Crustaceous lichens are the first foundation of vegetation. Though hitherto we have considered theirs a trifling place among plants, nevertheless, they are of great importance at this first stage in the economy of Nature. When the rocks emerge from the seas, they are so polished by the force of the waves, that scarcely any kind of plant can settle on them. However, the smallest crustaceous lichens begin to cover these arid rocks, and are sustained by minute quantities of soil, and by imperceptible particles brought to them by rain and by the atmosphere. These lichens in time become converted by decay into a thin layer of humus, so that foliose lichens are able to thrust their hyphae into it.*

When lichens start a job of repair work for nature, centuries must pass before finished stages appear. Then the mosses arrive—if, indeed, they have not arrived along with the lichens—and carry on the same action, constantly adding to the mass of plant tissue, beginning to clothe the once bare surface.

Lichens and mosses colonizing an otherwise bare rock

Larger lichens and mosses soon get a foothold where their predecessors have grown. As older plants die and disintegrate, their remains are mingled with the accumulation of crumbled rock. At the same time, wind-borne dust is caught and held by the mosses and lichens. As both add their share to the gathering layer of humus, fern spores carried in by the wind begin to germinate, until they dominate the scene. Thus, patiently, slowly, but as surely as time passes, soil is prepared for higher forms. Dead leaves, stems and branching parts arrest more dust from the air and mud from the water and make of these a soft bed for the next generation. Plants follow a succession, those of one group preparing the way for another. The next vegetation on rocks is made up of grasses, ferns, composites, pinks and other small herbs. (In the water it is made up of pond weeds, hornwort and related plants.) The second generation flourishes in greater abundance than the first, the third more than

Hairy Cap Moss, showing the ground litter that readily builds up about the bases of the plants

the second. Later still, the winged seeds of shallow-rooted trees, conifers, birches and maples gain a foothold and a mountain forest is started.

An anonymous nineteenth-century poet summed up the whole process rather succinctly in this passage:

A small sisterhood of plodding lichens
Wrought on the rock; the sun, the wind and rain,
Helping them gladly till each fissure filled
And fit for planting; mosses came in haste
And strewed small seeds among them, destined they
To clothe the stern old rock with softest verdure
With ferns and flowers, where yet the laboring bee
May find pasture.

The index of a lichen's success is whether it is "dominant," the sole or primary vegetation in a given area. Saxicolous (rock-growing) lichens are almost always dominant plants; they alone being able to colonize bare rock. Such lichens are influenced by the chemical composition of rocks, and also by the physical structure. (Granite, for example, often becomes dotted with circular lichens no larger than small coins, appearing dark gray

The roots of a tree, swaddled in moss and providing the ideal conditions for hardwood seedlings and polypody fern

and zoned with whitish rings: the Coin Lichen, *Crocynia zonata*.) Weathered surfaces are first occupied, but rocks weathering too quickly are almost entirely bare of lichens. The breaking up of the surface gives no time for the formation of either thallus or fruit. Close-grained rocks, such as quartzite, also have a poor lichen flora, the rooting hyphae being rarely able to penetrate and catch hold. But once they attach themselves to the surface of the rock, lichens begin the process of manufacturing their own food, drawing minute amounts of water and carbon dioxide from the air and at the same time beginning the long, gradual process of eroding the rock, particle by particle, preparing a soil on which more highly developed plants can grow. The surface of the rock inhabited by lichens becomes distinctly marked and corroded.

Some foliose species are regarded as rock destroyers, the underlying rock being roughened and gradually broken up into particles by their disintegrating effect. All lichens have the ability to synthesize a number of organic acids of the phenol type. Some of these acids are brightly colored, giving certain lichens a brilliant yellow or orange-red tinge and bitter taste. They may form crystals in the thallus. The chemical structures of nearly 200 lichen acids have been described, and their molecules have been found to have a unique pattern unknown in other plants. Such acids are secreted by the fungal component alone, *but only when it is part of a lichen.* Some acids are specific to certain species, but most are common to groups. The amount of acid varies from 2 to 3 percent to as much as 25 percent of the total solids in some of the Rucellae. Their peculiar chemical structure is presumed to result from some as yet unknown relationship in the mutual metabolism of alga and fungus. Recently the long observed weathering of rocks encrusted with lichens was interpreted by Dr. Carl Axel Wachtmeister of Stockholm as being due to the disintegrating, solvent effect of lichen acids.

Early in this century, Dr. E. Bachman recorded a study of the action of lichens on mica, garnet, quartz and calcareous rocks. Mica and garnet were rapidly decomposed; calcareous rocks were gradually dissolved by lichen action. Quartz, more resistant, was only minutely etched.

Some mosses perform in a similar way: A tuft of common Beard Moss lifted away from the stone upon which it is growing will reveal small corroded depressions around the place where the tiny stems of the colony have been growing. The rhizoids, embedded in loose particles of the rock, have secreted a fluid which tends to disintegrate it further. In this way the moss obtains mineral salts necessary to its growth, and the solid rock is gradually crumbled to dust.

Dr. E. J. Fry, a noted lichenologist, in some ingenious experiments explained the mechanical force exhibited by lichens in the disintegration of rock. She found that films of gelatin spread upon glass and dried, contract and tear away flakes of glass. This was also seen when films of gelatin were dried upon smooth, unwetted pieces of shale. The lichen thallus, when wet, is mucilaginous or gelatinous and on contracting when dry, strips off thin sheets of stone in the same manner as drying gelatin. The rhizines, too, anchoring the under surface of a lichen to the rock, expand as they absorb water from the atmosphere, penetrating crevices and prying away tiny particles. When drying, they contract, peeling off thin layers of rock dust.

Needless to say, the lichen does not discriminate between surfaces laid bare by nature and those sculpted by man. As a result, tombstones and mausoleums are especially prone to lichen damage. Any old cemetery contains gravestones whose engravings have been gradually corroded and rendered unreadable by lichen growth. Valuable stained-glass windows of ancient cathedrals have been damaged as colonizing lichens etched the glass surface; marble, alabaster and Florentine mosaics have been damaged.

It could be said, in fact, that in choosing a place to grow, lichens hardly discriminate at all. True, certain species have become so adapted to a special habitat that they never, or rarely, wander. Maritime lichens, the most specialized of any, grow near saltwater surroundings. They are mainly rock growing; the presence of seawater is the factor of greatest influence on their growth and distribution. Characteristic types grow at various distances from the shore, and at different heights on rock from the shore. They can thus be identified.

But others—called omnicolous—are true vagabonds in the lichen kingdom and settle on any substance affording a foothold: leather, iron, bones, pottery or earth. The "wanderers" are the same in every locality, passing easily from one support to another. Lecanora has been found growing on tar and charcoal. Old bones form a substrate for lichens; no effect of lichens on the bones has been detected. *Xanthoria parietina* (Yellow Wall Lichen) is one of the commonest wandering species. It has been seen on an old cannon lying near water and rusting away. Certain lichens often set up colonies on clinkers from burnt coal. Still other lichens prefer to form communities on bricks or roof tiles; china, earthenware and leather are attractive too; and pasteboard provides a lichen substrate. Lichens have set up colonies on linoleum, India rubber, felt, cloth, silk and various animal excreta. The "wanderers" are quick growers, and probably do not persist long in one area.

Lichens often accelerate their growth rate to take advantage of impermanent environments. Although some of the ground-growing lichens are the fastest growers, they are not commonly dominant. In certain conditions they may gain a permanent footing; in others they are only temporary, easily crowded out. They are generally in close contact with the ground and

Yellow Wall Lichen, *Xanthoria parietina*

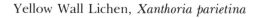

dependent on the nature of the soil and the water content. A calcareous soil attracts specific species, particularly the Lecanora. On siliceous soil there are other specific species, such as Cladonia. Very attractive, the Rosy Crust Lichen (*Baeomyces roseus*) gives a lovely rosy tint to bare stretches of rocky ground after a rain. Gray-green, fluffy lichen growth seen on the ground as "sod flakes," or reaching up on stones, stumps or trees is usually a primary thallus or mat of Cladonia, not identifiable until the vertical growth with stalk, goblets and colored fruits appear.

Sand dune lichens are included in the terricolous (earth-growing) communities, but they really represent communities found near the shore. They are under the influence of salt spray, but not within reach of the tide. Such are sun-loving lichens, and react to the strong light by producing the deep color of the thallus. Specific varieties are seen on shingle formations—a mixture of sand and stones—above the shore.

Mosses too are largely terrestrial; their distribution is governed by the type of soil available. Some authorities divide mosses into calciophiles (calcium-loving mosses) and silicophiles (silica-loving mosses). Mosses have also been classified according to whether they grow in acid, neutral or basic substrate conditions.

Like lichens, some mosses manifest a relationship to the organic content of the soil or to particular kinds of humus. Some may grow only on decayed wood. Certain mosses are termed nitrophiles because they prefer, or are able to tolerate, a very high concentration of nitrogen. These "wandering" bryophytes grow on decaying carcasses (Splachnaceae), on animal dung (Splachnums) or in less nitrogenous circumstances (Taylorias). *Bryum argenteum,* the common weed moss of gardens, is a nitrophile. It has been found to form coatings on hillsides covered with bird dung. Certain mosses and liverworts (Funaria, Leptobryum and Marchantia) grow readily in recently burnt-over areas and are undoubtedly nitrophiles.

Fire and smoke are lichen enemies, however. Lichens do not grow in burnt-over fields or forests, nor do they survive in industrial areas and large cities where man-made substances pollute the atmosphere. During the eighteenth century many lichens were reported and collected in London's Hyde Park and Hampstead Heath; these have long since disappeared. It may be possible to evaluate the degree of air pollution by measuring the abundance of lichens. The sulfur dioxide content in the air can be estimated qualitatively by studying the lichens growing on trees. A ten-point scale has been constructed and used in pilot surveys in England and Wales.*

A number of lichens grow well on dead wood, though none are wholly restricted to such habitats. These might reasonably be called "Dead Wood Communities." On worked wood uncovered by paint, such as old doors or palings, there is often an abundant growth of lichens, many preferring such substrate. Wood fibers loosened by weathering retain moisture and yield some nutrition to the lichen hyphae burrowing among them. Foliose lichens grow prolifically on trees, old roofs and fences, some with a preference for dead twigs of conifers. Some grow best on dead wood, or flourish on trunks of live trees. Scarlet Crested Cladonia (British Soldiers) with its bright red fruiting bodies will grow on trees or rocks, but prefers dead logs or decomposing tree trunks.

Lichens living on dead trees, stumps and decaying organic matter return to the earth and air the very substances that the trees took for their growth years before; they serve this function mainly by virtue of the fungus partner.

Truly arboreal communities are often dominant and represent the sole species of lichen in a given area. Strigula, for instance, an epiphyllous crustose lichen, grows on the foliage of evergreen hardwood trees in the southeastern United States, where it has little competition. In some localities there may be a considerable development of mosses and a mantle of algae on the trees. Most larger lichens are arboreal, though there are exceptions.

A subgroup of the arboreal lichens is called corticolous—that is, growing on bark. The type of lichen growth depends on the physical nature of the bark more than the kind of tree.

---

*Hawksworth, D. L. and Rose F. "Qualitative Scale for Estimating Sulfur Dioxide Air Pollution in England and Wales Using Epiphytic Lichens," *Nature*, 227: 145–148, March, 1970.

Smooth-bark trees such as hazel, beech, lime and younger trees in general, bear only crusty species, many with a very thin thallus, often partially immersed below the surface. As the trees become older and the bark more rugged and irregular, other lichen types gain a foothold, such as the thicker crustose forms or the larger foliose and fruticose species. Moisture collected and retained by the bark is probably the important factor in the establishment of thicker crusts. The rhizines are able to gain a secure grip on the broken, uneven surface, quite impossible on smooth-bark trees. Lichens growing on smooth bark are of particular kinds; those on rough bark are generally of different species. (Bark-growing mosses on the other hand, fall into two categories: those which grow around the base of trees where humus content is high, and those growing on the trunk and branches.)

A few lichens are partial to trees of open, cultivated areas such as parklands or roadsides, but verdant lichen growths are

Above, Puffed Shield Lichen, *Parmelia physodes;* below, Old Man's Beard, *Usnea florida,* two arboreal species

also found on the barks of trees in forests. The profuse spread of lichens is allegedly on the north side of trees, perhaps serving pioneers as a guide through the forest. Emerson's "Wood Notes" records: "The moss upon the forest bark was Pole Star when the night was dark." But actually, this may represent shade-loving lichens' tendency to avoid sunlight. Then, too, more dew tends to accumulate on the cooler north side of trees, and the shape of all lichen growth is influenced by available moisture. Most species grow in a concentric contour, but become eccentric owing to a more vigorous development toward the side of damper exposure. This can be seen in most Umbilicaria species (Rock Tripe). Where the forest grows thicker and moisture is plentiful, lichens will often girdle the whole trunk.

A more practical woodsman's guide is used to estimate the normal depth of snow cover in northern mountainous forested areas by noting the height of growth of certain brown Shield Lichens growing on trees. These are especially sensitive to

Wrinkled Shield Lichen, *Parmelia caperata,* on birchbark

prolonged snow cover and promptly disappear from those parts of the tree covered by snowfalls. Such information is useful in estimating watershed, irrigation potentials and probable snowfalls in mountain passes. It aids in solving railroad and highway engineering problems in regard to location of snow sheds and strategic location of snow fencing.

Orchardists and foresters have tried to prove that lichens damage trees. Though this has never been convincingly established, crusty lichens growing on the bark of trees may burrow with their hyphae among the dead cells of the outer bark, using up the material with which they come in contact. Certain species do have rhizinal hyphae, or rhizoids which penetrate the bark and woody layers of branches, and may inhibit growth. Old trees with thick bark are surely not affected, but as a careful search will show, lichen growth provides shelter for many potentially harmful insects. Taking no chances, European horticulturists often scrape lichens off the barks of citrus trees or spray them with fungicides.

Mosses' and lichens' versatility in their choice of environments is traceable to the fact that these plants "travel light." As a group, lichens have only a very few basic needs, one of which is light. The fungal component of the lichen has no chlorophyll, requires no light and grows very well in partial or total darkness, but the algal component still requires some illumination. Like other plants, lichens are sensitive to changes in illumination, some—as we have seen—being shade plants, others, sun-lovers and able to adapt themselves to varying degrees of light. Certain lichens grow in limestone caves, and in hollows and clefts of rock. As we have seen, lichens growing in forests receive abundant, though diffuse, light—rarely direct illumination. But very few plants remain normal in semidarkness, even though some few can grow in almost total dark.

Lichens growing in full sunlight are usually a darker hue. For instance, *Cetraria islandica* (Iceland Moss) growing in an open situation is darker than the same species growing in woods. The deepening of color is visible on exposed rock lichens and is very pronounced in alpine and tropical species, which grow best on full sun exposure, and whose cortex becomes thicker and more opaque. This thickened cortex checks water loss and is characteristic of desert species exposed to strong light and dry atmosphere. Sun-loving lichens continue to grow in the shade, but the thallus is reduced and the plant may become sterile. It is no surprise then, that many lichens prefer bare rock where there are no plants to overshadow them.

Mosses, more sophisticated, are also more sensitive to illumination. Basically, they are much more shade tolerant than higher plants and algae are even more shade tolerant than mosses. Experimentally, it has been shown that in caves lighted with electricity, ferns will grow nearest the light, the mosses next to them and farthest away, the algae. Two mosses *Tetradontium brownianum* and *Schistostega osmundacea,* are entirely restricted to caves. The atmosphere in caves, however, has a known higher carbon dioxide concentration which may make it possible for mosses to live and grow under dim light.

High humidity and abundant precipitation are conducive to moss growth. Mosses are able to do well on bare ground or under short grasses, but when a good cover of vegetation is established, they are at a considerable disadvantage. Bryophytes are absent on the ground in tropical forests where there is an almost continual falling of dead leaves, although they grow abundantly on the trunks and branches. In forests of the Northeast they are restricted to "islands" of rock or wood which protrude above the inches-deep flood of leaves each autumn. But whenever any change occurs which makes the environment unfavorable to the growth of herbaceous plants, both mosses and lichens are again in a favorable position to prosper. In forests, opening up by thinning or clearing, there follows a wave of growth of tree and ground lichens, previously unable to thrive. Newly planted trees may furnish homes for a new lichen community. The building of houses and walls with mortar attracts a particular species of lime-loving lichens.

If bare soil in a damp climate is temporarily exposed, mosses promptly appear. The sometimes annoying growth of mosses under trees and over lawns is due to the impoverishment of the soil rendering it more favorable for mosses than grasses. Similarly, in the frigid arctic regions a rich moss flora is often found where such belligerent extremes prevail that most vascular plants are excluded.

On the other hand too much light can overheat or dehydrate the moss, which generally prefers a cool environment. The mosses' tolerance for both heat and cold seems to manifest itself best under conditions of low humidity.

Mosses growing on unshaded mountain tops have evolved various devices to protect themselves against the intense light. Like some higher plants, they develop a reddish pigmentation (anthocyanin) which serves to shield the chlorophyll of the leaves. Common mosses which readily develop such pigment are the Grimmia and the Andreaea, which are less brown in shaded than in light-exposed places. Some of the Sphagnum or Peat Mosses develop a deep red color which deepens in proportion to the magnitude of intensity of the sunlight.

Excessive ultraviolet light has an inhibitory effect on the growth of moss plants, and in addition to becoming pigmented, mosses growing in a mountainous area often assume a low or cushion-like growth habit which may be due to this effect—but this low growth may also be a moisture-conserving mechanism. I have seen individual mosses growing partly out of and partly in clefts in rock; shades of color are seen ranging from pale green—the unexposed parts—to deep brown in the moss parts exposed to full sunlight. Another adaptation in mosses growing in light-exposed places is a glass-like, hyaline tip on many moss leaves which functions to reflect the intense rays of the sun away from the leaf. The familiar rolling in of the leaves of the Hairy Cap protects the delicate upper leaf surface, exposing only the brown, horny underparts of the leaf. But even Hairy Caps will die if a dark rock nearby absorbs enough solar energy to grow hot to the touch.

Along with all other plants, mosses and lichens require a certain amount of minerals to supplement their diet of water and carbon dioxide. Mineral substances necessary to lichen growth must be taken up in solution and are absorbed by the same rhizines, or "holdfasts," that absorb water. Crusty lichens growing on rocks may obtain inorganic salts from the mineral substances of the rocks themselves, as the acids loosen minerals for the lichens' nutrition.

Some rock lichens are changed to a rusty red color by infiltration of iron, often from a water medium containing iron salts. But clearly a "wanderer" living on porcelain or bone can draw no sustenance from these supports, or, at most, extremely little. Indeed, the color of "wanderers" that live growing directly on iron is unaffected, proving that the lichens are not getting any significant nourishment from their substrate. But these and other lichens obtain the salts they require from atmospheric dust dissolved in rain and from wind-borne particles deposited on the surface of the thallus, gradually dissolved and finally absorbed by the cortex. Certain lichens, for instance, grow especially well in rookeries of sea birds, where they obtain minerals from the droppings.

Inland Eskimos hunting the hoary marmot locate the burrows in talus slopes by spotting the bright yellow Xanthoria Lichen growing about the entrance, visible over long distances. The lichen's growth is accelerated by the feces and urine of the animals in the area close to the hidden entrance to the burrow.

Mosses, too, benefit from dust that travels through the air—not only along roadsides and in open plains—but also in mountain valleys and even in the ice fields of the north. Alongside a dusty road you will be almost certain to find mosses growing in small tufts. They will probably belong to the genus *Barbula* (Latin for "little beard"). On careful examination, pulling the leaves apart, the remarkable degree to which dust is accumulated and held by the tiny plant will be evident. As the older part of the moss dies, it develops a mucilaginous coat that adds to its tenacity in catching and holding particles of dust. Thus, in a sense, the moss collects its own soil to grow in.

Having fulfilled these two basic demands, mosses and lichens withstand a number of abuses that regularly kill higher forms of vegetation. Winds that cripple or dehydrate larger plants do not affect these smaller plants giving them an enormous advantage on the windswept barrens that are their favorite home.

The flat-growing crusty or leafy lichens are the least liable to wind injury. Their close adherence to their substrate, trees or rocks, shelters them. When wind carries sand, however, the tree or rock surfaces are swept bare of lichens. The terribly cold, high-velocity winds that blow round the North and South poles can be fatal to lichens that are not provided with a special protective cortex. Among these arctic species, the Cetraria and Cladonia are best fitted for weathering windstorms. Upright fruticose lichens are more liable to wind damage, but species like Ramalina and Roccellae don't suffer in temperate climates near the seashores.

The effect of wind on dissemination of soredia as well as thallus fragments is an important aspect of lichen propagation. It has been observed that lichens growing in open country are more abundant on the side of the trees that face prevailing winds; it may be that the soredia are more naturally carried to that side by the wind. On California coasts, a large and frequent species, *Ramalina reticulata,* is seldom found undamaged. The deciduous oaks are festooned by this lichen while the evergreen live oak, with persistent foliage, bears only scraps that have been blown onto it. Near the coast and southward the lichen grows on all kinds of trees and shrubs. (Lichens growing on the branches of trees do not long continue when the branches fall to the ground. This may be due to lack of light and air.) The fronds of Ramalina form a delicate reticulation and, when moist, are easily torn. In the winter, when leaves are off the trees, wind and rainstorms are frequent, and the lichen is exposed to the full force of the elements. Fragments and shreds are blown to other trees, becoming coiled and entangled in the naked branches and stumps on which they continue to grow and fruit. The next storm loosens and carries them still further. Branches of trees are often covered with tangled masses of lichens, not due to local growth but to wind-borne strands, and to coiling and intertwining of filaments owing to successive wetting and drying. It is thought that wind velocities of 77 miles per hour are not sufficient to cause pieces of lichen to fly off when they are dry. After soaking in water, the first pieces are torn off as the wind reaches a velocity of 50 miles an hour.

One observer thought these figures too high: Since evaporation occurs rapidly and thoroughly in high wind, it was found impossible to keep up the condition of saturation in experimental, artificially created wind. But in nature, of course, rain often accompanies gale-force winds, and thus it is the proper saturating combination of wind and rain that is obviously so very effective in ensuring the dispersal of these lichens.

The wind's influence on moss spore dissemination is, of course, of extreme importance. Very light in weight and small in size, moss spores may be air-borne great distances, or be carried in rain and snow. They even may be transported by avalanches!

If mosses and lichens will grow as long as their substrates remain unshaded, it would seem that the rock-growing communities would be the most long-lived of all. But this is not always the case. After a time, even the species of lichens growing on rocks begin to change. Some are naturally more vigorous and faster growing than others; the weaker, slower growing plants succumb. Crusty species are most subject to failure in this struggle for existence. Particles of their thallus are easily dislodged and bare places left, which in time are colonized again by the same lichen or some invading species. There may be a bewildering mosaic of different thalli and fruits

Common Twig Lichen, *Ramalina calicaris,* a tree-dweller

growing together in a rock-lichen community. This interspersion of lichens is readily seen, particularly on an especially "choice" rock face where light and moisture are plentiful. When mosses are added to such a competition, it becomes obvious that the rapidly growing plant has distinct survival advantage. Certain instances of association between mosses and lichens have shown that one or the other may simply overgrow, spreading over everything in its path—decaying mosses, dead leaves and other lichens. Some plants may overgrow other lichens and use up their substance as food material, but then a few lichens grow over and parasitize certain mosses!

A striking—and important—exception to such quick succession exists in the polar regions. As we have seen, lichens endure extreme cold even better than heat, but to do so, they dry up, lower their metabolism and assume a state of latent vitality. Severe cold slows lichen growth drastically. Here, a single plant may lie unchanged for decades.

Fruticose lichens, for example, grow apically, with continuous decomposition of the basal portion. Theoretically they have

Hairy Cap mosses growing in and among the sod flakes of Frayed Lichen

the power of unlimited growth though they rarely exceed eight inches in height. In arctic temperatures especially, lichens decompose very slowly due to slow decay and slowed biological processes; also the presence of lichen acids delays the action of saprophytic microorganisms in the soil. Below the living parts, the undecayed old growth of Cladonia species forms layers of "white" peat representing the accumulation of centuries.

On Axel Heiberg Island, located on the rim of the Arctic Ocean's permanent ice pack, 500 miles from the North Pole, the Jacobsen-McGill Arctic Research Expedition is using a technique devised by Dr. Roland Beschel to estimate the rate of retreat of glaciers. Beschel, of Queen's University, Kingston, Ontario, first conceived his idea while a young botany student at Innsbruck, Austria. With a magnifying glass he studied lichens growing on old tombstones in an Innsbruck cemetery. The lichens, spreading out in a thin crusty mat, grow very slowly on bare rock as soon as they are exposed to sunshine. Some require centuries to grow a few inches, and each species grows at a standard rate depending on the climate. The dates on tombstones indicate when the lichen growth began and the rate of growth can thus be determined. Further studies on old Greenland cemeteries allowed him to determine rates of growth for arctic lichen species.

Dr. Beschel is studying the lichens on rocks in front of Axel Heiberg glaciers. Glaciers function like monstrous bulldozers, pushing great masses of rock and earth—moraines—before them. The moraine farthest in front of the glacier indicates the point of its maximal advance.

The moraines of Iceberg Glacier, Axel Heiberg's largest, showed that the glacier front had moved back about three miles. In studying lichens growing on rocks three miles in front of Iceberg Glacier, Dr. Beschel found one small yellow and black lichen called Rhizocarpon, growing in rosettes never more than two inches across. Another species, Lecidea, a silver-gray lichen, produced growths five inches across. By applying growth-rate information he had acquired in Austria and Greenland, he determined that these creeping lichen plants had begun their slow growth about the year 1600. This is estimated as the date the glacier began to retreat, exposing the rocks in front of it and allowing the lichens to colonize and grow. Three and a half centuries passed since the glacier began to recede.

For medium-sized White Glacier, Beschel found quite a different story. Here he noted 2,000-year-old lichens just a dozen yards in front of the ice, showing that White Glacier had moved little in twenty centuries. This technique, if proved as useful as it now seems, coupled with other methods of estimating glacier and ice cap age and rates of movement, may provide very important scientific data regarding the earth's past and development and recession of the four known Ice Ages.

Quaking Bogs,
Peat Mosses and Liverworts

It is ironic that tiny plants perfectly adapted to survive drought should be in large part responsible for the creation, maintenance and altering of sizable bodies of water. But on mountain peaks or in valleys, lichen-covered soil collects the rainfall and, along with mosses, helps prevent excessive quantities of water from pouring down the mountainsides. Above timberline in the Rocky Mountains one may find, in depressions, extensive patches of bog moss (Sphagnum) and Reindeer Lichen (*Cladonia rangiferina*). These appear perfectly crisp and dry on the surface; yet in their matted underparts, they retain so much water that a slight downward pressure produces a trickle of perfectly clear water. The source of many brooks and streams may be traced to such an over-saturated bed in a mountain

75

forest. According to F. W. Holiday, smaller rivers which fall into Scotland's Loch Ness "are subject to the usual wide variations in volume-flow and temperature which are the lot of all rain-fed streams rising in the mosses of the Scottish Highlands. These rivers vary almost hourly." Just the weight of air is often enough to release moisture from the saturated mass: "The prevailing barometric pressure appears to have an effect on the flow delivered to the head-springs."

A native example of this kind of lichen work may be found today on Mount Marcy in New York State, 5,344 feet above sea level. The rock of the summit is variously colored by lichens growing on an otherwise naked surface. The rock beneath the lichen growths is more soft and scaly than elsewhere; spaces between the lower stem and leaves of the moss tufts are filled with accumulations of dirt and sand. The soil in most places is only a few inches deep and is composed of decayed vegetable matter. The only plants seen here are those mosses and lichens capable of surviving this unfavorable environment. Active soil making is still going on.

Further down the mountain there are two small marshy areas containing plants growing in soil that could have been produced only by the local mosses and lichens. The water in these marshes is supplied by rainfall and melting snows from the rocks above. A few higher species have invaded the area, but they are dependent on the lichens and mosses for their existence.

There is only one of the larger lichens that adopted a purely aquatic habitat, *Hydrothyria venosa,* North American Lichen. It grows on rocks in the beds of streams, often covering them with a thick felt. But other mosses and lichens derive important advantages from their proximity to running water—and not only the assurance of abundant moisture.

Lichens growing near streams or on boulders are subject to constant overflow of water and obtain inorganic materials from the water.

On limestone rocks near Niagara Falls and in some other places, there may be found mosses that obtain carbon dioxide from the decomposition of bicarbonate of lime dissolved in the water. As the lime is precipitated it encrusts the leaves and stems of the mosses until their lower parts are totally embedded. As these embedded lower parts die off, the plants go on growing at the tips. In this way banks of calcareous substance are formed, which have been known to reach a height of forty-eight feet, and in which it is estimated that mosses have been at work for 2,000 years. The water-loving mosses are capable of arresting and maintaining large quantities of the mud and fine sand carried by the rush of a moving stream. Once again, the tendency of the dead membranes to swell and become mucilaginous explains the effectiveness of this brake on erosion.

The foliage of one species, found in turbulent waters, becomes so impregnated with mud that only the tips of the leaf-bearing stems can be seen above the gray accumulated mass.

Hygroamblystegium irriguum, one of the water-loving Cedar Mosses (the specific name means "water-loving"), is a small moss ranging from dark green to black in color, that clings to rocks in streams and becomes so conglomerated with mud and sand that it cannot be freed of them until after it has been thoroughly dried and shriveled. Even after being completely washed it remains harsh and gritty to the touch. Streams in relatively level terrain are continually being diverted from their meandering courses by the conglomeration of debris that is the result of the action of mosses in arresting mud and sand. A pond may have its outlet so choked in this way that new outflow channels must be cut. An arm or bay may be sealed off, or a small lake divided into two by the accumulation of sand and silt held together at first by mosses and eventually anchored by the growth of shrubs and trees.

More widespread, and no less remarkable, is the work of the bog or peat mosses in reclaiming shallow water for the reestablishment of higher land plants.

Peat bogs occur mainly in the cooler parts of the Northern Hemisphere, especially in Ireland and northern Europe. The work of bog mosses may also be observed at high altitudes, for example, in the Shawangunk Mountains of New York, the Poconos of Pennsylvania and the Green Mountains of Vermont. The "peat" mosses are among the largest of the bryophytes, and are usually gray-green in color. A few interesting types are gray, dark red, yellow and even purple. They grow profusely over wide areas in swamp-like places in valleys or in declivities on mountain summits, changing colors with the change in humidity.

The plants on the surface of a peat moor grow at the top, dying away below. Thus, the tips and growing parts are really parts of the same plants whose underparts died away long ago. The peat moss soon loses any root-like part and grows year after year from the apex of the stem or from branches below the apex.

As the floating mat of dead stems grows and multiplies along the edges of a body of water, it extends further out over the water—a floating raft anchored to the shore. Dead parts of the moss are continually dropping off and disintegrating into the bottom of the pond or bog, and the moss raft gradually sinks as its weight increases—so gradually, however, that new growth usually remains just above the surface of the water. Leaves,

Fresh, wet specimens of Common Peat Moss, *Sphagnum squarrosum*. These plants are so different from their fellow bryophytes that many specialists don't consider them mosses at all

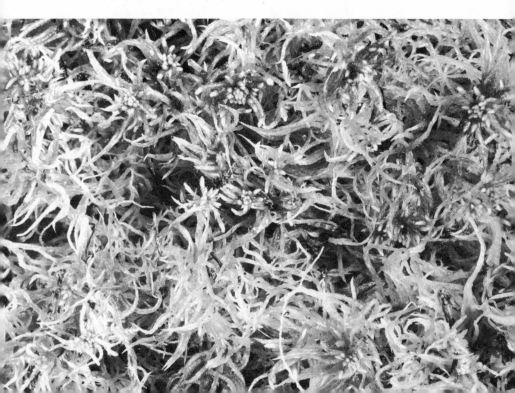

sticks and other vegetable matter wash in among the decaying stems. This process tends to pull the floating raft downward toward the gathering accumulation of vegetable debris on the bottom in which leaves, twigs and other plant remains mingle with those of the moss plants. Finally, the moss raft becomes thick—or deep—enough to reach all the way to the bottom. The weight of the mass on top and the decomposition in dead plant tissue convert the older moss plants into a solid, black compact substance that is burned as peat. Its combustibility as fuel depends upon the purity of the carbon produced over thousands of years of gradual decay.

As the margin of the peat moss raft extends outward from the shore toward the center of a pond, new plants continue to develop along the shoreline, sinking to form new soil and causing the water to become gradually shallower until the pond disappears altogether. One stage of this process produces what is known as a "quaking bog." It occurs when the moss has entirely covered the surface of the water, but has not completely filled in the bottom with debris. In the spongy mass of decomposing vegetation thus formed, a man may sink and be unable to rise again—whence the evil reputation that surrounds peat bogs generally. Ultimately, when the peat bog is completely filled in and built up enough for drainage, grasses move in and a meadow grows over the solid peat bed.

Peat bogs do not always turn themselves into meadows, however. Just as they carry the soil-building process inward toward the center, peat mosses may also grow outward from the water's edge, extending the marshy perimeter as the moss plants soak up water and invade the once solid ground, climbing slopes adjacent to the shoreline, carrying the marshy land up a hill. The marsh can absorb tremendous quantities of water, and as new mosses appear in the dead growth, the water-saturated remains of the dead plants form a secondary bog on the shore adjacent to the water's edge.

More than just ancient mosses have been recovered from such bogs. Tremendous logs have been dug out of peat bogs in excellent condition. The past two centuries have seen the recovery of about seven hundred human corpses from peat bogs in northwestern Europe. Because of a mildly antiseptic quality (acid formed as a by-product of decay) peat tends to act as a preservative. This was emphasized in May of 1950, by the discovery in Denmark of a number of peat-interred bodies believed to date to the Bronze Age—3,000 years ago. Other corpses in the same bog apparently dated to the Iron Age, at least 2,000 years ago—about the dawn of the Christian Era. The corpses showed remarkably little dessication, although the skin had been dyed dark brown by the surrounding peat. One male body was found curled up, resting on its side as if asleep—the facial expression could still be made out—eyes peacefully closed, but a quirk of irritation about the mouth. A noose of braided leather had been drawn tightly about his neck—strong evidence that the victim had not entered the bog either by accident or by his own free choice. He was unclothed except for a cap and belt, both of which were remarkably well preserved. It is surmised that this man, and most of the others whose remains were found in the same region, had been brought to the bog as a spring sacrifice in honor of a goddess of fertility, whose cult was widespread in prehistoric times.

The Tollund Man, who owes his remarkable state of preservation to burial in a peat bog, still bears the cap and noose with which he was strangled

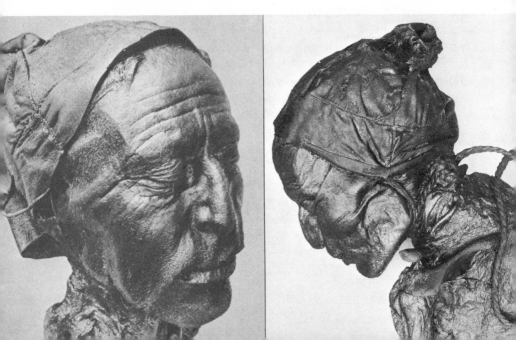

Criminals were once executed in the same manner, as is recorded by the Roman historian Tacitus. Writing shortly before A.D. 100, Tacitus remarked of the German tribes:

Traitors and deserters are hanged on trees; cowards, shirkers, and the unnaturally vicious are drowned in miry swamps under a cover of wattled hurdles. The distinction in the punishment implies that deeds of violence should be paid for in the full glare of publicity, but that deeds of shame should be suppressed.

There is a tradition that the body of King Abel, who died in 1252 and was buried in Schleswig Cathedral, would not lie quiet because he was guilty of murdering his brother. His body was disinterred and reburied in a peat bog near Gottorp, with a stake run through it to prevent his uneasy ghost from causing any further disturbance.

Besides being used in its decomposed and compacted form as fuel, peat moss has also been put to use as packing material—about the roots of live plants—and sometimes also for crockery—and is mixed with garden soil to increase the humus.

Laboratory frogs are often kept in a tank with a layer of damp Sphagnum. Other mosses are often used to pack moisture-loving live things, and while these species may not be preferable to Sphagnum, they may be more plentiful—and hence economical. In the western United States three mosses—*Neckera menziesii, Alsia abietine, Antitricha californica*—have been utilized as packing materials for vegetables. Leeches have been packed and shipped in *Hypnum tamariscinum*.

Botanical taxonomists commonly place the liverworts in the class Hepaticae, and the hornworts or horned liverworts in a separate class, Anthocerotae. As distinguished from the true mosses (Musci), however, they may be considered in three groups: the thallose liverworts, the leafy liverworts or scale mosses, and the horned liverworts or hornworts.

Thallose liverworts are conspicuously branched or lobed. Each division of the thallus is in two more or less symmetrical branches. Riccia is a common example; growing on moist ground, it often takes the form of a rosette.

Plants of the genus *Marchantia,* named in honor of a French botanist, are more complicated in structure. The thallus forms a broad, branching ribbon, anchored to the surface by many rhizoids. The upper surface is marked by diamond-shaped divisions, each with a chimney-like pore opening into an air chamber at its center. The side walls of each air chamber support the epidermis. On the floor of each air chamber are cells containing chlorophyll, whose function is to assimilate the gases entering through the pore, and to make possible the storage and transmission of food. *Marchantia polymorpha* (Latin, "many forms") is a widely distributed species. It may be found along wet stream banks, in swamps, often intermingled with mosses, in greenhouses, or in damp ashes remaining after a fire.

Abundant moisture also helps liverworts to retain the algal method of sexual reproduction. Sexual reproduction in Marchantia is carried on by male and female plants bearing antheridia and archegonia respectively. The male receptacles are stalked dish-like structures with scalloped edges; the antheridia are embedded in the upper surface. Early in their development the antheridia appear as rounded projections; later they are raised on tiny stalks. The female receptacles are also elevated on stalks and bear finger-like lobes, usually nine in number, around the margin, and resemble miniature umbrellas. The archegonia each containing an egg, develop in sections, al-

Close-up of a typical liverwort, *Marchantia polymorpha*

ternating with the rays, on the under surface of the receptacle.

In Marchantia, unlike some more highly developed bryophytes, fertilization occurs before the setae of the receptacles
begin to elongate. Rain or dew causes the antheridia to burst at
the apex, and the sperms are carried by the moisture to the
vicinity of the archegonia. With the union of sperm and egg, an
embryo begins to develop, eventually forming a spore case
whose contents are differentiated to produce spore mother
cells.

The spore mother cells are arranged in vertical rows, and
they undergo reduction-division to form haploid spores. As
they develop, elaters—slender, elongated threads with spirally
thickened inner walls—also take form. Next, cells lying between
the foot and the spore case divide rapidly to produce a seta,
which elongates, causing the enlarged archegonium to rupture.
The spore case then dries and opens, releasing a loose, cottony
mass of spores to be carried by the wind. It is the function of
the elaters to help in this process. As a result of their extremely
hygroscopic structure, they twist and coil as they dry, and their
abrupt, jerking movements propel the spores into the air. In

A colony of liverworts, *Marchantia polymorpha,* with the in-
evitable moss plants taking advantage of the moist conditions

the following season the spores germinate to produce a new generation of plants.

Marchantia, like many other genera of liverworts, also reproduces vegetatively. As the plant spreads over the soil, older parts gradually die away. Whenever this dying away occurs at the base of a fork in the thallus, the two branches become separate individuals. Under the conditions of a greenhouse, as well as in the open, Marchantia may exhibit yet another mode of reproduction—namely, by gemmae or brood bodies which are capable of developing into new plants without fertilization. Under a hand lens the gemmae may be seen as tiny discs, borne in small round cups with toothed margins.

Like all other bryophytes, Marchantia exhibits what is known as the alternation of generations. The thallus is produced by the germination of a spore, and bears antheridia and archegonia, as well as gemmae whenever they are present. This is the gametophyte generation. The spore case, seta and foot, which develop from the fertilized egg, constitute the sporophyte generation. The gametophyte may reproduce itself by gemmae or by fragmentation; the sporophyte, on the other hand, comes only from the union of male and female germ cells.

The largest of the thallose liverworts, *Conocephalum conicum* (Latin, "cone-shaped head"), commonly grows on moist earth or rocks, and may cover an area of several square feet. The pores are considerably larger than those of Marchantia, and the thallus is fleshier. When crushed, it gives off a pleasantly spicy aroma. The conical, spore-producing umbrella appears only in spring—usually late April and May—when the spores ripen.

Riccia frostii is a common and widespread thallose liverwort. Its close, forking habit of growth tends to form rosettes. When the plants are numerous and crowded, the rosettes merge into irregular mats. This species occurs along streams and roadside banks.

In the northeastern states liverworts of the genus Riccia persist through the winter. They are often seen in stagnant ponds or in moist, muddy places. *Riccia fluitans* (Latin, "floating") forms its branching ribbons in the shallow water of ponds, swamps and slow-moving streams, where it is often tangled with mosses. Its ribbons, which measure about 1/8 inch across and one or two inches in length, float or hang suspended in the water, where they may form intertangled mats. This species usually displays no rhizoids and no reproductive organs, except when the water subsides and the plant is left stranded. Then it develops both rhizoids and spores.

The leafy liverworts, commonly known also as scale mosses, comprise the largest of the three groups. They grow in profuse mats or carpets on damp soil, rotten logs, or the trunks or branches of trees. The plant body is dorsiventral—i.e., having a distinct upper and lower surface, and grows along an axis in the form of leaf-like expansions. These are entirely without a midrib, are frequently cleft or divided into lobes, and with few exceptions, grow in two flat rows, one on either side of the stem. In some species a third rank of leaves may develop from the under surface.

Liverworts of this group resemble the true mosses much more closely than those of the thallose group, and may be confused with them. A close look at the vegetative structure of a leafy liverwort, however, will make the difference clear: True mosses are radially symmetrical with leaves attached all around the stem, a pattern found in none of the leafy liverworts.

The reproductive organs of a leafy liverwort appear on the upper surface of the thallus. Antheridia arise at the base; the archegonia more commonly at the tip of a leaf. The antheridia—which are not easy to see—are spherical, borne on short stalks opposite a leafy tuft that is a lighter green than the rest of the leaves. The archegonia are borne on very short branches and are usually cylindrical at maturity.

The young sporophyte consists of a foot, a seta and a capsule which splits into four valves or sections. It is usually enclosed in a protective case from which it emerges at maturity.

The scale moss or leafy liverwort *Frullania eboracensis* forms pleasing traceries of dark brownish-green on the bark of beech and birch trees. It is a plant at once so common and so striking in appearance that further description is hardly needed. The details of the tiny, inflated-looking leaves can readily be made out with a hand lens. Another common and closely related species may be found growing on rocky surfaces.

Porella platyphylla (Latin, "flat leaf") perhaps best typifies the leafy hepatic or scale moss. It differs from Frullania in being larger, and is also usually more noticeably green in color. The plant consists of branching projections at right angles to the recumbent stem, which they often overlap so as to conceal it. The side branches may branch in turn, and the margins may be toothed, fringed, curved, or rolled inward, with an apex that may be either blunt or pointed. Porella may form a thin mat or a thick cushion. The younger growth covers a thatch of the older parts, which die and fall away in the absence of light. The largest of the leafy hepatics, Porella has a remarkable ability to resist drying, and quickly revives after long periods of drought.

Radula complanata, which is as common as Porella, grows in dark green mats on walls, stones and the roots of trees. The leaf is two-lobed, but there are no under-leaves. The rhizoids project from the lobes, rather than from the stem as in most bryophytes. The capsules can be easily seen with a hand lens.

Bazzania trilobata (Latin, "three-lobed") is another of the larger members of the group. It commonly grows in cool, moist ravines, woods and swamps; in New England it forms a soft green mat over stones, earth or old logs. The ascending stems are from two to five inches long and bear leaves that are oblong in shape and three-pronged at the apex, as the specific name suggests. The size of the plant varies a good deal with the circumstances of growth. In favorable conditions Bazzania may form mats as large as two feet in diameter.

Other species of leafy hepatics show further variations, but they should be identifiable from the characteristics they share with these common examples.

The hornworts or horned liverworts are the least numerous of the three groups. The best known, belonging to the genus *Anthoceros,* grows commonly on damp soil. The thallus is small, lobed and circular, with no suggestion of either stem or leaf. Male and female sex organs are borne on the thallus, where they are deeply embedded in the plant tissue. The sporophyte develops from the fertilized egg into a tapering, spike-like spore case borne an inch or more above the surface of the thallus. At the base of the capsule, and extending downward to the deeply embedded foot, is a sheath formed from the tissues of the thallus. At maturity the capsule splits into two valves, releasing the spores.

Anthoceros laevis is very common throughout the continent, and is most frequently found growing on damp soil. The wholly leafless thallus is small, lobed and approximately circular. The pod-like, usually erect, much elongated spore case opens into two valves, disclosing the spores within.

Liverworts have few uses, particularly today when the Doctrine of Signatures is no longer in vogue. (See Chapter VIII.)

Leafy liverworts are used to pack living plants in the tropics, but only because they are common and plentiful. The plant's extremely moist, fleshy nature makes it difficult to preserve, and its requirements would make it hard to cultivate commercially, even if there were any reason to do so. Most likely the liverworts will remain an intriguing subject for the student botanist and a bane to the professional florist.

"Wretched Food in Barbarous Countries"

BACK in prehistoric time a wooly mammoth made a meal out of a small portion of cold Siberian tundra. Shortly thereafter he became entombed in ice. Thousands of years later he was removed and his well preserved body was sent to the Natural History Museum in Paris. The contents of the stomach were examined and fragments of three mosses—Hairy Cap and two species of Hypnum—were recovered, the earliest known instance of mosses used as food.

In addition to nourishing other, higher plants by their organic remains, lichens and mosses provide foodstuffs for a wide spectrum of the animal kingdom, up to and including man himself. First in "line," of course, are the bacteria and one-celled organisms who habitually prey on plant tissue, living or dead.

The next higher class of enemies these small plants have to deal with are the insects and land molluscs that, next to the lichens themselves, are among the most ubiquitous of living things.

Dr. George A. Llano, one of America's most distinguished lichenologists, reported that several invertebrates—mites, caterpillars, earwigs, snails, slugs and black termites—have been known to feed partly or wholly on lichens. An interesting minor series of scientific experiments regarding the feeding of such invertebrates was reported by Annie L. Smith. Some workers reported that the lichen acids shielded the plants against attacks by animals, but a series of experiments with snails disproved this hypothesis. Offered slices of potato smeared with pure lichen acids, the snails readily ate the potato. The crystals of the acids passed unchanged through the alimentary canal of the snails, and were found in masses in the excreta. Another worker reported that snails and caterpillars consume most lichens with impunity, and that the bitter taste attracts rather than repels them. Large slugs have been seen devouring a bitter crustaceous lichen "with great satisfaction." How a slug shows satisfaction is not clear—perhaps with a smile.

Indeed, snails do not eat lichens when they are dry and hard; but on damp or dewy nights and rainy days, all kinds of snails, both large and small, emerge from their shells and devour lichen thalli softened by moisture. Amusingly, one worker reported that a certain gelatinous lichen was unharmed by snails. The slippery surface of the molluscs' own "feet" prevented them from getting a foothold on the thallus. These lichens do not contain acid, and if dried and reduced to powder, are "eagerly eaten" by both snails and wood lice, according to the study.

Mites, wood lice and caterpillars (also many butterflies) live on lichens, though with the exception of caterpillars, they eat them only when moist. Certain moth caterpillars not only feed on lichens, but take on the color of the lichen they affect, either in the larval or in the moth stage. This protective resemblance to lichens makes them extremely difficult to detect. There are several perfect examples of such mimicry, in which moths have been found at rest on lichen-covered bark, from which they can hardly be distinguished. Robert Browning knew of this protective coloration as shown in his "By the Fireside" where he referred to "boulder stones where lichens mock the marks on a moth"; he also appreciated *Cladonia cristatella*.

Another lichen study was reported by Paulson and Thompson (quoted by Annie L. Smith):

> *Mites of the family* Oribatidae *must be reckoned among the chief foes of these plants upon which they feed, seeming to have a special predilection for the ripe fruits. We have had excellent specimens of* Xanthoria parietina *spoiled by hidden mites of this family, which have eaten out the contents of the mature fruits after the lichens have been gathered. One can sometimes see small flocks of the mites browsing upon the thallus of tree dwelling lichens, like cattle in a meadow.*

Some theorists have gone so far as to "explain" the abundance of lichens in arctic regions by citing the scarcity of snails and insects to interfere with the normal and continuous growth of these plants. However, this is certainly far from established fact.

Though insignificant in size, lichens are important as forage plants for wild as well as domesticated animals in the arctic and subarctic regions. This is because of their massive accumulation under special conditions, where other plants cannot survive. Late in winter, animals eat lichens for want of better fodder. *Usnea barbata,* one of the Old Man's Beard lichens, for instance, is a famine food for northern white-tailed deer. On over-browsed ranges Usnea is often completely cleaned out as high as the animals can obtain it on the trees. When trees are felled, however, tame deer feed on this same lichen.

Mosses, for the most part, are depleted by birds and browsing mammals (such as the wooly mammoth mentioned at the beginning of this chapter). When insects are scarce in Colorado streams, rainbow trout eat several algae and mosses. Capsules of Bryum and Hairy Cap form an important part of the food of Norwegian grouse chicks. Scottish red grouse are fond of capsules of moor-inhabitating mosses, and Wyoming sage grouse include small amounts of moss in their diet. Snow buntings eat capsules of *Bryum pendulum,* and probably other mosses, often depleting the food supply in certain areas of Scandinavia. The moorhen, blackbird, song thrush and the fieldfare all eat mosses.

Man makes essentially no use of mosses as food. Even though Laplanders have used Sphagnum as an ingredient in the composition of bread, the use of Sphagnum is described in an ancient medical and economic botany book as a "wretched food in barbarous countries." Peat moss is included in the list of famine foods published in China. Dr. A. J. Grout thought spore-filled capsules of Hairy Cap might be eaten by a person starving in the wilderness.

Lichens, however, have been used for human consumption as far back as history goes. Prehistoric remains near Lake Constance in Switzerland at the Abbey of Schussenried provide some proof of use of lichens in antiquity. Under successive beds of peat and crumbly-turf, there was discovered a layer, three feet thick, containing flints, reindeer antlers, bones of various animals and, along with these, masses of Reindeer Lichens.

Archeological studies of Norse remains in Greenland disclosed an abnormal wearing of teeth as compared with present-day Eskimo skulls. This suggests that in the latter period of settlement the inhabitants may have subsisted on lichens or seaweed.

Lichens, with few exceptions, are nonpoisonous, but just how appetizing a lichen can be depends on the species and how it is prepared. Some serious study has been made of lichen food value, and the results vary widely from one kind to another. Some lichens have cellulose, but the nutritive value of lichens as fodder is due to substances synthesized in the thallus. The principal nutrient substance is the carbohydrate, lichenin; proteins are present in 0.5 to 3.0 percent, and fats, 1 to 2 percent amounts. Vitamin C is found in most lichens, and Vitamins B and G in certain lichens of Alaska. Reindeer Lichen contains more Vitamin D than other lichens, but the content is very low compared to yeast and molds. Most lichens are poor in minerals, though certain minerals have been noted in lichens, in special habitats, not ordinarily occurring elsewhere. In the western United States, selenium (in quantities sufficient to poison sheep and cattle) has been reported. Beryllium was detected in *Parmelia saxatilis* (one of the Boulder Lichens) and *Xanthoria parietina* (the Yellow Wall Lichen).

The starch, lichenin, is the most important component. It is a cellulose-like complex of sugar molecules. Isolichenin is a starch-like complex sugar, occurring with lichenin, and differs from it in that it is easily soluble in cold water and stains blue with iodine, as does starch. Lichenin itself is soluble in hot water and gives a colloidal solution easily hydrolyzed by dilute acid to yield ordinary glucose.

It is the starch, of course, that makes lichens desirable as food for man and beast alike. (It is probable that wild animals digest the cellulose of lichens by bacteria in their digestive system, rather than with their own enzymes.) A crusty lichen once called "Earth Bread" by the Kirghiz Tartars contains starch enough to serve as human food. (Curd Lichen, *Lecanora subfusca,* another of the Earth Bread lichens, is found throughout the United States on mountain rock at high elevations.) Ancient Egyptians ground up lichens for flour in bread-

Curd Lichen, *Lecanora subfusca (N.Y. State Museum and Science Service)*

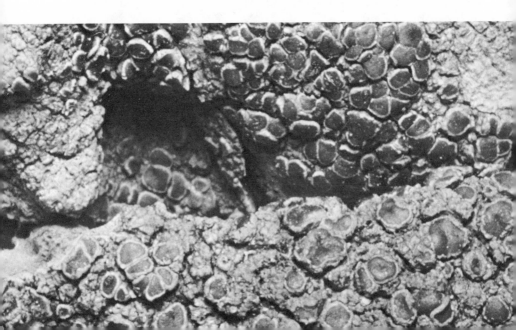

making, and years ago in Sweden people made bread of Reindeer Lichen flour. But balancing out this positive quality are the lichen's acids, all of which have a bitter taste and some of which have proven quite irritating to the intestine.

Where low-acid lichens and imaginative (or hard-pressed) cooks abound, lichens have been served as a delicacy.

The Central Eskimo of northern Canada is said to eat lichens found in the stomach contents of caribou and musk ox; this half-digested mass is taken as a treat, as warm food immediately after the hunt or frozen for later use. It may be the only source of plant food for many high arctic Eskimos.

In Japan certain species of Rock Tripe are a gourmet item and sold as "Iwatake" or "rock mushroom." The market price is high. In India one of the Parmelia is used as food and medicine; it is prepared as a curry powder and called "Rathipuvvu."

Ernest Thompson Seton, famous author and naturalist, describes the preparation of Rock Tripe:

> *First gather and wash it as clear as possible of sand and grit, washing it again and again, snipping off the gritty parts where it held on to the Mother rock. Then roast slowly in a pan till dry and crisp. Next boil it for one hour and serve it either hot or cold. It looks like thick gumbo soup with short, thick pieces of black and green leaves in it. It tastes a little like tapioca with a slight flavoring of licorice.*

Another similarly behaving and edible lichen is the Lung Lichen (*Lobaria pulmonaria*) so called because its pitted surface resembles that of a normal human lung. This foliose lichen is not encrusted to the bark where it grows but clings lightly to its support. On drying it curls up its white under surface to protect the gray-green upper mat.

Dr. Edward Tuckerman, a famous lichenologist, described a by-product of the Lung Lichen as a "yellow, nearly insipid mucilage which may be eaten with salt."

In early Scandinavian literature, recipes are found for preparation of lichens for human use. Iceland Moss, *Cetraria islandica,* whose erect, leaf-like growth habit gives it the appearance of moss, was long a source of food in Iceland, Norway and Sweden. It probably ranks first as human lichen food. It is pale or grayish-brown when moist but light gray when dry; pleasant and nourishing to eat. It contains about 70 percent lichen starch. Some have said it contains more starch than potatoes and more good food than oatmeal. Iceland Moss prevents a form of scurvy known as Iceland Scurvy; in fact, vitamin C has been detected in the lichens. In a few seasons of scarcity, the poorer people of Iceland have had little else to eat. In Norway B. Lynge quoted a tradition "that there was no starvation at Modun in 1812 as long as there was bread moss (Bröd-mose) left in the forest."*

In preparing it for the table Iceland Moss is first boiled to remove foreign material as well as the bitter taste. It is then dried, crushed to a powder and made into cakes or bread, or boiled with milk to form a jelly. It is the basis of various light and easily digested soups and other delicacies. It can be made into bread, porridge or gruel (recipes follow). It is often mixed with mashed potato and cereals. It can also be made into candy by mixing the hardened jelly of Iceland Moss with lemon juice, sugar, chocolate and almonds.

---

*Smith, A. L., Presidential address. "The relation of fungi to other organisms." *British Mycological Society Transactions,* 6:17–31, 1918.

A top view of the Lung Lichen, *Lobaria pulmonaria*

The lichen powder was often mixed with ship's flour, making the bread less friable and less subject to weevil attack. It has long been considered a food and tonic for convalescents.

To make porridge, a cooking container is filled with one-third Iceland Moss and water; the mixture is boiled three or four times and stirred frequently until thick. Top broth is skimmed off and the rest is salted to taste. This may be allowed to cool and harden, and is eaten with milk as a cereal.

"A gruel is made with one pound of finely cut lichen; add 1½ to 2 quarts of water; cook slowly until half the water is evaporated; strain while hot and flavor with raisins or cinnamon. After boiling and separating the broth, the residue is eaten with oil, yellow of egg and sugar as a salad, and the most pretentious person will like it."*

More often, however, lichens appear on the record as famine food. In northern Finland, for instance, in famine times Reindeer Lichen and rye were made into a bread tasting like wheat bran but leaving an unpleasant sense of heat on the tongue.

"Tripe de Roche" or Rock Tripe was so named by the French Canadian fur hunters of boreal America who used it in

---

*Llano, George A. "Economic Uses of Lichen," *Smithsonian Report for 1950,* p. 395, Smithsonian Institution, Washington, D.C.

Rock Tripe, *Umbilicaria dillenii,* showing apothecia

emergency. Rock Tripe (Umbilicaria) contains enough lichen starch to be useful as emergency food. Sir John Franklin recorded in his diary that this lichen saved him and his party from starvation in the arctic seas in 1829. He recorded in his log that Smooth Rock Tripe was more pleasant to eat than other types. His men boiled Rock Tripe with fish roe and other animal sources of food, finding it agreeable and nutritious. The complete report of the Franklin Expedition, however, states that the species of lichens used caused severe illness. (The men were also boiling and eating the leather of their equipment, and so could not have found this species of Rock Tripe an enormous delicacy.) It seems likely that the often-quoted success of Franklin's expedition in using lichens as food should be tempered and not adopted until further knowledge is gained regarding selection of lichen used and methods of preparation.

The Manna Lichen (*Lecanora esculenta*), a desert species of Crusty Lichen, probably fed the Israelites in their plight in the desert. It is still eaten by desert tribes, who mix it with meal to one-third of its weight and make it into bread. In southwest Asia, it is used as a substitute for corn.

This lichen grows lavishly in mountainous districts of many countries of both North Africa and western Asia, where it spreads rapidly, being only loosely attached to the rock on which it grows. As the plant grows older the crust is torn and separated from the mountain rock. Crust edges curl over to form an elliptical, warty body the size of a hazel nut. The outer surface is grayish-yellow, wrinkled and warty; it is white as popcorn inside. Wind and rain carry great quantities down mountainsides. Blown by high winds, the lichen thalli form little hummocks in the valleys below.

The primitive—and often hungry—peasants in certain regions of North Africa have supposed it to be "bread rained from heaven." Ancient travelers in Tartary, Algeria and other parts of northern Africa have noted and recorded four noteworthy and extensive "rains of manna." There was an abundant fall of this "manna" in Turkey as late as 1891. One of these "rains" may have been the event of "miraculously" supplied manna to the Israelites in the wilderness.

In recent times a remarkable deposit of lichens occurred in Mesopotamia during a violent hailstorm. When the hail melted, the ground was covered with lichens; specimens were sent to a scientist named Errera who identified them as *Lecanora esculenta*. His opinion was that two kinds of manna are referred to in the Bible; in one case (Exodus XVI:4) it is the sweet gum of the tamarisk, a graceful evergreen shrub or small tree, with slender, feathery branches in southern Europe and western Asia; the other kind (Numbers XI:7–9) plainly refers to the lichen.

An extensive account of the Manna Lichen is given by a certain General Jussuf who tested its value in the Sahara Desert as food for soldiers. Bread made from the lichen alone was friable and without consistency, but when mixed with a tenth portion of meal, it was similar to the ordinary bread eaten by soldiers. General Jussuf also used it as fodder for horses, some being fed with the lichen and a mixture of barley for three weeks, with no ill effects. It is also said that camels, gazelles and other quadrupeds eat it with advantage; however, it cannot properly be regarded as other than famine food.

There is, however, one neat biological trick that man (among other carnivores) has been using to gain nutriment from inedible substances: If you can't eat it yourself, then eat an animal who can.

Lichens as extra food for domestic animals, particularly swine, has been recommended. Young pigs have been found to thrive on a combination of "svinamose" (swine moss) and ordinary feed better than with the latter alone. Icelanders feed Iceland Moss to cattle, pigs and ponies, and the richness of the milk of small cows in northern Scandinavia is attributed to this food. The nutritive value of such nongrassy feeds lies in their high content of lichen starch (lichenin). The bitter quality, due to lichen acids, can be removed by soaking them in hot water, rendering them palatable for domestic animals. But of course it would be much better to find some creature that doesn't need its lichen dinner so lavishly prepared. And fortunately for the Lapps, such a beast exists in the form of the reindeer, who is particularly suited to make use of lichen fodder.

Over those ice-free areas of Greenland that have enough moisture for lichen growth, as well as Siberia, northern Scandinavia, Iceland, Alaska, the Northwest Territories of Canada, the archipelago of the Arctic Sea, and Labrador, many thousands of square miles provide nongrassy range feed in winter for caribou, musk ox, wood buffalo and other wild herbivores, as well as for domesticated reindeer. (Though lichens are by far the predominant plants in Antarctica, they are not as richly developed as in the Arctic. Moreover, there are no herbivores in Antarctica, rendering it less important economically. The extreme southern tip of South America, lower Patagonia and Tierra del Fuego, is included in this type of pasture rangeland). Such ranges lie north of the tree line and above timberline but may extend into timber along mountainsides. They are best developed in subarctic regions but may extend into moderate temperature zones.

Reindeer meat is served throughout Finland and Scandinavia. The hide is used for leather goods, and since reindeer hairs are hollow and provide optimal insulation, hide with the hair left on is made into boots, shoes and high-quality sleeping bags. Indeed, a reindeer culture developed through the centuries in Lapland; the Lapp depends on reindeer and the latter depend on lichens for subsistence.

Reindeer culture is not peculiar to the Lapp, but from ancient times was the way of life of many nomadic tribes living in lands bordering the Arctic Sea from Murmansk across and down into Siberia, where evidences of present-day and ancient reindeer cultures have been found.

Lapps keep goats or a cow in addition to reindeer but it is common for a Lapp to own several thousand of the latter. Keeping his property close at hand, the Lapp herd owner has always followed natural migration of reindeer herds. In summer the animals migrate to the highlands or near the coast, partly to avoid insect pests and partly to feed in fresh pastures. But during the rugged Scandinavian winter, they move away from the windy coasts and down from the icy highlands to the snow-covered lowlands. This constant, natural rotation of caribou and reindeer prevents over-grazing on any one part of the available range, but it is is during the critical winter period that lichens play their most important part in the reindeer's diet.

This is not to imply that the wild animals are entirely dependent upon lichen forage for winter grazing. Grassy range feed is often available in the lowlands, and the American caribou and Old World reindeer have learned the habit of pawing away snow-cover to obtain better grazing. Reindeer actually take lichens the year around, but during a short period of each winter when the snows are the heaviest, the reindeer feed almost entirely on the lichens that protrude on snow-free pastures.

Lapps have formulated their own Lappic term for various types of reindeer grazing lands and lichen species, clearly differentiating between lichens and mosses, since reindeer seldom eat the latter. (Reindeer do graze upon Hairy Cap, *Aulacomium turgidum* and *Hylocomium alaskanum* and, of course, on vascular plants.)

"Jaegel" refers to field lichens on which reindeer fatten; "Gadna" grows on stones and trees and is taken if no other food is available; "Lappo" are the "Beard" forms growing on trees, for which the animals have great fondness. The herders also recognize the cycle of prompt, successive lichen formations that occur in a severely burnt-over pasture.

Oddly enough, lichens are far from ideal food for reindeer. A. Kursanov and D. D'Yachkov, Russian scientists, described rather severe nutritional illness in reindeer forced to spend the long winter on lichen fodder alone. Critical dietary deficiencies of protein, fats, minerals and vitamins occur, partly because of the low content of these substances in the plants and also because of their low digestibility. Reindeer, because they are snow eaters, have only distilled water as fluid from the time of the first freeze-up to the spring thawing of lakes and streams. Hence they are salt-depleted by April and May; they will kill lemming and mice with their forefeet and eat them; they eat young birds as well as eggs. They also have a peculiar craving for human and dog urine, and it is a custom of Eurasian hunters, as well as the central Eskimo of Canada, to use urine and lichens as bait over snow-covered pitfalls to attract the wild reindeer. Reindeer also gnaw on old bones, and on reaching the sea, wade in and drink seawater. Perhaps we should not blame the lichens too much; these dietary habits alone may account for sick reindeer.

Reindeer absorb up to 28 percent of the carbohydrate of lichens; even so, lichens are not a nutritious food. But oddly, experimental exclusion of lichens from their diet brings on diarrhea; this may explain why reindeer eat lichens even in summer. Small amounts of these plants seem somehow essential to normal digestive function.

In any case, the Lapps gather large quantities of lichens for their domesticated reindeer. The most useful fodder species are Reindeer Lichens, which they grow in extensive carpet-like masses to a height of six inches. Lapp women do the harvesting by hand or with hand implements. Dry "moss" is brittle and pulverizes readily, resulting in large losses, and for this reason the lichen is most economically harvested when it has a water content of 40–70 percent by weight. After gathering, the lichens are stored in straw-covered shelters. In winter they are taken to drying houses where water content may go down to 14 percent of the dry weight.

Brittle and chalky when dry, Reindeer Lichen, *Cladonia rangiferina* is strikingly beautiful when moist. As its name implies, it is a frequent winter fodder for arctic reindeer

Ironically, lichen harvesting is another area in which man is more clumsy and destructive than the animals. Reindeer, feeding on fruticose lichens in the wild, crop the lichen close but leave enough of the thallus for future growth. Hand or implement harvesting, however, uproots the lichen thallus too; it may require ten or more years for regeneration and growth. This situation has been alleviated by regulations imposed by local governments.

With current increases in both native and white populations in arctic and subarctic regions, the demands for food, especially meat, are increasing beyond the available wild-game supply. But the attendant increase in northern European reindeer population has resulted in restriction and international laws controlling herds crossing Norwegian, Swedish and Finnish boundaries, and has necessitated study of the use of northern pastures. Meanwhile, problems are arising for present-day Lapps, some of whom have given up their nomadic life and, hence, their main source of revenue. Swedish, Norwegian and Finnish governments are trying to maintain the economics of Lapp reindeer culture in several ways, notably by encouraging lichenologists to make studies and surveys of lichen flora in those countries.

Whenever man has discovered a natural source of starch, his first response has been to make bread with it. His second—in virtually every corner of the globe—has been to ferment it and make liquor. Lichens have by no means been overlooked by the enterprising distiller, and have long since joined the potato and the grape. Indeed, the manufacture of alcohol from lichens is an ancient art.

The Lung Lichen (*Lobaria pulmonaria*) was used in beer manufacture, substituting lichen for hops in the brewing process. Its use was confined to certain monasteries in Europe and Siberia that had the reputation of serving bitter but highly intoxicating beer to the traveler.

French and Scandinavian chemists employed both Reindeer Lichen and Iceland Moss in the manufacture of alcohol. The method is as follows: Lichens are treated with sulfuric or hydrochloric acid, transforming lichen starch into sugar. The sugar, allowed to ferment, produces alcohol. Two pounds of lichens furnished about one pint of alcohol. In Stockholm in 1868 S. Stenberg published a report on production of lichen brandy. He included detailed plans for setting up a distillery with figures of possible production levels. Preparation of spirits from lichens was recommended in 1870 as a means of saving grain otherwise used in the production of alcohol. Two pounds of lichens would yield five liters of 100 proof alcohol.

In 1872 R. Arendt reported that the Swedish discovery was being applied in the Russian cities of Arkhangelsk and Pskov Novgorod. Distillers exhibited samples of lichen spirits at the Russian Industrial Exhibition in Moscow in 1872, lauded by French and English visitors. And by 1893 brandy manufacture from derived lichen-alcohol had become a large industry in Sweden. The industry failed, though, in 1896—due to exhaustion of the supply of lichens!

During the war years 1942-1943, the two Russians, A. Kursanov and D. D'Yachkov developed a method for the extraction of "glucose molasses" and glucose from certain lichens. Beet sugar was scarce and Russia needed to conserve grain and potato starch for alcohol manufacture for military purposes. The method allowed processing of some thirty to thirty-five tons of lichens annually, with a total daily production of 220 pounds of glucose. Though the harvesting cost for lichens was low, the equipment, fuel and processing chemicals, lime, sulfuric acid, potash and activated charcoal were expensive; the cost of the finished product compared to glucose extraction from the sugar beet was rather high.

The amount of glucose obtained in percentage of dry weight of the plants varies with the species. The most productive were species of Alectoria, 82 percent; Cetraria 78 percent; Cladonia 75 percent; and Usnea 74 percent. Glucose molasses from Iceland Moss has a sweet caramel flavor, and is transparent with a brown tinge. Lichen glucose is described as "superior" to beet sugar. It is also used for typographical purposes in a printing plant in Kirov. It is difficult to remove bitter-tasting substances from some species, however, and these lichens are better used to produce alcohol.

If lichens can be economically treated to obtain glucose or other nutrients, we may someday see lichens being harvested and grown on a wide scale—and not just for distilleries or reindeer. Professor Hanstien, chief lecturer in the Agricultural School, Aas, Norway, long ago "prophesied that lichens are destined to become the great popular food of the masses because of their cheapness and nutritive value." But there has been little effort to investigate this possibility. Lichens have many assets as a crop: They grow and flourish in the most arid regions and can be preserved indefinitely. They grow in cold and dry or moist and warm climates; dried lichens shrink to a fraction of their moist size, facilitating storage; and most interesting is the contribution lichens could make in arctic agriculture, a new and important science.

There is no predicting what lichens might offer in formal cultivation. Their greatest defect for agriculture, of course, is their very slow growth, but then, millions of acres are currently seeded with trees that frequently take longer than ten years to become ready for harvest.

With less than one-fourth of the earth's surface actually tillable, and the human population growing in geometric progression, what a contribution it would be to have an edible crop growing on scorched deserts and arctic tundras!

Botany and Medicine

THE main incentive of early botanists was to find plants useful as food, medicine or in the household. Thus, early man's interest in mosses and lichens was utilitarian. Initial considerations when he observed a plant were, "What is there about it for me? Can I eat it? Will it poison me? Will it cure my ills? Will it clothe me?" Among the higher plants were materials in abundance for food, shelter, clothing and medicine. Inconspicuous in color, size and form, mosses and lichens were generally neglected.

But not always: Stems of common Hairy Cap Moss often grow twelve to eighteen inches in length, sometimes longer. The central core of the stem, when cleaned, is a pliable tough strand well suited for the manufacture of brooms, brushes and plaited articles; mats, rugs, baskets and hassocks. This was quite an ancient art. One of the oldest known examples is a partially finished Polytrichum basket found at the bottom of a ditch in an early Roman fort at Newstead, Roxburghshire, England. An indication of the age of the basket is given by the date, A.D. 86, of some coins in the same ditch. Of about the same age are a "four-ply plaited object" and a "fringe-like structure" made from the long stems of Hairy Cap Moss, found near an excavation of the Lochlee Crannog in Scotland.

In general, it has been the "uncivilized" peoples of the far north who have made the most imaginative use of mosses and lichens. The very climate that inhibits trees, grasses and other useful plants is one in which these remarkable plants thrive, often growing to large—and quite noticeable—size. Being the dominant vegetation on much of the tundra, these plants could hardly be overlooked!

The Cree Indians used *Dicranum elongatum* for lampwicks. Eskimos of northeastern Labrador employ *Rhacomitrium lanuginosum* for the same purpose. The Chukchi Eskimos, a Mongoloid people living in northeastern Siberia on the shores of the Arctic Ocean and the Bering Sea, fashion wicks of "reindeer moss" and fuel stove lamps with blubber oil.

Alaskan Eskimos still use lichens as kindling material. *Cetraria richardsonii*, a loose, coarse tumbleweed-like lichen, is gathered for priming wood fires.

According to Laplanders, Hairy Cap Moss is excellent for bedding. They select a large patch of plants, cut out an area large enough for a bed and separate the mass of intertwined mosses from the soil; a similar portion of the moss patch serves well as a cover. The moss bed may be rolled up and carried from place-to-place. Linnaeus in his wanderings often slept on such a bed.

The Indians of Mendocino County, California, use a moss, Alsia, as a bedding material especially for babies. Moss was used in old Eskimo burials as a bed upon which to lay bodies of the dead. In northern England Hairy Cap mosses were used to stuff mattresses and upholstery. Native moss "Tuida" (probably Sphagnum) was employed by Fiji Islanders as stuffing for pillows. Pillows have been stuffed with certain Hypnums in the belief that the mosses were capable of inducing a trance-like sleep. Actually, the Greek word *hypnum,* "sleep," possibly refers to the prostrate growth habit of most Cedar mosses.

Use of lichens in medicine is traced to distant antiquity. The common species of Oak Moss (*Evernia furfuracea*) was found in an Egyptian vase from the eighteenth dynasty (1700-1600 B.C.). Egyptians used Oak Moss to preserve odor of spices employed in embalming mummies. (The lichen was sold on the Cairo drug market under the name of "Kheba." It is still imported to Egypt from Europe and sold with Iceland Moss as a foreign drug.)

The earliest written references to lichens are unreliable, being generally described with similar plants as "Muscus" by the earliest writers.

The Greek philosopher, Theophrastus, who lived from 371 to 284 B.C., a disciple of Plato and student and successor of Aristotle, wrote some imperfect descriptions of lichens. In his *History of Plants,* one of the earliest known botanical texts, he described Old Man's Beard (*Usnea florida*), a common tree lichen growing in fringes from branches of oaks and evergreens. (Hippocrates had prescribed the Old Man's Beard Lichen for uterine ailments, and interestingly, the natives of the Malay Peninsula still use a closely related species for treating colds and to promote strength after confinement!)

Theophrastus also mentioned a lichen now called *Roccella tinctoria,* as yielding a blue and purple dye, the same one referred to in the Old Testament as a dye. Lichen colors are indicated by the prophet Ezekiel in his denunciation of Tyre: "Blue and purple from the Isles of Elisha was that which covered thee." (Exodus 25:4, and Ezekiel 27:7) Theophrastus used the term "lichen" to describe a growth on olive trees; his reference, however, was to liverworts rather than lichens.

No further references to lichens have survived until the first century of the Christian Era; Pedanios Dioscorides (circa A.D. 68), Greek physician and founder of medical botany as an applied science, gave the term "lichen" to true lichens in his *Materia Medica.* He thought they resembled the skin of people with leprosy (hence "lichen," from the Greek for "leprous") and supposed the lichen to be specific treatment for this disease.

Though Dioscorides wrote of lichens, he had little appreciation of what they were. His book had an illustration of a lichen, *Lobaria pulmonaria,* probably the first drawing of a true lichen; he also described the Bryum mosses.

Gaius Plinius (Pliny the Elder, A.D. 23–79), a Roman naturalist who perished in the volcanic eruption at Pompeii, mentions lichens. Like Theophrastus, he described *Roccella tinctoria* as yielding oricello, the blue and purple dye of the Old Testament. In his book *Phycos Thalassion,* he referred specifically to the lichen Roccella, "with crisp leaves, used in Crete for dyeing garments." Though oricello was in use long before the first century of the Christian Era, knowledge of the dye's use was lost before the fall of the Roman Empire. Pliny also uses the name *Bryum* to describe the mosses that bear that name even today.

In the fourteenth and fifteenth centuries A.D., there arose in Europe and Britain a philosophic concept known as the Doctrine of Signatures. This doctrine was an explanation for the paradox of God's inhumanity to man. Providence, having created man and also pestilential diseases to destroy or maim him, provided natural clues or signs to indicate remedies or palliative essences by which man could cure his disease or ease his pain. On various plants there seemed to be "signatures"— more or less vague resemblances to parts of the human body or diseases to which humans were subject—thus indicating that the plants provided specific remedy.

In the fifteenth century a constant attempt was made throughout Europe to follow nature's guidance in the study and treatment of disease. Several lichens had popularity in treating disease and were looked upon as God's Signatures.

A yellow papery lichen (*Xanthoria parietina,* Yellow Wall Lichen) growing on stones was once popular for the cure of jaundice, because of its color similarity to the skin of jaundiced people. The Lungwort or Spotted Lungwort (*Lobaria pulmonaria,* Lung Lichen) was first included among medical plants in 1540 by Dorstenius, a professor at Marbury who gave directions for its preparation as a cure for disease of the lungs. In England it was recommended by a famous Dr. Nicolas Culpepper (1652) who believed in astrology even more than in signatures. He wrote: "It is of great use with many physicians to help the disease of the lungs and for coughs, wheezings and shortness of breath which it cureth both in man and beast. Jupiter seems to own the herb."

A century later Dr. John Hill, physician and naturalist, stated that the great tree lungwort has been at all times famous in diseases of the breast and lungs; but by that time, "it was not much used owing to change in fashions." A decoction of the common Hairy Cap, *Polytrichum commune,* was used to strengthen and beautify ladies' hair.

The name "liverwort" was originally applied to a common member of the thallose group (the genus *Marchantia*), because of its division into lobes and sections whose form and texture suggested those of the animal liver. It was, of course, regarded as a specific antidote for disease of the liver—whence the Latin name Hepaticae, the German Lebermoose, and the English "liverwort." Specifically, *Marchantia polymorpha* was used in the treatment of pulmonary tuberculosis and infections of the liver; what success was achieved seems unreported. From an old herbal comes the following statement concerning Marchantia. "It is a singular good herb for all the diseases of the liver,

The underside of the Lung Lichen, *Lobaria pulmonaria,* clearly showing how it got its name—and why it became a staple item in the medieval physician's Doctrine of Signatures

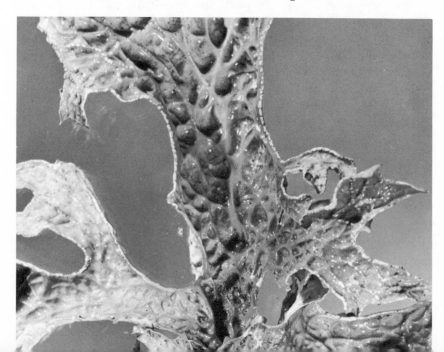

both to cool and cleanse it and help the inflammation in any part and the yellow jaundice likewise."

The Doctrine of Signatures reached the height of absurdity with the inordinate value given to a lichen found growing on human skulls, "MUSCUS CRANII HUMANI" or "MUSCUS ex cranio humano." Many lichens grow at random on a variety of substances, and not rarely on bones lying in the open. This skull lichen (common name Boulder Lichen, *Parmelia saxatilis,* Stane Raw, Scots.) "brought its weight in gold as a cure for epilepsy." Parkinson, in 1640, wrote in all confidence,

> *it groweth upon the bare scalps of men and women that have lyen long—in former times much accounted of because it is rare and hardly gotten, but in our times, much more set by, to make the "Unguentum Sympatheticum" which cureth wounds without the local application of salves—but as Crollius hath it, it should be taken from the skulls of those who have been hanged or executed for offences."*

The same gruesome plant is "celebrated by several authors as useful in hemorrhages" and it is said to be an ingredient of the famous "Unguentum Armarium," reported to have been invented by Paracelsus.

Few really scientific observations were made in the Dark Ages until the sixteenth century. With an awakening of scientific interest all over Europe, the printing press came into use and many books on medical botany were published, most containing references to lichens. The first book on Natural History in England was the *Grete Herball,* translated from a French work, *Hortus Sanitatis,* published by Peter Treveris in Southwark in 1526. One herb recommended for various ailments is "Muscus Arborum," the "Tree Moss," *Usnea barbata.*

One good scientific observer of the sixteenth century, Moisan, expressed the opinion in 1590 that "lichens represent secretion products of soil, rocks and trees."

The best known botanical book of the sixteenth century is the *Herball* of John Gerard (1597) of London, Master in Chirurgie, who had a garden in Holborn. He recommended as medicinally valuable Usnea and *Cladonia physiata* (Goblet Lichen), for which he coined the name "Cuppe or Chalice-moss."

Samuel Doody, a London apothecary who was in charge of the Garden of the Apothecaries' Society in Chelsea, had as his chief interest Cryptogamic Botany, a branch little regarded before his day. He wrote extensively on lichens. Among Doody's associates were Reverend Adam Buddle, James Petiver and William Sherard. Buddle was a collector; his herbarium, including many lichens from all parts of the world, is incorporated in the Sloane Herbarium at the British Museum.

The Society of Apothecaries was founded in 1617; the members acquired land on the riverfront at Chelsea which was later extended and made into a Physick Garden. James Petiver was one of the first Demonstrators of Plants to the Society in connection with the garden. One of his duties was to conduct the annual "herborizing" tours of the apprentices in search of plants. He collected a large herbarium on annual excursions as well as shorter visits in the immediate neighborhood of London. He wrote many tracts on Natural History subjects, including many on lichens.

Sherard, another of Doody's friends, studied lichens and was full of enthusiasm for Natural Science. It was he who brought Dillenius, the great German botanist, to England and finally nominated him for the position of the first Sherardian Professor of Botany at Oxford University.

Robert Morison, a Scotsman from Aberdeen, made the greatest advance in this period. He studied medicine at Angers in France and superintended the Duke of Orleans' garden in Blois; on returning to England in 1669 he became keeper of the botanic garden at Oxford. In a book published posthumously, the lichens were put for the first time in a separate group which he called "Muscofungus."

Johanan Jakob Dillenius is famous for his book *Historia Muscorum,* which was finally published in 1741. It includes an account of all the then-known liverworts, mosses and lichens. However, he still considered the lichens as mosses. His herbarium of lichens still exists at Oxford, mounted with the utmost care and neatness.

Dog Tooth Lichen, one of the papery lichens, grows in moist places with its dark green, velvety ruffles spreading over the ground, rocks or dead trees. The ruffled edges are set with erect fruiting discs curled in such a manner as to resemble dog's teeth or tiny brown fingernails. When dry, the ruffles are a drab gray, turning to a lovely dark green when moist. This plant is called *Peltigera canina,* meaning "teeth of a dog." It was listed in the London Pharmacopaeia as a remedy for the cure of rabies, and sold as the celebrated "pulvus antilyssus." The lichen was dried, finely powdered and mixed with red pepper. (The history of the Royal Society of London records that several mad dogs belonging to the Duke of York were saved by this powder.)

Dr. Richard Mead recommended, in about 1741, the following prescription for humans stricken with rabies:

> *Let the patient be blooded at the arm, nine or ten ounces. Take of the herb called in Latin, Lichen cinereus terrestris, in English, Ash-coloured ground liverwort, clean'd, dry'd, and powder'd half an ounce. Of black pepper powder's two drachms. Mix these well together and divide the Powder into four Doses, one of which must be taken every Morning, fasting; for four Mornings successively in half a Pint of Cow's Milk, warm. After these four doses are taken, the Patient must go into the cold bath, or a cold Spring or River, every Morning fasting, for a Month. He must be dipt all over but not stay in (with his head above water) longer than half a minute, if the Water be very cold. After this he must go in three Times a Week for a Fortnight longer.*

Dog Tooth Lichen, *Peltigera canina,* which was once used as a remedy for rabies—hydrophobia

In 1777, Lightfoot refers to this medicine as "the once celebrated 'Pulvus antilyssus,' much recommended by the great Dr. Mead." He adds that

> *it is much to be lamented that the success of this medicine has not always answered the expectation. There are instances where the application has not prevented the Hydrophobia, and it is very uncertain whether it has ever been at all instrumental in keeping off that disorder.*

Belief in the efficacy of the powder died out before the end of the century, but the echo of the famous remedy remains in the lichen's name.

Linnaeus (Carl von Linne, 1707–1778), the great Swedish plant taxonomist, called the lichens "rustici pauperrimi" or "the poor trash of vegetation." However, Linnaeus gave Iceland Moss (*Cetraria islandica*) the important place it held in medicine for many years. It was used in chronic diseases as an emollient and tonic. It would have been the "Divine Gift to Man" it was claimed to be, had it proven as effective as its prescribers reckoned. A tea made of Hairy Caps was purported to dissolve stones in the kidney and gallbladder. Peat tar extracted from peat was said to possess antiseptic and preservative properties. Sphagnol, a distillate of peat tar, was used for the treatment of skin diseases, also recommended to relieve itching due to insect bites, and even to prevent them.

Dr. Boerhaave, the famous Dutch physician, described Lung Lichen as an excitant, tonic and astringent, and recommended it for hemorrhages and asthma.

A Stalked Lichen (*Ramalina calicaris,* Common Twig Lichen) was useful in "treating chilblains and chapped hands."

The utility of moss in building was well known to North American pioneers, who filled the chinks of their cabins with it to keep out the wind. The nineteenth-century explorer Dr. Isaac Hayes, who reported finding moss as far north as Booth Bay in Greenland, at a latitude of 76° 30', also described a hut built by his party in a crevice of rock, thatched a foot thick with moss—which they dug with dinner plates from under two feet of snow. They also improvised moss candles which, dipped in oil, provided both light and heat. In certain sections of Europe the water moss *Fontinalis antipyretica* was used for filling spaces between chimneys and walls; this practice based on the erroneous belief that this moss will not blaze, thus the name, antipyretica, meaning "against fire."

Gilbert White in his *Natural History of Selborne* wrote of another use of Hairy Caps.

> *While on the subject of rural economy it might not be improper to mention a pretty implement of housewifery that we have seen nowhere else; that is, little neat Bosoms which our foresters make from the stock of the Polytrichum commune or the Great Golden Hair which they call silk wood and find plenty in the bogs. When this moss is well combed and dressed and divested of its outer skin it becomes a beautiful bright chestnut color and being soft and pliant is very popular for the dusting of beds, curtains, carpets, hangings, etc.*

The group of lichens called Usnea, (Old Man's Beard) was "endowed" by man with many wonderful powers, most of which are fictitious. Albert Schneider, M.D., PH.D., seventy years ago published an interesting account of the many uses to which the "Beard Lichens" were put. They were administered as a sure cure for catarrh. They had transient popularity in the treatment of dropsy; boiling the plant in beer was a necessary part of the prescription. They were an excellent "spring tonic." Listed under their many uses are: "astringent;" "diuretic;" an anodyne for whooping cough; cure for "scald head;" useful in scrofula, an old name for glandular tuberculosis; also for "hair powders, perfumes and the preparation of explosives." The long filaments of Old Man's Beard were used to promote hair growth.

A species of Stalked Lichen (*Evernia prunastri,* Flabby Lichen) was used by the Swedes to poison wolves. The lichen was powdered and mixed with powdered glass, to which it undoubtedly owes any effectiveness it had in wolf disposal. The mixture was then smeared over a dead animal and placed in a locality frequented by wolves. It is probable that the finely ground glass made multiple tiny wounds in the wolf's stomach and intestine, giving access to very toxic and irritating lichen acids.

Professor Luyken of Holland in 1809 thought that lichens were composed of air and moisture. In the early nineteenth century, botanic scholars thought lichens an example of spontaneous generation. Philosophers regarded them as the ultimate origin of all plant life. It was said that, "spontaneously, inorganic stone became living plant." In 1819, a learned man named Friedrich Hornschuch wrote,

Algae, lichens and mosses may develop without seed from decomposing water. The decomposition of water induced by warmth and sunlight gives rise to the common ancestral type of lichens and mosses. This ancestral type is a vegetable infusorium known as monas lens, which, when acted upon by light and air undergoes an evolutionary form of transformation into algae, lichens and moss.

It was thought that the so-called "primal substance" or "green substance of Priestly" (probably algae) developed into lichens, mosses and other lower plants. What plant finally evolved was determined, presumably, by the varying atmospheric influences and the chemical nature of the substrate.

Nees Von Esenbeck, a great teacher in Holland in 1820, enjoyed taking students to an old castle at Pottenstein to demonstrate "before their very eyes" how the "green substance" or "primal substance" growing on rocks (rock-loving algae) could be transformed into lichens, on being placed in water!

In 1866 Anton DeBary first proposed the true nature of lichens, concluding that the lichen is a dual organism, both alga and fungus. The concept of spontaneous generation was not dislodged, however, and his work was not accepted. In 1867 a Swiss botanist, Simon Schwendener, repeating this research, confirmed DeBary's view and added incontrovertible evidence of the dual nature of the lichen.

He believed the mutual relationship to be a parasitism of fungus on alga. Until then, lichens had been regarded as simple organisms intermediate between algae and fungi, and many species had been so described. But if symbiosis is used in its accepted meaning as "harmless but intimate cellular association between at least two individuals belonging to different species," then it was J. Reinke who proposed the theory of lichen symbiosis. His term "consortium" was used to define two partners living peaceably together, each working for the common good of the whole complex organism.

Controversy about lichens never ceases, and even today there is not general agreement. Though Schwendener's landmark work and his theory of the nature of lichens was beyond criticism, he was loudly denounced throughout the nineteenth century; his concept of the dual nature of lichens, and his idea of the fungus parasitizing the alga was hotly contested by many lichenologists of the day. Lauder Lindsay dismissed the theory as "merely the most recent instance of German transcendentalism applied to the lichens." W. Nylander wrote in fury, "all these allegations belong to inept Schwendenerism and scarcely deserve even to be reviewed or castigated—so puerile are they—the offspring of inexperience and a light imagination. No true science there!" J. M. Crombie agreed in his estimate of "these absurd tales" and added his rejection of the whole subject as a "Romance of Lichenology, or the unnatural union between a captive algal damsel and a tyrant fungal master." At a later time he was even more comprehensively contemptuous: "Whether viewed anatomically or biologically, analytically or synthetically, it is instead of being true science, only the romance of lichenology." *Someone* was wrong, and as time has shown, it was *not Schwendener!*

Dried Sphagnum was once for sale in herb shops in China. The whole plant was boiled in water and the decoction used to cure acute hemorrhage and eye diseases. Country people in Britain used it in the treatment of boils and discharging wounds, and Alaskan Indians still make a salve for cuts by mixing Sphagnum leaves with tallow or other grease.

Sphagnum has long been used for absorbent bandages. American Indians used dried Sphagnum as diaper material. (Chippewa Indians used another moss, *Dicranum bonjeani* as an absorbent.) It was highly recommended during the Napoleonic and Franco-Prussian wars for use by army surgeons.

The value of Sphagnum in surgery was not fully appreciated until World War I. It was estimated that using Sphagnum in place of cotton resulted in a saving to the British of $200,000 per year. (Equally important was the release of scarce cotton for use in explosives.) In the United States 500,000 Sphagnum dressings were made by the American Red Cross from March, 1918, until the war's end in November, when the total British output was estimated at one million pounds per *month.*

The Germans were more active than the Allies in utilizing Sphagnum, which was very common on the Russian front. Allied prisoners of war reported that part of their work in German prison camps was to gather Sphagnum from the bogs.

During World War I, an American surgeon, Dr. J. B. Porter,* listed a number of advantages of Sphagnum over cotton for surgical use:

A.   It absorbs liquids more rapidly (three times as fast) and in amounts three or four times as great as cotton.
B.   It retains liquids much better, thereby reducing the number of times the dressing needs changing.
C.   It distributes absorbed liquids uniformly through its mass.
D.   Sphagnum dressings are cooler, softer and less ir-ritating than cotton.
E.   These dressings are produced more rapidly and cheaply. Besides, the slightly antiseptic properties of Sphagnum are retained in the dressing.

The Sphagnum leaf has two kinds of cells, small green cells forming a network and large empty hyalin cells communicating with one another, occupying the meshes of the network usually perforated with pores. Pore cells of leaves and those of stems and branches are responsible for Sphagnum's being able to absorb and retain 95 percent of its dry weight in water.

In creating a "quaking bog," the Sphagnum moss frequently prepares the way for the more primitive cousins, the liverworts and hornworts. Liverworts on the whole tend to prefer moister

*Porter, J. B., "Sphagnum Surgical Dressings," *International Journal of Surgery,* 129–135, *1917.*

habitats than mosses. In greenhouses, where the humidity is high and Sphagnum is frequently used to hold moisture around the roots of cuttings, liverworts can often spread quickly enough to qualify as weeds. So it is in the wild: Only the most humid areas are able to host these strange and little-known bryophytes.

Belief in lichens' medicinal powers has persisted right up to the present day. Among the collections of the late Dr. O.F. Cook were found two packets of lichens purchased by him in the Indian market of Sicnani, Peru. One had the following information written on it: "Intisuncja, mealy beard of the sun, grows on the ground in high summits near the glaciers; taken as tea for coughs, etc." The other was "from the same places" but named "Pachacuti, a medicine for fevers." Both were Roccella, the famous dye lichen.

George Llano reports a correspondence with a person who used Reindeer Lichen as treatment for "anemia and a general run-down condition." The individual attempted self medication on the advice of a Norwegian professor who recommended the treatment as an old-time remedy. He reported "a gain of seven pounds in one week and return of normal skin color. There was return of physical strength and resumption of an extremely active life." It is not known how the lichen was prepared. The supply was obtained from Norway, though it is a common plant in North America. It is unlikely that the lichen was of any real benefit.

There may, however, be some foundation in fact in the medical use of the Lung Lichen. Dr. Florencio Bustinza of the University of Madrid in Spain reported that lichen extract in a solution of one part in fifty thousand inhibits growth of tuberculosis bacteria in the test tube. We might profitably examine methods and concepts of our less well informed ancestors in the light of modern science. In 1944 Burkholder assayed the antibiotic properties of twenty-four different lichens; he ground up the thalli of the plants, extracted them with water and added the extracts to cultures of bacteria growing on agar plates. Two common bacteria, *Staphylococcus aureus* and *Bacillus subtilis,* were significantly inhibited by most of the lichen extracts. Extracts of many lichen species of the temperate zone will inhibit bacterial growth. In most cases the active principle is a specific lichen acid.

Dr. C. V. Barry at University College, Dublin, has reported the same growth inhibition for tuberculosis bacteria by certain lichen extracts. Barry used an acid extracted from the Manna Lichen (*Lecanora esculenta*) and found that it completely inhibited tuberculosis bacilli growth in the test tube at a dilution of one part to five hundred thousand. The most active of such compounds are being tested in animal protection experiments. Similar studies were made at Andhra and Delhi universities in India, at the University of Illinois and the University of Madrid.

Gram positive bacteria as well as the tuberculosis bacilli are inhibited by protolichesteric acid, usnic acid and a few orcinol derivatives. The same acids inhibit the growth of certain fungi.

In Finland lichen antibiotics have been marketed commercially. Usnic acid is extracted from *Cladonia rangiferina,* the Reindeer Lichen, incorporated in a salve called "USNO." It is said to be more effective than penicillin in treating external wounds and burns; it has been used to treat mastitis in cattle. In Germany a commercial preparation called "USNIPLANT" is presently being marketed. Usnic acid and streptomycin in combination has been used with inconclusive results in the treatment of patients with tuberculosis.

The Great
Lichen Industries

Since lichens have aromatic substances blending well when extracted, it was as early as the sixteenth century that several lichens, including Cladonia, Parmelia and Usnea, were used as raw materials in the perfume and cosmetic industry. At first plants were dried, ground to powder and crudely combined with other substances. "Cyprus Powder," a mixture of three lichens (one of which was Old Man's Beard, seemingly out of character), was scented with ambergris, musk and oil of roses, jasmine or orange blossoms for use as a toilet powder in the seventeenth century. It was used to whiten, scent and cleanse the hair. As manufacturers acquired more skill the materials were blended into toilet powders, scented sachets and perfumes of considerable value.

The trade had a variety of names for these lichens, somewhat foreign to unromantic biologists, such as muscus arboreus, lichen quercinus viridis, acaciae et odorante, Eichenmoos and Mousse de Chêne or oak moss and scented moss. These lichens are universally used today in the creation of "deep tone" scents, the very stable perfumes of modern manufacturers.

Oak Moss or Flabby Lichen (*Evernia prunastri*), a lichen of Europe, is collected in shaded, damp regions, mountain ranges of Central Europe, the Piedmont of Italy and forests of Czechoslovakia. The "parfumeur" differentiates between those plants growing on oak (greenish) and those found on conifers (grayish). Those growing on conifers may include resins, rendering them less desirable for the trade. (Many essences and extracts may be due to the diversity of locations in which lichens grow. Certain pleasant odors are associated with lichen oil from plants growing on oak but not from those on beech or birch.)

The crop is gathered by peasants and shepherds and pressed into large bales for export. Before World War II the American supply was exported from Yugoslavia. It amounted to a few tons yearly at a cost of 5 to 7$\frac{1}{2}$ cents a pound, f.o.b. New York City. Sufficient quantities are now available in northern forests of the United States and Canada to supply the domestic trade.

Use of dried, pulverized Oak Moss is restricted in the perfume industry. The principal sale is of extracts, essences or resinoids. Addition of alcohol gives an "extract of oak moss" which may be used in this form or may be further concentrated to obtain a semi-fluid substance.

The professional parfumeur speaks of abstract lichen qualities enhancing his product. Extract of Oak Moss or scented moss "agrees" or "harmonizes" in the "happiest" manner with many other essences. It gives "flexibility" to tarragon, coriander, yland-yland, and vanillin; "contributes stability and depth" to patchouli, coumarin and musk, and "elevation" to alpha ionene. Oak Moss is an indispensable ingredient in such perfumes known to the trade as Chypre, Fern and Heath, and in many bouquets called "Fancy" as well as for Oriental perfumes. Reindeer Lichen has been recommended by parfumeurs because they are white in color, readily dried and "occur abundantly in open healthy places."

Essential oil of Oak Moss (concrete, as it is called in the trade) is used as an impalpable powder in soap. The powder, having an agreeable odor, is mixed with soap. If the powder is not perfectly impalpable, the soap has a sandy texture. Soap cakes, to be adequately scented, have 1–1^1/$_2$ percent by weight of lichen powder. Oak Moss "concrete" improves, strengthens and renders less expensive, lavender-scented products. It is essential in higher grades of cosmetics in combination with other aromatic oils such as jasmine or orange blossom. Iceland Moss (*Cetraria islandica*), used as food and medicine, is a source of glycerol in the soap industry. Because of its lack of odor it is used in cold cream manufacture.

Paper and dye industries use quantities of sizing made from lichens for filling pores in the surface of paper, fiber or plaster.

A gum was extracted from Ramalina for use in "Calico printing," an early dyeing process, by the Arabians about A.D. 800. French and German industrial research has probed the chemical nature of extracts, gums and mucilages from lichens.

During Napoleonic wars the French had a monopoly of Senegal gum; Lord Dundonald of England at this time tried to introduce lichen mucilage in place of the French product. There is no evidence that the British market became interested. At Lyons the French successfully substituted lichen mucilage for gum arabic in the fabrication of dyed materials. R. W. Minford investigated lichen gums and mucilages and found Iceland Moss and other lichens to be excellent raw material for the manufacture of high-grade gelatin, isinglass and similar gelatinous products, corresponding to those obtained from vegetable products for this purpose.

Sizing is used in bookbinding to apply color, gold leaf or the like to book covers. This lichen product is useful to dress, glaze and stiffen silks, and to print and stain calico.

Cladonia is employed by architects to represent trees in various miniature table-model outdoor scenes, model buildings and dioramas. These lichens as well as many others are used extensively by taxidermists as decoration in animal and plant groups.

Dicranum scoparium and *Hylocomium splendens* is used by florists to form banks of green in show windows.

In Sweden lichens are woven into lovely wreaths by poorer

farming classes and sold in the cities. They are used for many home decorations as well as the more utilitarian purpose of providing insulation between storm windows and the permanent window. Lichens are made into funeral and grave wreaths in Scandinavia, partly as a tradition, also to save the expense of out-of-season flowers. English florists fashioned Climacium into wreaths and crosses; moss roses have been made from *Hylocomium proliferum.*

Women's hats a half century ago were decorated with bundles of Climacium dendroides. Students of mosses wrote in 1874,

> *And a ladies cap which we saw in a window was in no wise adorned by having sprays of artificial moss tacked all over it—nor is a bunch of moss which has died of thirst suitable for trimming a bonnet. The chief beauty that bonnets at present possess is their being fresh and clean. Dry moss is particularly fusty looking and is not improved by being dyed a leather color or a violent blue-green, the latter being the worst as being a bad match, for moss is never blue-green.*

All of these applications are dwarfed, however, by the lichen dye industry—an enterprise that virtually revolutionized medieval textile commerce and which dominated international trade for over 600 years.

It was circa A.D. 1300 that one Federigo, a Florentine of German parentage, rediscovered the method of preparation and use of the Rocella dye. Traveling in the Levant, he noted that urine (very likely his own, as he relieved himself on a Mediterranean beach) imparted a fine purple-blue color to certain lichens. Experimenting successfully, he founded the very lucrative dye industry which established his family name and gave to his native city a monopoly existing until the discovery of the Cape Verde Islands in the fifteenth century where lichen grew in abundance. Federigo achieved great success and became the head of a distinguished family, the Rucellai, also known as Oricellai. From these names, orseille, one name of the dye, is derived; the generic name of the lichens is from the family name.

Carol Woodward has cited references to "archil" and "orchil" in Shakespeare's *Richard II* and *Richard III*. The Spanish dye terms "orcigilia or orchillia" and Portuguese "urzela" were likely derived earlier than the Italian.

Of all the lichen dyes used by man none achieved so much commercial and historical importance. The English knew the rediscovered Rocellaceae dyes as orchella moss, orchella weed, orchil paste or liquor; the French, as Orseille; and the Germans, as Persis. Lander Lindsay states that,

> *We may practically regard Orchil as the English, Cudbear as the Scottish, and Litmus as the Dutch name for the same substances. The first is manufactured as a liquid of a beautiful reddish or purple color; the second as a powder or cake of red color, and the third as small cakes of a blue color.*

The commercial article was prepared first in paste form. Because of the Florentine merchants' monopoly, other nations imported dye as paste from Florence.

For about two centuries, Italy supplied the world with orseille derived from lichens collected on islands of the Mediterranean Sea. The dye industry was controlled entirely by the Rucellai and other merchants of Florence, but with discovery of new lands, the monopoly was broken. Abundance of plants was found along any warm sea coast. Trading centers then became Portugal, France and Holland.

Even so, methods of preparing and using dye was traditionally kept a close trade secret by small groups and the chemical components of lichen dyes were not understood in the early development of the industry.

The actual coloring substances extracted from the dye lichens are the various and numerous acids peculiar only to lichens. Many different species were used, some of which had far more of the coloring substances in them than others. Orchil, for instance, can be extracted from some twenty different lichens, but the Rocella yields the most abundant dye. The color of the lichen thallus gives little indication of its coloring properties. Crustaceous species growing on rocks near the seashore are most likely to yield red and purple dyes; yellow lichens yield a brown to yellow dye. August was recommended as the best month for gathering dye lichens; the accumulation of acids in the plant was said to be at a maximum just after the season of greatest light and heat.

The old English method was to cut the lichen to bits or pulverize it to a powder and pass it through a sieve. It was then placed in iron drums provided with paddles. The mass was moistened with stale human urine and the mixture stirred once a day. (The use of human urine was commonplace, being the only early source of ammonia. Saltpeter and certain other salts of ammonia were often used in the process.)

With additions of soda for five or six days at a temperature of 35–45° C., fermentation proceeded. It was checked frequently until the coloring matter, a dove gray, ceased to increase. The product, orchil paste, was placed in wooded casks and covered with limewater until needed by the dyer.

To make "orchil liquor" the lichen, treated with water and urine, was allowed to ferment. Fibrous matter was removed next and the "liquor" collected and stored. Dillenius in 1741 "reckoned the color more beautiful than the Tyrian blue" when first dyed.

New sources for the "weed" were rapidly found. It was gatnered from the Cape Verde Islands, East Africa, Zanzibar, Ceylon, the East Indies, Australia, Madagascar, Chile, Peru and the West Coast of North America. Shiploads were gathered from lower California and adjacent islands; old importers were close with their secrets regarding origin of their best supplies. *Roccella tinctoria* of the Cape and South America was said to be "6 to 8 inches long and as thick as goose quills." It was highly regarded by the dye merchants. In the 1750s Cape Verde and the Canary Islands exported one hundred tons annually to England. The industry reached a zenith in the nineteenth century when the "weed" became an article of international exchange comparable to spices. By 1818 the cost had leaped from £40 to £200 per ton, depending on quality. De Avellar Brotero of Lisbon wrote in 1824, referring to the dye:

> *Its uses have been much extended for it serves as pigment to dye wool, silk, cotton and various other fibers; it serves in paints and to color marble; it is needed in wines, liquors, oil, grease and wax.*

Dr. George Bancroft in 1832 described the infusion of orchil as "of a red crimson color inclining to violet." He recommended the use of ammonia instead of urine, and of hogsheads to facilitate agitation. He regarded the practice of adding arsenic and alum as useless and dangerous.

Specimens of Roccella were exhibited at the London Crystal Palace in 1851, at which time the price was quoted at £380 per ton. Lander Lindsay described the industry in 1854–55, noting that manufacturers recognized different qualities in urine in producing coloring matter—

> *Hence I have been informed that some English manufacturers who continue to use this form of ammoniacal solution have learned by experience to avoid urine from beer drinkers, which is excessive in quantity but frequently deficient in urea, ammonia and solids, while it is abundant in water.*

Lindsay pointed out that the field was new and open to many possibilities; he urged that lichen resources of Scotland be explored. "The speculation [investment] of substituting home for foreign dye lichens promises to be remunerative as the Rocellas have frequently reached the high price of £1,000 per ton in the London market." He reemphasized that

> *if commanders of ships were aware of the value of these plants, which cover many a rocky coast and barren island, they might, with a slight expenditure of time and labor, bring home with them such a quantity of these significant plants as would realize considerable sums, to the direct advantage to themselves and ship owners; and consequently to the advantage of the State. Indirectly, a multiplied trade in dye lichens might scatter the seeds of civilization; and place the means of a comfortable existence at the command of the miserable inhabitants of many a barren coast or island; at present far removed from the great centers of social advancement.*

In 1886 a stable supply was obtained from Ceylon where Roccella grows luxuriantly on the palm trees. The price settled at £50 per ton.

Northern countries of Europe have long used brown and yellow lichen dyes. In sections of Scotland, such as Aberdeenshire, every small cotter's farm had a dooryard tank or barrel ("litpig") of stale, putrid urine ("graith"). It was the task of the mistress of the household to macerate lichens ("crotals" or "crottles") to prepare dyes for trousers, dresses, homespun stockings, nightcaps and other clothing. Ammonia in urine, an obviously ever-present source of ammoniacal solution, was the substance extracting the dye. The urine-treated macerated lichen mass and woolen cloth were boiled together until the desired color was obtained, usually brown. This took several hours, producing fast dyes without need for any fixing agent. This dye method was used in Iceland and Scotland to prepare the famous homespun Harris Tweed.

A. R. Horwood reported that in the Shetland Islands lichens were harvested in May or June after rain. In autumn or winter a metal scraper was used for rock lichens. Plants were washed, dried in the sun and powdered. They were then shipped to the London market in casks as "cudbear." The term "cudbear" is a corrupt pronunciation of the name of Dr. Cuthbert Gordon, a Glasgow chemist who patented his process of preparing lichen dye.

The manufacture of "cudbear" flourished in Leith and Glasgow, lichens being plentiful in the western Highlands. They provided the chief source of income to poor Highlanders. Cudbear was also manufactured in England, where the "orchil makers" imported lichens from Norway and Sweden.

The cotters mixed the "crottles" with "graith," working it into small balls or cakes with burnt shells or lime. The cakes were wrapped in dock leaves and hung up to dry over peat fires. The peat smoke odor was thus imparted to fine homespun Harris Tweed. Dye in such cakes kept for over a year, was dissolved in warm water when ready for use.

The colors of cudbear and orchil are practically indistinguishable. Lichen dyes were often mixed or had other substances added to vary the color. Addition of indigo to the dye of the Lung Lichen (*Sticta pulmonaria*) gives a permanent black dye. Addition of acids or alkalies changes the color: Acids produce yellows and alkalies produce blues; lead acetate gives a crimson color and calcium chloride, red.

Because of their low production cost, synthetic dyes have now largely replaced the lichen dyes; also they generally surpass the natural products in fastness. Though the lichen dyes were renowned among peasant dyers for their color and high quality, today they are the least known. Some are still popular in rural districts of Great Britain, Iceland, Scandinavia, Germany and France. In the *National Geographic Magazine* of February, 1947, Margaret Shaw Campbell reported that in the Hebrides, "lichens from the rocks [still] supply a dye of misty brown." The fishermen do not wear this color while in their boats, believing that "what is taken from the rocks will return to the rocks."

In Scandinavia the Hemslojd (Home Industries Association) is reviving interest in lichen dyes. The Irish government is trying to reestablish the art of lichen dyeing in the poorer farming and fishing districts.

There is sound economic reason for such revival. The production of Harris Tweeds, the luxury cloth of high quality and great demand, originally depended upon lichen dyes. Wool dyed with lichen dyes is not invaded by moths; this may in part account for the durability of the cloth. An attractive aspect of home-dyed and -woven cloth is not only the dye utilized in its manufacture, but also the individuality of patterns evolved by a particular household or community. When these are standardized for greater volume and less expensive production, they lose much appeal to retail trade. Under production control, prices tend to rise beyond their true value, even for hand-made things.

From 1925 to 1939 the Harris Tweed industry expanded considerably, mainly in the export trade; it was necessary to use synthetic dyes because of decreasing availability of lichen dyes. The Harris Tweed Association of Great Britain reported in 1948 that

> *just prior to World War II a certain amount of the dye used in making the Crotal shade (brown) of Harris Tweed was produced from lichens; during and since the war, economic conditions have altered so that dyeing by lichens is impractical. It takes a person nearly a whole day to collect sufficient lichens to dye 50 to 60 pounds of wool.*

Kemp, Blair and Co., Ltd., of Galashiels, Scotland, reported an interesting note:

> *Considerable knowledge existed in the Hebrides with the use of other vegetable growths such as heather tips and roots, but the quantities in use are practically negligible. It is likely that the quantities of Crotal used will gradually increase again, but it is doubtful if it will ever reach its pre-war quantity.*

Miniaturized Gardening

EVEN if lichens are never used for commercial food crops, it is likely that the future will see them used increasingly in gardens. Mosses too, as people are just starting to realize, are interesting and wherever there is soil they will grow and reproduce themselves. They also take up very little space and are easy to keep an eye on.

A garden may be only a little dirt in a dish with a dozen different species of plants growing; or no more than a foot of land in a window box; or it may be a large garden formally laid out and tended. Any family may have a garden: The joys and satisfaction of gardening do not depend on size or cost or the unusual nature of the plants; in fact, the gardener will have much more fun and be more creative if he has no rigid, arbitrary opinions regarding what a garden should be. Helping plants grow should be his chief delight and satisfaction.

Despite their great potential, mosses and lichens are little used, if at all, in gardening. The indices of eleven books on gardening show mosses mentioned only once—and that was not a significant reference—and so, still today they go largely unappreciated! But both mosses and lichens are readily cultivated the year around, through sunshine and rain, snow and sleet, heat and cold, indoors and out—and have a certain "immortality," remaining attractive throughout all seasons. Their endurance and vitality are remarkable. They are unusually free of parasitic fungi or animal foes. In damp weather they grow with surprising rapidity and in dry or frozen periods, simply stand and wait. The stems die below and grow above, adding new plant-supporting soil of vegetable origin.

As long as 1,000 years ago, the Japanese were confronted with chronic overpopulation of their urban areas. Land and space for cultivation were at a premium. And so they decided to miniaturize nature and bring it under control. Naturally dwarfed trees were collected from mountain crags and infertile soil where wind, drought and inhospitable conditions had produced gnarled trunks and branches and knotty exposed roots that are usually found only on far larger and older specimens. Just as a haiku poem expresses an entire environment, so does a bonkei sai suggest the full grandeur of a mature tree.

Mosses and lichens are used regularly in bonsai, of course, but only as an accessory to the potted tree. Moss is encouraged to grow over the roots, both to lend age and to serve as an indication of when the tree needs watering. But miniature trees often need to be watered at least once a day, and as a result, the moss can often overgrow, piling up upon itself and sometimes frothing down the side of the pot like the "head" on a glass of beer. Moreover, such rich, moist, dense mats of fiber inhibit root growth and lend themselves to explosive growths of fungi—and the bonsai enthusiast may discover a black, tarry sludge spreading throughout his collection. For these reasons, most bonsai experts advise removing the moss each autumn.

A good bonsai, or potted tree, may take as long as 150 years to reach perfection. For the gardener who wants quicker rewards, bonkei—or dish gardening—or terraria may be the answer. The Japanese, again, were the first to make dish gardens and constructed them as decorative, artistic efforts, requiring training, as in music, painting or sculpture. This technique is ideal for illustration of some geographical area, modeling of a landscape or scene, or simply creation of a tiny garden. Mountains, lakes, deep forests, canyons, all can be recreated in pots a few inches across. One brings the outdoors indoors and the joy of real woods and streams in miniature is on your table or in a sunny window. Dish gardens and terraria are superb outlets for creative self-expression in gardening on a miniature basis, and an excellent outlet for children or for the convalescent or shut-in—real garden therapy. They are a novel variation for indoor or porch gardening, and the charm of growing things is never more interesting and exciting than in this context.

Strangely, mosses or lichens have not been used in dish gardening, though they obviously lend ideal proportion, simplicity and balance to a dish garden or terrarium. The many species of mosses provide a superb choice of "bushes, trees, undergrowth, grass, fields" and other landscape items.

Hairy Caps growing among Frayed Lichen, *Cladonia degenerans*

To make a terrarium—the most easily kept form of such a miniature landscape—in a brandy snifter, glass bowl or glass aquarium, one should first lay out all the materials needed on a plastic tablecloth in an orderly fashion: scissors, pencil, a few small sticks, the plants, pebbles, soil and charcoal. Small stones and pebbles are placed in the bottom of the terrarium for drainage and many small pieces of charcoal added. Then mix the soil with some charcoal and add it to a depth of about one-third the height of the bowl or container. Next the soil is tamped down with small sticks or a pencil; contours are prepared and formed in the soil. Then moisten the soil with a fine spray of water until it is quite firm. There should be a slight slant to the soil, sloping toward the viewer. The taller plants are best placed in the background with smaller plants in front. Among the mosses Leucobryum, Sphagnum, Hairy Caps, *Bryum roseum* and the Dicranums are especially beautiful in a terrarium. Lichen-covered twigs, *Cladonia cristatella* or any of

The Giant Bryum, *Bryum Roseum,* largest and showiest of its group, is nearly leafless except at the end, where its large leaves form a single rosette

the Cladonia fairy-cup lichens add special charm. Tiny ferns, rattlesnake plantain, and partridgeberries are all commonly used. Miniature ceramic animals, mirror ponds, pieces of driftwood or lichen-covered stones lend unusual interest. Lastly the finished planting is sprayed with a fine mist of water, wetting it down well. It should be kept in a cool place in the home, in good light but avoiding direct sunlight.

On the other hand, one of the delights of bonkei—open-dish planting—is the landscape's "sculptural" quality. Follow the above directions, but plant your garden in a shallow ceramic tray—and don't forget to water it at least once a day. Schools of dish gardening still exist in Japan; it is regarded as belonging with the art of poetry, and every tiny landscape is like a poem, painting or song. In building a dish garden, one visualizes, plans the picture and then works it out for himself. By reversing the terrarium process—putting small plants in the rear and large ones in front—amazing illusions of perspective can be created. There may also be small figures of people,

Mealy Goblet Lichen, *Cladonia chlorophaea,* showing the characteristic sod flakes—plus a few Hairy Cap mosses, as usual

animals, a few stones and a stream either actual or mimic (i.e., in the mind's eye of the designer is a "painting" and a scene is produced utilizing mosses and lichens for the background scenes).

Special attention may show certain mosses to have a tropical appearance or to mimic trees or plants in faraway places. Seashore, seasons of the year—autumn, winter, spring—may be worked out, or an especially well-loved corner of the world may be created in miniature in a dish garden. Settings from books, plays, mythology or fairy tales may be recreated. One called "A Fairy Ring" was reproduced in which *Baeomyces roseus* was used as the mushroom fairy ring.

A good idea is to play around with your stones a bit before adding soil: They may suggest boulder-strewn pasture far better than the palisades and waterfall you may have been contemplating. Remember that in nature, broken, jagged rocks are the emblem of mountains and abrupt outcroppings. Fat, round rocks have usually lain for years in a field or riverbed to get their smooth polish. Use soil as you would mortar in building a stone wall—to enclose each rock, making sure it appears to rise out of the soil. Then when your landscape is ready, and only then, you can apply the moss.

Wrinkled Shield Lichen, *Parmelia physodes,* completely enclosing a fallen twig

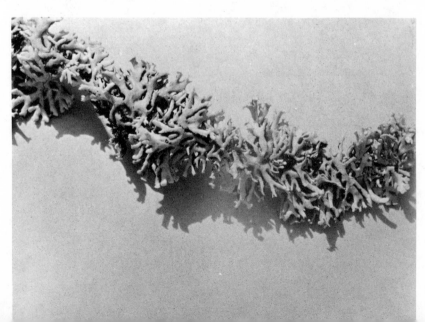

Rules of thumb: Mosses do best in crevices, along flat, sloping rocks where rainwater drains *horizontally* (each drop, therefore, does double duty)—and do poorly on the proverbial round and rollable stones which shed their water readily. If you are planting one of the flat, creeping Sphagnums on a rock, be sure to wet the "toupée" thoroughly before applying it to the rock, and exclude all air. No matter how often you water, the layer will not flourish if drying air is allowed to get underneath.

In general it is better to transplant mosses and lichens to an environment similar to that from which they have been taken. Their preferences as to soil moisture, exposure, temperature or climate can be judged by the area from which they are removed.

For planting in soil, try to place the bottom of the individual stems at or slightly below ground level. Many mosses that form "carpets" put down minute rhizines, and trap bits of soil in their stems. As a result, after loosening with a flat trowel, a whole colony of moss may come up in one single slab, and the gardener may be tempted to think he can just put it back down again wherever he wishes. Unfortunately, the soil held by the moss and the substratum he wishes to place it on are seldom of the same consistency. When the planting dries out, the moss

Moss clumps that have just been pried up. The excess soil needs to be scraped away before they are planted

"rug" often curls up, pulling away from its underpinnings. The only answer is to remove as much of the original soil as possible without having the entire moss colony dissolve in your hands. *Bryum argenteum,* the Silver Moss, for instance, forms a mat that, when wet, handles almost precisely like linoleum. But the rhizines, a delicate red in color, often trap enormous quantities of the clayish soil that is argenteum's favorite habitat, and the clay will not mix with any other soil. The best way to deal with this species is to place its mat upside down on a flat surface and then wash away the clay with a fine spray of water. When a dark-reddish, iodine-looking fabric of hairs appear, the silver moss is ready for planting. Remember, though, that since mosses have no real roots, a clump will not "take" on any patch of ground until the edges have had a chance to colonize the surface immediately adjacent, thus "tying down" the original graft. This is why some Japanese experts recommend drying and then breaking each individual clump into fragments and "seeding" them down on bare soil. This latter method produces perfectly adhering mosses, but it also takes weeks longer, and the fledgling bonkei must be even more scrupulously protected from wind, sun and excessive dryness.

Once established, the moss will give every indication of health by spreading in every direction. *Bryum argenteum* seems

A clump of Hairy Caps in fruit

to propogate sexually; Hairy Caps hardly ever spread in dry soil, but when they do, they appear in a charmingly dwarfed form. Fern and Cedar mosses will usually overgrow their neighbors, often to a most beautiful effect.

To begin and maintain such a landscape, it is absolutely essential that the bonkei soil itself be kept, if not always moist, at least cool. The dampest moss will shrivel if the temperature remains constantly above 70° F. Put bonkei outside during hot-weather nights and don't leave them where drafts blow.

Anyone who has seen the wild enthusiasm of a pot-bound moss may well want to grow mosses out-of-doors. Mosses and lichens may be distributed throughout the garden mixed in with most other plants. A wildflower garden with ferns and wild grasses is made particularly attractive and natural with mosses and lichens interspersed. (Mixtures of mosses and lichens grow well together, of course.)

Areas of the garden, such as steep slopes, that would otherwise be problem locations or eyesores can be converted into unique beauty spots using mosses and lichens. Homeowners have increased the beauty of shady walks by encouraging moss

A single plant of Mountain Fern Moss, *Hylocomium splendens,* showing the odd branching that gives it its common name. It is found abundantly on rocks and logs in cool, moist mountain woods

growth, and a growth of mosses on new buildings will give them that "old look."

Specific plants may be selected for placement almost anywhere in a garden, from trickling rills of fragrant coolness to full exposure in bright sunlight. Striking, large or colorful lichens that lend themselves especially well are the Cladonia (most species), Cetraria, Sticta, Umbilicaria, Evernia, Peltigera and Ramalina, also *Xanthoria parietina.* Particularly attractive and very available mosses would be the Polytrichum (several species); Dicranum; Leucobryum, Sphagnum and Climacium. Large boulders in a garden lend themselves exceedingly well to observation of plant succession; first the lichens, then mosses, then ferns and shallow-rooted plants.

Wall gardens may be made standing free with two sides for planting. A concrete foundation is often used—or a boulder wall against a bank is effective. Mosses and lichens grow very well from a vertical rock face—the cliff dwellers.

The rock garden is generally a site for the growth of alpine and rock plants, and thus, is especially effective for mosses and lichens. They are optimally displayed in such an appropriate setting. Mosses and lichens often do better than alpine plants because the length of the growing season in most rock gardens is so much longer than that which the plants experience when growing wild. They render the rock garden much more natural, blending with surroundings and scene. Locally available stones should be used in most instances and rocks may be selected which already have good growths of mosses and lichens on them. A boulder rock garden is especially attractive with extensive moss and lichen plantings, and provides a winter activity for the gardener, too, as mosses and lichens grow effectively even under the snow, surviving cold and frost. If not planted along the cracks of shady stone walls and paths, then mosses and lichens can even be given their own corner of the garden where a few choice specimens may be allowed to run riot. But to attempt to cultivate mosses *al fresco* means exposing these plants to dangers and drawbacks that have kept most gardeners before you from succeeding.

Again, for a model of a true moss garden, we must look to the Japanese. In Kyoto, where trees have been planted closely together, the ground beneath is often covered with yards of green velvet, brilliantly beautiful where a shaft of occasional sun strikes through the branches. Flat pieces of stone are set into the moss so that admirers and gardeners can make their way through the garden.

Mosses will survive in partial shade, but only when ample moisture is available from below. Therefore, the rich, well-drained soil that every gardener's encyclopedia recommends will do them no good until their mats have grown thick enough to act as sponges. Similarly, shrubs or some other form of windbreak should surround the Bryums, if only so that dust, leaves, and other ground litter are not blown into hollows in the diminutive topography. Conifers—pines, hemlocks and spruces—produce *excessive* shade, however, and the copious amounts of dead needles they release will strangle the hardiest tuft. Tupelo, tulip tree, ash or maple provide the best shelter.

The moss gardener will soon understand one reason why enormous stretches of "pure" moss are rarely encountered in the wild. The deeper recesses of a tuft offer almost perfect germinating conditions—moisture, air and dark—for weed and grass seeds, and whether or not a moss is under cultivation, it continues to pave the way for higher, if less desirable, forms of life. The first weeds will appear about two weeks after a moss garden has been created; the problem will persist as long as there are seeds left in the soil immediately underneath to be aroused by the moisture and darkness.

Obviously the best preventive method is to sterilize the soil, but even then, moss plants are ideally suited to trapping wind-borne seeds. Besides making a real effort to install windbreaks, the gardener should definitely plan his garden around rocks or tiles on which he can sit or stand comfortably when weeding—this will be a particular chore the first season or so. Plants that have germinated in moss tend to put their roots out *horizontally*, again thanks to the plant's superb water-retentive qualities. Thus, weeds which would normally have only a long taproot and which could be pulled as smoothly as a carrot will suddenly be found to have long side roots that take up horribly wide swathes of moss with them as they come loose. The best answer, of course, is preventive—clip off the seedlings' nourishment by removing the cotyledons and seed's leaves as soon as they are borne aloft on the stem. The remaining root will die.

But if the plant has grown ground level (as in the dandelions and most grasses), the whole plant must come out. Straddle the stem with your fingers or gardening fork, and push down as you pull up the weed with your other hand. This way the roots come free with a minimum of disturbance and the moss immediately surrounding the weed stays in place. For deeply-rooted, stubborn weeds, it sometimes pays to cut around the weed in a circle with a sharp trowel and lift weed, moss, soil and all out as a single "plug." Then the root comes loose easily by pulling *down* on it from below, the leaves vanish into the root-hole, and the entire plug can be neatly replaced.

It is better to leave weeding wounds open (the moss will quickly heal over) than to fill them with soil and take the chance of introducing several weed seeds where there was one before.

Although it is true that no animal is likely to lunch directly on a moss planting, birds are one of the moss garden's worst despoilers. A flock of starlings or even a solitary bluejay will wantonly tear up tufts that have taken laborious hours to plant, scattering the pieces in every direction—all in apparent search of the insects and worms that so frequently inhabit the mosses' thick underlayers. The only real solution, short of unsightly netting or aluminum pinwheels, is to exploit the birds' natural claustrophobia. Again, dense planting can not only shade and shelter a moss garden but can make it difficult and uncomfortable for a bird to land, let alone forage. A variety of miniature evergreens are available in specialized nurseries (one particularly fine selection and catalogue is available from Mayfair Nurseries, Nichols, New York), and the moss gardener can protect and enhance his plantings with a number of exquisitely and naturally dwarfed cryptomeria, juniper, hinoki cypress, chamaecyparis and heather—all of which can be kept under a foot tall with a minimum of clipping. Their slow growth keeps ground litter to a minimum, and if one imagines them as full grown trees, the surrounding moss will come to appear in scale as grass. The final result is likely to be a full-scale miniature landscape, with white-veined rocks representing a waterfall and yucca, shrubbery and flowers recreated in miniature by saxifrage, maidenhair fern, spleenwort and *Cladonia cristatella* respectively.

Though water gardens are the most difficult of all to maintain, they are extremely interesting either as part of a larger plan or as the primary garden. Such water-loving mosses as Sphagnum and Fontinalis can be grown in either running water or still-water pools. These bog dwellers are especially attractive and colorful. A pseudo-bog may be created and the process of bog formation observed on a miniature scale. Mosses mix well with such plants as water lilies, irises, forget-me-nots and water snowflakes. Even if all of these possibilities fail, you can always go back indoors and try growing bonkei (dish gardens) and specific species in a greenhouse.

Popularity is increasing for large plants from tropical humid forests, used indoors and out; the glamorous ginger plants, orchids and bromeliads are increasingly seen as indoor and entryway decoration. They cry out for some green foliage nearby (other than the weed wood sorrel which grows unwanted in their pots). Water flowing indoors is increasingly attractive architecturally, and lends itself well to use of water-loving mosses, Sphagnum and Fontinalis. An extensive growth of mosses cools an area, and with increasing use of vines and trailing plants, mosses, too, can be planted on trellises and indoor walls. Climacium, Hypnum, Brachythecium, Hylocomium and Sphagnum are always available and survive such transplantation well. The liverworts do not lend themselves as effectively, however, since their "raw" appearance and need for constant moisture keep them from being appreciated indoors.

Broom Moss, *Dicranum scoparium,* makes a good "meadow"

Key to Common Lichens
by Growth and Structure

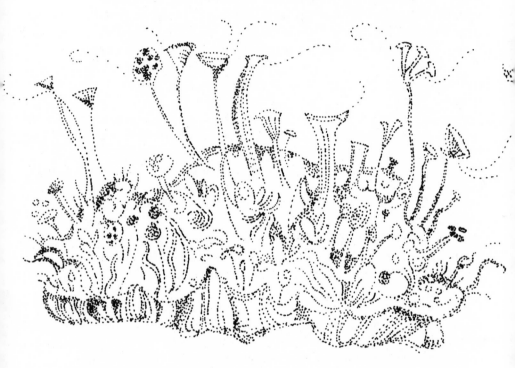

THE classification and specific naming of lichens is a near impossibility because they are not really individual plants. For this reason taxonomists have had great difficulty deciding on names, the question being, should the lichen be named for the alga component or the fungus partner? Botanical taxonomists have always named lichens as though they were not two plants but a single entity, but since we know the lichens now as definite composite plants, the older nomenclature is improper. The International Code of Botanical Nomenclature forbids naming a plant made up of two or more different plants. However, at an international meeting of botanical taxonomists in 1954, it was arbitrarily decided that the old lichen names were to refer only to the fungus component.

Had this decision not been made, it would have been necessary to coin literally thousands of new names for lichen fungi. For example, the common British Soldier Lichen, *Cladonia cristatella,* is composed of a fungus and the well-known alga, Trebouxiae. However, the scientific name refers only to the fungus, whether existing separately or as the lichenized fungal form. Obviously, this arbitrary ruling is a matter of necessary convenience and is not factually accurate. It depends on the unproved assumption that every species of lichenized fungus is different. The International Code accepts this convenient fiction as a necessary evil. The most current and best system of classification is that proposed originally by Lutrell, for fungi, and modified by Santesson for lichens. Despite the seeming state of chaos that characterizes lichen classifications, rather precise identification of the common lichens is quite possible and can be simply done by an untrained person.

Lichens can be collected at all times of the year. They are the simplest of plant specimens to collect and preserve, since they keep in good condition for years. Plants collected in damp places in a moist atmosphere are more beautiful and complete than dry ones. The best specimens available are taken; some should be in fruit since the fruits are helpful in identification.

The tools needed are a heavy, sharp knife to scrape foliose and fruticose species from bark or rocks; a geologist's hammer and chisel to chip off crustose rock species; and a hand lens to examine the lichen where it is growing. Crustose lichens on bark should be cut with a thin layer of bark underneath, and the margin of the thallus carefully secured.

Dry specimens can be stored indefinitely, wet specimens must be air-dried to prevent molding. A few notes should be taken in the field about each specimen regarding its habitat, the date and place of collecting and observations made at the time.

Later in preparing the lichens for a collection or herbarium, the specimens should be well moistened, pressed flat gently between blotters, dried and placed in paper packets about 3 × 4 inches and opening by a flap. Each species has a distinctive look, and when naturally dried, pressure should not be great enough to flatten the plant beyond its normal form. Small boxes may be more satisfactory for small fruticose specimens. A label should be pasted on the flap or the box showing the common and specific name of the specimen, the locality found, the collector and the date. A sample specimen label is as follows:

DOG TOOTH LICHEN, Peltigera canina, *bank of mountain stream, Mt. Mansfield, altitude 2,700 ft., Stowe, Vt. 9/30/69. Collected by: J. W. Smith   Determined by: J. W. Smith*

Lichens are not eaten by moths or carpet beetles and usually will not shrink or discolor.

Both fresh and dry material should be available for comparison. If only dry lichens can be found, they can be freshened by soaking in clean water in a small dish or watch glass. One then can learn as much as possible with the unaided eye about the color, texture, fruits, margins of the thallus and the rhizines.

The author examining lichen flora along a riverbank

A piece of plate glass, twelve inches square, placed on a table over a piece of white paper makes gross examination of lichens easier. Thallus and fruits stand out more clearly against a contrasting background.

Because lichens are small plants, and parts to be examined are tiny, the strong magnifying hand lens is an important part of study apparatus. For ordinary work a lens of from six to twelve diameters is needed (lichen fruits are best observed in this way). For finer details a lens of thirty or more diameters is necessary. Small hand microscopes about the size of a fountain pen, having magnifications of from ten to forty diameters are obtainable from optical supply houses or toy stores.

To use a hand lens best the lichen should be held with a thumb and forefinger of the left hand, and the lens with the right hand. Then by resting the right hand on the left, the lens can be focused without difficulty. It is best to let the thumb of the right hand lie on that of the left. If the hands do not touch, it is often difficult to hold them steady enough to keep a high-powered hand lens in focus. A stand to hold a hand microscope steady can be made of a wire coat hanger, thus leaving hands free to manipulate the specimen. If one is serious about studying lichens, he may want a binocular dissecting microscope. A small microscope lamp is useful, as direct light should be avoided. Any small light, a small clip-on reading lamp, is satisfactory.

A pair of fine forceps is helpful in separating plant parts for closer observation. Hemostats are used to handle specimens; two dissecting needles, bought at surgical supply houses, are useful to skewer fruits and thalli for close scrutiny, or to tease apart and identify the fungus and algal components. A scalpel is needed for cutting cross-sections of the thallus or the fruits. The preferred scalpel is one with replaceable blades, but a razor blade or old-fashioned straight razor serves as well. Map tacks are handy for finer dissection.

To make slides of fruits or thalli, grasp the plant between thumb and forefinger, and slice across it with a scalpel or razor blade. Another very effective method is to place the plant part between two small pieces of balsa wood and press tightly together; then sections are cut as thinly as possible, cutting *both*

Tools for collecting and examining lichens in the field: a geologist's pick, knife, chisel and pocket magnifier

The tools for detailed examination of lichens at home: scissors, tweezers, glycerin solution and eyedropper, map tacks, razor blade, scalpel, dissecting needles and glass slides. The whole ensemble is mounted on a pane of glass set on blocks, so as to facilitate illumination from below

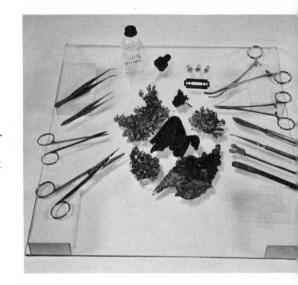

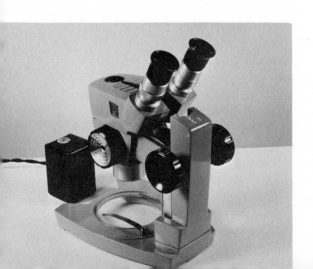

A binocular microscope

the balsa wood and the lichen. Make a number of sections, and among them some will be found showing the structure. These are floated off in water in a small dish or watch glass. Sections are then fished out and placed on a slide, and mounted in a 10-percent solution of glycerin. Since the plant tissues and glycerin are often nearly at the same refractive index, even better visualization of the component parts is obtained by mounting in a general protoplasmic stain to produce contrast between the components of the plant, the best being acid fuchsin in lactophenol. The section is then ready for examination by a small microscope or hand lens. A permanent mount and slide is made by ringing the slip cover with clear fingernail polish and letting it dry.

The small microscope and hand lens are best carried into the field on searching expeditions for lichens. Two blank slides, two rubber bands, a pair of fine-pointed forceps and a small bottle of water may be carried in the pocket, to enable one to mount slides on the spot. This may save the trouble of carrying home useless materials, or leaving a good thing behind because it is not recognized. The rubber bands are to slip over the two slides and keep them in place when objects are mounted between them.

Unfortunately, there is a lack of accurate manuals with comprehensive up-to-date keys and illustrations for identification of lichens. An amateur lichenologist (and, often enough, a specialist) cannot hope to arrive at critical identification. The recommended book for more advanced study is *Lichen Flora of the United States,* by B. Fink, University of Michigan Press, Ann Arbor, Michigan.

The following steps will serve to identify most lichens encountered by the beginner using this book:

1. Determine the growth form: crustose, foliose, or fruticose. Look carefully for such characteristics of the surface of the lichen as color, texture, wrinkling and type of margin. These characteristics will often allow separation of genera.

2. Look carefully with a hand lens for soredia, isidia or soralia. These characteristics often allow identification of a species.

3. Inspect the under surface or margins of lobes for rhizines or cilia and other surface characteristics.

4. Check the lichen with descriptions, illustrations and photographs under appropriate category: crustose, foliose or fruticose. Good specimens may be sent to lichenologists in museums and universities for precise identification, but lichens can usually be placed in the correct genus on sight after only a little practice.

Each member of the broad categories has growth characteristics and specific fruiting manifestations aiding identification. There is some overlapping among the three large categories. For instance, a flaky, frosty green growth is often seen about the base of fruticose lichens, sometimes spreading over fairly wide areas. This is called "sod flakes," and it is from this thallus or flat-growing part of the lichen that the stalk or podetia and branching parts arise.

As we already discussed, the crustose or flaky lichens are the most primitive type; the fruticose, stalked and intricately branching ones, are the most highly developed; the foliose or papery lichens are an intermediate form. Some primitive forms which are simply dust-like are difficult to recognize unless you know what you are looking for. Almost any pale gray, olive green, greenish-gray, mineral gray, black or brownish-red, yellow, brown or slate-blue growths on rocks, decaying logs in woods, on trees, or earth, any chalky or mealy growth coating old fence rails, spreading over rocks and cliffs or extending over soil is usually a lichen.

CRUSTOSE LICHENS

This group of lichens consists of numerous, more or less independent flakes or crusts with a papery structure, not organized into rosette form. Usually an upper and an under surface different in color and texture can be made out, but the under surface is sometimes so tightly adherent to the rock or wood upon which it grows that it cannot be observed or described. There are seemingly innumerable lichens in this group whose form, mode of growth and color blend one into the other. No good purpose, except for the specialist, is served by attempting to completely differentiate them. Some may consist of a sod of flakes for years, and then stalks may arise from them. They may have some of the characteristics of the papery lichens, superficially, though they are always very tiny. These are the least developed and the lowest forms of lichens.

The Sod Lichens are found on the ground about the bases of trees and on stumps throughout the eastern United States. They are common, and grow as greenish-gray flakes usually about $1/16$ inch long and about as wide. There may be toothed or finely-divided lobes crowded together into a dense frosty looking sod extending sometimes over an area of twelve to eighteen inches in diameter. The erect edges and the under surface are white and appear dusty with a mealy substance. One of this group called the Burn Lichen is found on tree bark and dead charred wood in pine barrens and mountains. Fan-shaped scales or flakes are seen. They may be scattered or densely clustered, much like shingles. The flakes grow downward with the lower edge usually projecting somewhat from a vertical foothold. When crowded, the flakes stand out almost horizontally.

The Stud Lichens are found on rocks, particularly granite, on exposed areas throughout most of the United States. Fruits are commonly button- or pie-shaped, dark brown or black in color and very dry looking, with a rim colored like the lichen. They grow tightly adherent to the rock and the central fruits are prominent. There may seem to be radiating lobes from the central areas of the lichen. The fruits project upward and suggest shirt studs.

The Zoned or Coin Lichen is found on rocks in dense, shady, wooded areas. Common but easily overlooked, this lichen grows as a circular, blackish-gray area, commonly $1/4$ to $1/2$ inch in diameter covered with radiating clusters of granules. At the outer edge the granules are whitish but going centrally from the edge they turn dull green or blackish. A second and sometimes a third growth may spread later making two or three concentric zones of whitish tips against the much darker central tips. They also grow so tightly adherent to the rock that they cannot be separated.

The Common Yolk Lichen is found on rocks and dead wood throughout the United States. It is readily recognized by the egg-yellow granules scattered or heaped over it. Older plants sometimes blacken and only the youngest granules remain yellow. Fruits are frequent, disc-shaped or somewhat irregular, but very tiny. A hand lens is necessary to see them. They grow most profusely on dead wood and are more scattered when seen on rock, particularly granite. They often tend to grow over other flaky rock lichens.

The Blood Lichens are found on tree bark, preferring that of balsam fir usually at high elevations. They consist of a white, cream-colored or gray crust which is granular or powdery. The plant may spread four to five inches, often growing in a circular manner, sometimes bridging separations in the bark with cottony cords. Fruits are usually plentiful and button-like or disc-shaped, being light red when young. They are approximately $^1/_{16}$ inch in diameter. The fruit may have a sparsely toothed white rim.

The Rock Button is a lichen found on rocks in many parts of the United States. The crust or flaky part of the lichen is seldom seen and may show as only a few scattered granules. The fruits appear to grow directly from the rock and are the most prominent part of the plant. They are disc-shaped and button-like in character. The middle part of the fruit is a dark brown color.

The Tar Lichen grows on the ground and on rotten wood. It is a dark brown or blackish growth of very minute particles which make a felt-like surface oftentimes growing two or three feet across. The fruits are frequent, tiny and disc-shaped or bead-like, sometimes clustered and lumpy. They may be seen on damp sandy or peaty soil along roadbanks. The black patches suggest that tar has been spilled there long ago. A hand lens will show the felt-like surface and a black undercrust. The fruits become apparent when observed with a hand lens.

FOLIOSE LICHENS

Foliose lichens most commonly appear in rosette form, spreading leaf-like expansions of one or many lobes which adhere in varying degree to the substrate on which they grow. The upper surface has a tough cortex made up of densely packed lichen hyphae, beneath which is the algal layer or gonidial zone and the medulla. There is also a lower cortex usually of a darker color from which project downward rhizines or "root hairs" made of tough strands of hyphae that serve mainly as a means of attachment or anchoring for the plant. Foliose lichens generally have two different growth forms, the most characteristic being leaf-like and lobed and anchored to the substrate by many rhizines projecting downward from the greater part of the under surface, e.g., Parmelia and Peltigera. The less common or umbilicate form is roughly circular in form and attached to the substrate by a single central cord-like structure, e.g., Umbilicaria or Rock Tripe.

The foliose lichens are mostly greenish-gray or yellow-gray, though many shades of color other than bright green occur. Their mats of finely wrinkled paper-like structures are usually radiating with branching parts flattened tight against the substrate and only the tips and peripheral edges lifted from it. Ascocarps in fruits are common and often brown in color, saucer-shaped and occurring in the central part of the upper surface, sometimes at the tips of the lobes. Foliose lichens include the most conspicuous, more or less circular patches of lovely pale green embroidery which lie target-like on the darker back of trees or soften the ruggedness of boulders with their delicate traceries. They will probably be the first lichens one sees as he starts on a lichen walk.

Genus Parmelia   The Boulder Lichen or *Parmelia conspersa* is the most abundant of all papery lichens. In size it varies from tiny rosettes two or three inches across, to mats spreading more than a foot over a rock. There is little to show whether it is all a single plant reviving again where old and broken parts are seen; or if it represents several plants. It may appear to be several lichens tangled together when growing in large mats.

The Boulder Lichen is found on stones, boulders, cliffs and sometimes on the roots of trees. It does not do well on trees, and degenerates on dead wood. It is leaf-like and papery when moist, pale green or straw-colored above and blackening below. The margins are elevated but the rest of the plant is tightly adherent to the rock. The fruits are easily seen. They are common and many will be observed as saucer-shaped round discs, brown to chestnut in color, generally situated in the central portions of the plants.

The name *Parmelia* is from the Latin, *parma* (small, round shield). It is derived from the resemblance of the saucer-like fruiting bodies to a small shield. The specific name *conspersa* (besprinkled) refers to the appearance of the surface of the lichen which looks as if it had been sprinkled with tiny grains. This feature may be another identifying evidence. If you glance at a rock covered with a papery lichen and say that it is *Parmelia conspersa,* you will be right at least 50 percent of the time!

The Puffed Shield Lichen (*Parmelia physodes*) is very common on dead limbs of pines and hemlocks. It attaches itself lightly to its support. It often completely encircles the smaller twigs, giving the tree an especially attractive appearance. It grows on trees by preference. Occasionally it grows on rocks in the highlands and pine barrens through the northern United States. The Puffed Shield is particularly plentiful in the mountains.

When growing luxuriantly on green branches and twigs, it may stand out from them a half inch or more. This lichen is freely branching and varies from a zigzag forking to finger-like branching. The branchings have a puffed or inflated appearance which gives them the name *physodes,* (from the Greek, meaning "like a bellows").

The upper surface is smooth and greenish-gray and the under surface is black to brown about the tips of the branchings. The branchings usually curl upward showing conspicuously the color of the under surface. Fruits are rare but when they do appear are less than $1/16$ inch in diameter, are saucer-shaped and brown in color. This lichen is small but conspicuous with well-marked distinguishing characteristics. The puffing of the tips separates it from all other types of Parmelia.

The Wrinkled Shield Lichen (*Parmelia caperata*) is found on tree bark, dead wood and rocks throughout the United States. It is very common, forming light, pea-green wrinkled wavy mats. The upper surface is frequently covered with a very light green powder, the soredia. The under surface is black with a reddish-brown margin and scattered rhizines. Though fruiting is rare, the fruiting organs are cup-shaped with wavy margins. The Wrinkled Shield Lichen is a conspicuous object of beauty on the bark of roadside oaks and maples, easily seen from a passing automobile. The delicately wrinkled surface readily separates it from similar lichens. There are other shield lichens but these three plants characterize the entire group and the overlappings of individual species are minor.

Genus Cetraria   The Spanish Shield Lichens (*Cetraria*) grow on trees and more rarely on rocks or earth. The color on the upper surface is bright yellow, greenish-yellow, straw, olive or brown. The flat-growing part of the plant is expanded, leaf-like and gives a shrubby appearance. The branches are compressed or channeled and the lobes, flattened and broad. The Spanish Shield Lichens are related closely to the Parmelia or ordinary Shield Lichens. The Spanish Shields, however, are more shrubby in appearance and not as flattened or rosette-like. It would seem that the Spanish Shield Lichens are a little further advanced and beginning to become stalked or branching but have not yet attained this characteristic of growth. The rhizines on the under surface are few or absent. The disc- or saucer-like fruits are not as common as in the Parmelias. They occur at the margins of the plant rather than on the central portions. The "saucers" are brown in color. The name *Cetraria* is from the Spanish *cetra* (shield).

The Pitted Cetraria (*Cetraria tuckermanii*) is found plentifully on trees and old fence rails. It is very easily detached. It is also called the Lettuce Lichen and grows in tufts resembling lettuce. On the upper gray-green surface there is a pattern of tiny pits or small wrinkles. The old species name, *lacunosa (pitted), has reference to the pitted surface of the upper part of the plant. Fruits are* $1/16$ to $1/2$ inch in diameter. They are disc-shaped, brown and irregular, occurring along the margins. The Lettuce Lichen is a conspicuous but variable lichen.

Iceland Moss (*Cetraria islandica*) is found on soil and rocks throughout the northern United States. It is common only in the north. It forms tufts and tangled masses $1/2$ to 2 inches high, appearing as though it were becoming a stalk or branching lichen. However, the tufts are paper-thin rather than being real stalks. These curl, particularly in drying, so that the upper surface becomes a kind of trough. The surface is usually smooth but may be slightly wrinkled. Iceland Moss is brown to olive or gray when dry, and olive green when wet. The under surface is a little paler than the upper. Fruits are borne along the margins of the enlarged tips. They are oval, irregular and dark brown in color. Iceland Moss is one of the most important lichens and has been used for centuries in the northern countries both for human food and animal fodder. It can hardly be mistaken for any other lichen. It represents a transition stage between papery and stalked lichens.

The name, *islandica,* refers to the fact that the lichen is so very abundant in Iceland.

Genus Umbilicaria   Rock Tripes (*Umbilicaria*) are fascinating papery lichens, leathery in consistency, occurring in more or less circular sheets attached to rocks at a single central point. The name Rock Tripe derives from the resemblance of the under surface of the lichen to the cells in the stomach of cattle and pigs from which the Boston delicacy tripe is made. The shape may be very irregular with deeply cut contorted lobes. There are rhizine processes on the under surface but they do not function as rhizines. The plant is firmly fixed to the rock by a strong central umbilical attachment. The majority are found in mountains, being particularly abundant above timberline. Some species descend to altitudes of 1,000 feet, however, or even may be found at the seashore.

They grow best on exposed cliffs and dry boulders depending on the air for moisture. Fruits are not common but are disc-shaped and scattered over the upper surface, sometimes closely clustered in groups. Peculiar furrows and convolutions give the disc an unusual appearance. The name *Umbilicaria* comes from the Latin *umbilicus* (navel), and has reference to the single point of support in the lichen's center.

The Smooth Rock Tripe (*Umbilicaria mammulata*) is one of the most common of the Rock Tripes. It is seen in abundance on cliffs and boulders at elevations from 1,000 feet up in the northern United States and may be seen below 1,000 feet in the Northeast. It is a flat, somewhat wrinkled, contorted, leathery sheet, varying in size from a few inches in diameter to fifteen inches. It is attached to the rock at a single central point and there are no lobes. The margin may be torn and ragged in appearance. The upper surface is smooth, dull and usually powdery, brown or grayish when dry and live green when moist. The under surface is striking, being coal-black with a dense black, ragged nap less than $1/16$ inch deep. Toward the point of attachment this hairy coating may pass into a few flat, radiating, branching strands clinging to the under surface. The fruits, not commonly seen, are attached, button-like, to the upper surface.

The Blistered Rock Tripe (*Umbilicaria papulosa*) is common on exposed cliffs and boulders. It grows in more or less circular sheets often as much as four to five inches in diameter. They are firmly attached by a central attachment to the rock surface from which parts of the somewhat crumpled area may be lifted. The indented and torn edges often curl back. Interesting knob-shaped blisters as much as $1/8$ inch across and $1/16$ inch high occupy most of the upper surface. These are arranged in roughly radiating lines. The lichen gives the appearance of blistered paint. The color is olive green when moist and brown or gray when dry; the under surface is buff or pale brown, black when old. The fruits are plentiful and are seen on the upper surface as black disc-shaped areas between the blisters. The Blistered Rock Tripe is the most plentiful of the Rock Tripes at moderate elevations. It will not be mistaken for any other lichen. The name *papulosa* is from the Latin (blistered) and refers to the knob-like protrusions on the thallus.

The Fleecy Rock Tripe (*Umbilicaria vellea*), the third common Rock Tripe, is found on rocks at high elevations in various parts of the United States. It is pale, often nearly white or very pale blue-gray. The under surface is dark brown rather than black. A fascinating aspect of this plant is that its under surface is very hairy or may have soft granules instead of hair. They are large, leathery and strongly attached by the central umbilicus. The Latin name, *vellea,* means fleece, referring to the hairy under surface of the plants.

Genus Peltigera   The Toothed Lichens (*Peltigera*) appear crudely saucer-shaped or fan-shaped. Most of them are leathery in appearance and brittle when dry. The upper surface is some shade of brown or gray, usually blackening when old and wet. The under surface shows an interesting fine felt netted with thick vein-like structures from which spring large, cottony branching rhizines. The striking characteristic of these lichens are the fruits, which appear to be tightly glued against the upper surface of elongated tips at the margin of the plant. When they are mature they curl with the brown spore layer outward to form a cone-shaped or tooth-shaped projection. This may strongly suggest brown fingernails to some. The name *Peltigera* comes from the Latin *pelta* (shield), and *gerere* (to carry), and has reference to the fruits which are shield-shaped with a more or less scalloped border.

The Dog Tooth Lichen (*Peltigera canina*) is found on the ground throughout the United States and also frequently about the bases of trees and along the edges of rocks. It reaches its highest development in the dense shade of damp woods and along stream banks. It is not commonly seen in exposed places but is very common and will not be overlooked. It frequently grows among mosses and liverworts in extensive patches of large greenish-gray or brownish plants.

Their resemblance to dogs' teeth resulted in their specific name *canina,* from the Latin (dog). The under surface is a fine felt, white to pale brown covered with a network of thickened, white, brown or blackish veins which usually do not reach the tips. Fruits are common and most of them mature in spring and in autumn. The narrow fruiting lobes spring upward from the tips of plants at first curling to form a hood over the young fruits. Later the fruits become flat on the upper surface of their lobes and finally roll into a cone-shaped structure with a reddish-brown or blackening spore layer outward. There are many species of Dog Tooth Lichens. This group is easily recognized.

Many-Fruited Dog Tooth Lichen (*Peltigera polydactyla*) is similar to the ordinary Dog Tooth Lichen except that it has slender fruiting lobes, on the tips of which are several fruiting bodies rather than one. This gives the appearance of several fingers and hence the Latin name *polydactyla* (many fingers). The plant is smooth above and sprinkled with brownish warts. It differs from the Dog Tooth Lichen by being smooth above and nearly naked beneath.

Genus Lobaria   The Speckled Lichens (*Lobaria*) are lichens of an irregular rosette growth habit resembling Shield Lichens. They differ in several important respects. The under surface is downy; a closely related genus *Sticta* has its under surface speckled with pale dots or tiny cups, called cyphellae, resembling large recessed pores. The name *Sticta* is from the Greek *Stiktos* (dappled), and refers to the striking spotted appearance of some species. No other papery lichens show cyphellae and Lobaria is thus separated from Sticta. The thallus of Lobaria is leaf-like, but with the lobes wide and rounded or elongated. The under surface is covered with short, soft rhizines. Fruits are shield-like, elevated and located near the margin of the thallus.

The Spreading Leather Lichen (*Lobaria quercizans*) is found on the bark of large trees, rarely on rocks. It frequently grows in the mountains, forming rosettes sometimes eight inches or more in diameter. It grows flat with wavy margined lobes or branchings, resembling a very large oak leaf; the specific name *querizans* is taken from the Latin word *quereus*, referring to the oak tree. The upper surface is smooth with no wrinkles. It is usually pinkish-gray or pearl-gray when dry and dark green when wet. The downy under surface is a pale buff at the margins and a darker brown near the center. Fruits are frequent and plentiful, xeing light red when immature and brown or black with age. They are saucer-shaped, crowded and irregular, with a smooth pale rim. The Spreading Leather Lichen is easily recognized by the red, saucer-shaped fruits. No other papery lichen of large size has similar fruits.

The Lung Lichen (*Lobaria pulmonaria*) is found on trees and occasionally on lime-bearing rocks in the mountains. It forms regular open rosettes of a leaf-like, leathery, tawny or olive-colored growth, loosely attached to the surface on which it grows. It is lobed and the lobes are large and entire, with a netted looking, deeply pitted under surface. The under surface is pale to white with rounded prominences outlined with slender hairs. The margins are lifted from the surface on which they grow as much as $1/2$ inch. The color varies from pale greenish-gray to brown or even black when dry, to olive green when moist. The pitted surface is the most striking characteristic and there seem to be rounded ribs between the pits forming a network. The lifted margins and sometimes the rib-like places may be studded with dusty gray powder, the soredia.

The under surface is exactly the reverse of the upper because the lichen is paper-thin, and like paper which has been impressed with a seal. The pits of the upper surface become the lumps of the under surface and the ribs of the upper surface become grooves of the under surface.

Genus Xanthoria   The Shore Lichens (*Xanthoria*) are rosettes or lobed single sheets, are usually some shade of orange and have orange fruits. The brilliant color is distinctive enough to separate this lichen from all other papery lichens. This group grows leaf-like or scale-like but occasionally may have ascending or shrub-like branchings. The fruits are yellow and shield-like.

The Yellow Wall Lichen (*Xanthoria parietina*) grows on trees and rocks, usually near bodies of water. The plant is leaf-like, pale yellow to orange above and white below. It is attached loosely to the surface on which it grows. The margins are frequently loose and ascendant. Fruits are small orange discs with entire margins. The name *parietina* is from Latin (wall), and refers to the lichen's habit of growing on stone walls.

Genus Physcia   The Blister Lichen (*Physcia*) is a papery lichen in rosette form or sometimes straggling, is frequently small, is not particularly conspicuous and has prominent branching parts. It may look somewhat star-like on the stone. The fruiting portion is shield-shaped with its surface covered with whitish powder. The name comes from the Greek *physcia* (blister) and has reference to the inflated appearance of the plant. The upper surface is dull and dusty looking rather than shiny. It is gray, brown or whitish—never yellow.

The Plume Lichen (*Anaptychia speciosa*) is frequently found on tree barks and mossy ledges in open woods throughout the northeastern United States, growing in rosettes up to three or four inches in diameter. Their graceful branches have feathery divisions, the tips being slightly lifted. The upper surface is greenish to ashen-gray or almost white. The upward curling margins break into pale blue or white, mealy-looking soredia.

These are often crescent-shaped, seeming to cap the branching lobes. The under surface is white and there are white rhizines. The fruits are not commonly found, but are brown and cup-shaped.

THE FRUTICOSE LICHENS

Genus Cladonia   Cladonia, from the Greek, *klados,* branch, includes a large group of lichens with great diversity of form, making them the most fascinating and baffling of all lichens. They are difficult to separate completely into individuals because there are many overlappings in fruit color, presence or absence of cup-like processes, and branchings of varying shapes and forms. However, there will be no question about recognition of the general group Cladonia for they are unmistakable. The common and striking members are easy to find and name, and the rarer ones more difficult to categorize.

The Cladonia group are often distinguished by a sod of frosty green flakes at the base of the plant. This may or may not persist. The horizontal growth may be scale-like or more rarely granular.

From this sod hollow, stalks arise. These are thin shells surmounted by bright-colored, lumpy fruits which are also hollow. Some of this group have been called Shrublet Lichens because of their habit of branching. The fruiting branches are hollow with occasional pores opening to the outside. They may appear leathery, cup-shaped or funnel-shaped, sometimes shrub-like and much branched. The fruiting organs are lumpily modeled, hollow within and variously colored, but never black.

The Brown-Fruited Cup Cladonia (*Cladonia fimbriata,* v. *amplex*) grows freely on stumps and earth. The horizontal thallus is scale-like and variously lobed. Fruit-bearing branches rise erect from the larger, broader sod flakes growing horizontally. Greenish-gray or brownish stalks are at first goblet-shaped and later branch by extensions from the lip of the goblet. These extensions may be strap-shaped, often forking once or twice, or may develop into goblet-shaped extensions of a second or even third tier. The fruits are brown or purplish in color and are borne on the lip of the goblet on extensions from it. This lichen is common and easy to recognize.

The Scarlet-Crested Cladonia Coral Fungus (*Cladonia cristatella*) is a common lichen growing on earth, tree bark, dead wood, fences and woods and along roadsides. The sod 'flakes are usually tiny and toothed. From among the sod flakes rise stalks (podetia) commonly ½ to 2 inches high; they are thick rod-shaped or branching and tree-shaped. The surface is smooth or slightly warty and covered, sometimes densely, with flakes like those of the sod. The color is a frosty greenish-gray, slate gray or whitish. Fruits are bright red, globular and lumpy in appearance. These scarlet knobs are the most striking part of the plant and have given rise to the name, British Soldiers. The name *cristatella* is suggested by the bright fruits. It is derived from the Latin, *crista* (crest).

The Cornucopia Cladonia or Red-Fruited Cup Cladonia (*Cladonia cornucopioides*) grows freely on earth. It is branching and horn-like in form with the hollow, elongated, top-shaped, warty branches. There are scarlet knobs on the tips of the fruiting branches which are horn-like or cup-like. The name *cornucopioides* is suggested by the fruiting bodies and means, of course, horn of plenty, -*oides* meaning resembling.

Reindeer Moss or Reindeer Lichen (*Cladonia rangiferina*) is not a moss, but a freely branching lichen. It is found on soil and particularly above ledges of rock in exposed places throughout the northern United States. It covers extensive areas as a shrubby, grayish-white branching plant. The tufts of growth suggest a sponge shape of densely intertangled stalks, springing from a gray, granular, crusty horizontal growth. The crust soon disappears or escapes notice. The stalks are tiny, delicate and hollow. Most of the branching tips turn downward, subdividing into several tiny drooping fingerlets. The surface resembles a fine felt, grayish-white or silvery in color.

On close inspection there are tiny, lumpy, brown fruits at the tips of all the branches. A hand lens readily brings this out.

The plant is brittle and easily crumbled when dry and quite resilient when wet. The name *rangiferina* is from the Latin word *rangifer,* for reindeer. It is called Reindeer Moss because reindeer feed upon it in the wintertime. It is the poet's "Wiry moss that whitens all the hill."

The Ladder Lichen (*Cladonia verticillata*) is found through-out the United States on the ground, in shady edges of old fields or in sandy, earthy places. The sod flakes are greenish-gray on the upper surface and white beneath. Stalks rise to a height of two to three inches, broadening upward from a thickness of less than $^{1-}16$ inch. A cup-like expansion grows and from the center of this may spring one or more similar stalks with the cup-like expansion supporting a further branching, and so upward several stories high. About the margins of the tray-like branchings brown fruits may be seen. The stalks are greenish- or bluish-gray. This lichen is unmistakable because of its ladder-like form. There are many species of Ladder Lichen which merge one into the other.

The Frayed Lichen (*Cladonia degenerans*) is found on the ground in the northern mountains. Sod flakes are usually not seen and the lower parts of the stalks blacken, suggesting decay. Cluster of stalks may take irregular shapes only recognizable as vague contorted goblets or trumpets growing in tiers somewhat branching. The outer rind may be stripping off, exposing the fibrous pith on the inside of the stalk showing a net-like pattern. Small flakes and granules occur on all parts giving the lichen a ragged, frayed appearance. These grow on the pith as well as the rind. The general color is light greenish-gray, tinged brownish or olive and in places, blackish. The Frayed Lichen, though a distinct species, has the appearance of a partly decayed and reviving Spoon Lichen. They are easily confused.

The Mealy Goblet Lichen (*Cladonia chlorophaea*) grows every-where throughout the United States on the ground, stumps, logs, tree bases and rocks. It is very common. It differs in having the stalks largely covered with fine granules. This Goblet Lichen will always be seen growing among a plentiful growth of sod flakes of the same species of plant as itself. The forms vary from the simple goblet of many forms and sizes to branched and contorted modifications with many special names such as Cup Moss, Ladybird Cup Moss, Stick Cup Moss and Fringed Cup Moss. Some are densely overgrown with flakes, some have a second tier of goblets springing from the center of the summit instead of the margin. There are many other goblet-shaped lichens but the Mealy Goblet is by far the most common. Some grow fruits along the margins of the goblet.

The Spoon Lichen (*Cladonia gracilis*) is found on the ground and among mosses or rotten wood throughout the United States. It is more common in the North and at high elevations. Sod flakes may be seen in abundance growing all about the base of the lichen. The stalks of the Spoon Lichen are extremely variable, reaching a height of 2½ or 3 inches and expanding upward, and are trumpet-shaped with the summits cup-shaped, spoon-shaped or irregular. There are seldom more than three tiers each springing, not from the centers of the trumpets, but commonly from their tooth edges. The surface is smooth gray-green and may become brownish. Stray flakes may grow from the sides of the stalk. The regularly occurring brown fruits are borne singly on the tips or the edges of the "trumpets." There are many similar species, but this one is readily distinguished.

Genus Stereocaulon   The Easter Lichen (*Stereocaulon paschale*) differs from Cladonia in that it has solid stalks rather than hollow ones and springs from a real sod of flakes. The stalks are covered with tiny, ashy-gray lobules. Sod flakes, however, are only rarely seen near the base of the stalk. The vertical stalk growth becomes shrub-like or even tree-like, with fruit-bearing branches. Fruits are tiny disc-like, dark brown or black bodies at the ends of the branches. The Easter Lichen is found on rocks or soil throughout the northern United States in exposed places. Stalks branch freely with granules and flakes on the upper parts or upper side of leaning branches. When dry, the color of the upper branches is a shining silver-gray, turning green when wet. The name *stereocaulon* is compounded of the Greek words *stereos* (solid) and *kaulos* (stalk). The specific name, *paschale,* is the Latin for "passover" and hence is appropriate to that season. The Easter Lichen is said to have been the first plant to develop upon the volcanic lava of Vesuvius. Wild animals feed on it when Reindeer Moss is scarce.

The Beard Lichen (*Usnea florida*) is a common, shrubby lichen growing on tree bark, old tree branches or dead wood in swamps or mountains. It hangs pendulous or beard-like and is unmistakable once seen. It is slender, flexible and blows freely in the wind, sometimes reaching a length of eighteen inches or more. The main stalks are usually less than $1/16$ inch in diameter. The surface is smooth and covered with prongs and granules. There are tiny branchlets springing nearly at right angles from any part. It is greenish-gray in color, becoming black on older stalks.

The structure of the stalk is unique. One may pull it until it breaks and see definite layers like a telephone wire with a tough white core surrounded by this more brittle "insulation." The stalks, because of this arrangement, are quite tough. One may see this in nature where the outer layers have been stretched or broken by ice or climbing animals while the core held firm. The cracks fill gradually with a growth of pith. This does not occur in other stalked lichens which are either hollow or have no such strong core.

This cosmopolitan lichen is the Beard Moss or Tree Moss of the poets, the "idle moss" of Shakespeare. Fruits, though rare, are shield-like, distributed along the branches rather than on the tips. The fruit disc is pale gray or buff-colored and the rim is fringed with long thread-like fibrils. The name *Usnea* is from an Arabic word *achneh,* meaning lichen.

Genus Ramalina   The Twig Lichens (*Ramalina*) are the most common of the stalked lichens growing on trees. Because of their small size they are not the most frequently observed. Stalks are typically flattened, somewhat like irregular noodles, hard and rather rigid when dry. Those commonly seen are small, dense tufts, almost like burrs on the barks of various trees and shrubs or among their twigs. In the far West they form beautiful lace curtain-like draperies in the trees. Stalks are variously flattened, angled or channeled. The thickness may vary from that of paper to that of blotting paper. There is never much difference between the two sides of the flattened stalks—which may be twisted and tangled, branching by forking to tips that are either pennant-shaped or divided into slender branchlets. The color is pale greenish-gray. Fruits are commonly found along the thin edges of the branches or near the tips. They are at first saucer-shaped with a smooth rim and as they become older may present a swollen, lumpy appearance overgrowing the rim.

Genus Evernia   The Oak Moss (*Evernia*), sometimes called the Flabby Lichen though a stalked lichen, has some of the characteristics of the papery lichens. It is found on trees and dead wood in the mountains of the northeastern United States and northward. It may grow two to five inches in length, spreading or hanging downward or plastered against the bark, the wider part of its branches expanding to about ¼ inch across. The surface of the branches appears to be sprinkled with a mealy substance. The color varies from gray-green to bluish-gray. A related lichen is the noted yellow "Ulfmossa" (Wolf's Moss) of the Swedes. It was so named from the popular belief that the plant was poisonous to wolves.

All members of this group contain fragrant, essential oils valued as bases for perfumes. It remains an established article in the perfume industry. The name Oak Moss comes from the fact that the oils are said to be the most fragrant when the plant has been growing on oak, though it is often found on pine or fir. It may look at first glance like a wilted Ramalina.

Key to the Mosses
by Habitat

MOST of what has been described about collecting and studying lichens is equally true of the mosses. They are among the simplest of plant specimens to collect and preserve, and will remain in good condition for years. Wherever possible, fruiting specimens with spore cases should be collected. The peat moss, *Sphagnum,* is one of the few that can be identified without spore cases. Mosses collected in the field are best placed in herbarium packets, made by folding a good grade of bond paper in such a way that the specimen rests loosely within it, and later pressed between two good-sized books. This is all the weight they need; too much may render them unfit for study.

The packets are then labeled and pasted in rows to herbarium sheets of a good, stiff paper stock. Labels should include the common and scientific names of the specimen, the habitat, locality and date of collection.

The appearance of an entire colony may be a strong clue to identification. Once this has been noted, however, an individual plant should be separated from the others and examined under a hand lens. The spore case, its shape, position and angle with the seta, the stem and leaf arrangements can be easily seen with the naked eye; the shape of the leaves and their relationships to the stem are made out with the hand lens.

Although specimens are best studied while they are still fresh and moist, dried specimens can be examined after soaking in water, or preferably, in a 10-percent solution of glycerin. As the first step in examining a spore case, the cap is lifted off and the specimen is observed under a hand lens. Then the case is cut lengthwise and the two halves placed on a slide, one with the inside and the other with the outside of the case facing up.

Permanent mounts of leaves, cross-sections of leaves and stems or sectioned spore cases may be made by placing the section on a slide cover suspended in a 20-percent glycerin solution. A small amount of glycerin jelly is then placed on a second slide cover and lowered, one edge before the other to exclude air bubbles, over the first cover. The two sections adhere tightly, and can be kept indefinitely.

For a layman, habitat is the most satisfactory method of classification.

In the simple key that follows, the frequently descriptive common names are given, together with the scientific names of typical species. No effort has been made to enumerate and distinguish among *all* the species of any given group; this is a matter of concern only to specialists. Nearly all of the common species can be assigned a name according to the places in which they are found. Some, for example, flourish almost exclusively on decaying logs; others on the trunks of living trees; still others on boulders, on cement or stone walls, or on bare exposed rocks of mountainsides. Some live only in water—in bogs and swamps, in still or stagnant ponds, or in fast-moving streams. Some mosses are most at home in the cool, damp soil of woods; others do best in the drier soil of open fields; a few are partial to dusty roadsides. But for those less specialized sorts that may grow under more than one set of conditions, there are cross-references to the major description.

In this key, the five main groups are as follows:

Group One Mosses growing on or about decaying logs, wood or fallen trees, or that prefer moist, shady places among dead, decaying leaves, plants and peaty humus.

Group Two Mosses characteristically found in fresh water, either partly or completely submerged.

Group Three Mosses growing on the bark of trees, frequently well above the ground.

Group Four Mosses growing on boulders, stones, cliffs, cement and abut the bases of trees.

Group Five Mosses growing on soil of any kind.

GROUP ONE

MOSSES GROWING ON OR ABOUT DECAYING LOGS, WOOD OR FALLEN TREES, OR THAT PREFER MOIST, SHADY PLACES AMONG DEAD OR DECAYING LEAVES, PLANTS AND PEATY HUMUS

The Fork Mosses (of the genus *Dicranum;* from the Greek *dicranos,* "fork" or "flesh-hook") are found growing on the ground, on rotten logs in humus and occasionally around the bases of trees. They stand erect, with forking stems, to a height of anywhere from $3/4$ inch to several inches, crowded closely together in thick, wide tufts or mats. The color may be either dark green or a glossy yellow-green. The leaves are narrow and lance-shaped, and are turned to one side of the stem as though blown in that direction by the wind. The spore cases, borne on tall, erect setae, are curved and slightly inclined. The veil (calyptra) only partly encloses the spore case which is most conspicuous in autumn when the spores mature. The American Indians gave these mosses a name meaning "women's heads," because of their ability to spring up promptly after being trampled underfoot. They are easily recognized, and there are many species. Only the most common are described here.

The Broom Moss (*Dicranum scoparium*), a large species that may reach a height of up to four inches, grows in dense, shining tufts or sods on decayed wood and soil in shaded places. The long, beaked brown spore cases, tilted to one side, usually point in the same direction as the leaves. To the imaginative they may suggest the heads of ducks flocking toward the water, or a company of troops tilting their lances. One of the commonest of mosses, this species is distributed throughout the Northern Hemisphere. Florists sometimes use it as a background for window displays.

The Wavy Broom Moss (*Dicranum undulatum*) grows abundantly in loose, wide tufts of a bright yellow-green on peaty humus and soil where there are decaying wood and leaves. The largest of the group, it reaches a height of from three to ten inches. The leaves have a silky luster and are toothed toward the apex. The spore cases are bent in a bow-like curve and are produced in clusters, drooping or nodding on long reddish setae. The Wavy Broom is easily distinguished from the preceding species by its larger size and yellowish hue.

The Whip Fork Moss (*Dicranum flagellare*) is very common, fruits freely and is most commonly conspicuous in summer. It grows on stumps and old logs in moist woods. It is small—stems about one inch long; the leaves are curved and turned to one side and are yellowish to bright green. It most resembles the Little Fork Moss, (Green Hair Moss), *Dicranella heteromalla*.

The Little Fork Mosses (of the genus *Dicranella;* from the Latin, "little fork") are very small—two inches or less in height—and are hardly branched at all. The spore case, borne erect or slightly inclined on its seta, is short with a beaked lid. When this is removed the sixteen hair-like teeth that protect the opening may be seen. The leaves are narrow and silky.

The Green Hair Moss (*Dicranella heteromalla*), the only common member of this genus, grows in wide mats or tufts on the banks of shaded streams. The plant is ½ to 2 inches high, and the stems are forked. The leaves, which have the habit of turning to one side (whence the Latin name *heteromalla*—literally, "hair on one side"), range in color from bright yellowish-green to dark green. The setae are yellow and stand erect. The oblong or ovoid spore case is slightly bent or curved.

After the spores mature, in November or December, it stands dry and empty, deeply furrowed and brown in color.

The Humpbacked Elves (species of *Buxbaumia*) are so distinctive, that once seen, they offer little problem in identification. For some time after their discovery in 1712 by the German botanist J. C. Buxbaum, for whom they were later named, they were classified as fungi. Small and almost stemless with few or no leaves, the "Elves" appear as patches of greenish-black, which in fact constitute the protonema. The flattened, asymmetrical, egg-shaped spore case, which is large in proportion to the rest of the plant, is red-purple, obliquely placed and topped by a small conical veil. Such leaves as develop are almost invisible.

Bugs on a Stick (*Buxbaumia aphylla;* Latin, "without leaves") are all but unmistakable to anyone lucky enough to discover them growing in peaty soil or humus, or now and then on decaying wood in moist, shady places. The leaves are few, and are clustered at the base of the seta; they disappear as the spore case ripens. The mature plant consists of a few rhizoids, the roughened seta, and the spore case, whose appearance gives this odd plant its name. Borne on a seta about 1/2 inch high, it inclines nearly to the horizontal, and is flattened above and angular about the edges. The name "Bugs on a Stick" was proposed by A. J. Grout.

The Powder Gun Moss (*Diphyscium foliosum*—new name *Webera sessilis*) is no less odd than the above, and considerably more common. July is the best time to look for it growing densely in broad, dark green mats dotted with gray-brown spore cases, along shaded stream banks. The plant hugs the ground closely, and is almost sessile, with a short, scarcely visible seta. The leaves, unlike those of *Buxbaumia,* are both abundant and persistent. Immersed among them, the spore cases resemble large grains of wheat. A lichen almost always grows in association with the Powder Gun Moss, giving a mottled appearance to the colony. The new botanical name is in honor of the German botanist Professor Weber, who recognized and described this moss.

The Bryum Mosses (of the genus *Bryum,* Latin for "moss") are the most difficult to separate into species—of which there are about 500. Members of the group, however, can be readily identified. The Latin name *Bryum* was used by Pliny the Elder, the first-century Roman naturalist. These mosses were also described by the Greek physician Dioscorides, called the founder of botany. All are small, measuring from $1/4$ to $1/2$ inch in height, and all grow erect in dense tufts. The leaves range in shape from oval to lance-like. The setae are typically long, reddish or brownish in color, and twisted when dry. The spore case is nearly always inclined or drooping; when dry, it may show a well-marked neck. Careful observation with a hand lens will disclose a double row of teeth inside the mouth of the capsule. There is a hood-shaped veil that splits up one side. Without the spore case, these mosses are very difficult to identify.

The Silvery Bryum (*Bryum argenteum*) grows nearly everywhere, and at almost every altitude. Colonies form densely tufted sods or cushions, whose texture suggests the pile of a coarse velvet. A lack of chlorophyll in the cells of the upper leaves produces in the mature plant the silvery look that has given the species its name. The young plants, however, are pale green. A robust plant despite its small size—$1/2$ to 1 inch high—it is most at home on decaying wood, but may also flourish on firm, compact soil, and is no rarity between the cracks of city sidewalks. The leaves are closely overlapping and end in a slender bristle. The small, pendulous spore cases mature in the autumn, but are recognizable in almost any season. The slender setae are red and grow erect. The plant fruits freely, and a student of mosses is likely to find this one on almost any expedition.

The Giant Bryum (*Bryum roseum*—new name *Rhodobryum ontariense*) is the largest and most conspicuous of the group. The name *roseum* is a reference to the rosette of leaves that crowns the otherwise virtually leafless stem, which arises from a stolon or creeper running along the ground. The Giant Bryum forms large mats on rotten logs or in rich humus about the bases of trees. It seldom fruits; instead, reproduction is carried on mainly by the stolons, which send up plants at regular intervals.

The Matted Bryum (*Bryum caespiticium;* Latin, "matted") is undoubtedly the commonest of the group. It may be found on decaying wood or in open fields, old ash heaps and spots of bare soil. It often grows intermingled with other mosses. The leaves have an extended midrib that ends in a long bristle. The spore cases, which are produced abundantly, are inclined or pendulous.

The Nodding Moss (*Pohlia nutans*) is found throughout the world, growing in moist, swampy places or on rotten wood, where it forms soft cushions of yellow-green. The plant is from $1/2$ to 2 inches tall, with a red stem that grows simple and erect. The leaves near the apex are toothed, with a full midrib, but without a bristle at the tip. The slender yellow seta bears a spore case that may be horizontal or pendulous. The generic name honors a professor of botany, Dr. Pohl of Dresden, Germany; the Latin word *nutans,* "nodding," refers to the spore case.

The Mnium Mosses (of the genus *Mnium,* Greek for "moss") are related to the Bryums, but are generally larger. The many members of the group are generally handsome plants, found growing in cool, damp places. The leaves are large and translucent, and characteristically end in a rosette. The spore cases may be single or multiple, nodding or pendant.

The Pointed Mnium (*Mnium cuspidatum*) is found on lawns and in moist, shaded places, growing on the soil or on rotten logs. An expanse of its upright green sporophytes is one of the earliest signs of spring. Colonies may be loosely or closely tufted. The stems reach a height of half an inch, and are green or yellow-green. The leaves at the bases of the stems are small, but above they grow larger and are crowded into rosettes. The Latin name *cuspidatum,* "point," refers to the leaves which may have an oval shape and are sharply pointed. The spore case is egg-shaped and pendulous. Under a good hand lens, when the lid is removed, two rows of teeth may be seen; the inner row has a peculiar orange color.

The Fern Mosses (of the genus *Thuidium*) are easily distinguished by their delicate, fern-like form. *Thuidium* is the Greek word for a resinous evergreen; and indeed, the Fern Mosses are also often called Cedar Mosses for the resemblance of a single plant to a tiny cedar tree. Mosses of this widely distributed group may be found growing on tree trunks, rocks and soil. The stiff, robust plants form yellowish or greenish mats or cushions. They are as regularly branched as the pinnae of a fern. The leaves tend to curve when dry, and are spreading and erect when moist. The cylindrical, bow-shaped spore cases, borne on long setae, are inclined and become constricted below the mouth when dry.

The Common Fern Moss (*Thuidium delicatulum*) grows in large, beautifully intricate, fern-like mats that are often many feet across. Their usual habitat is in moist, shady places, where they spread over rotten logs, rich humus or even stones. The plants are bright green above and darker below. The large, curved, cylindrical spore cases, which are produced only in small numbers, mature in early autumn. They are borne on long, stout setae. The leaves about the foot have long, hair-like processes (cilia) on their outer margins. The Latin word *delicatulum* refers to the finely branching leaves.

The Wiry Fern Moss (*Thuidium abietinum*), another common species, may be found not only in moist habitats, but also in drier ones, growing in soil among the grass or on rocky ledges. The plant is coarser and more rigid than other Fern Mosses, but branches in the same regular, feather-like way.

The Mountain Fern Moss (*Hylocomium splendens*) grows abundantly in cool, moist mountain woods, forming greenish or yellow tufts over stones or old logs on the forest floor. Larger than others in this group, it is one of the most strikingly beautiful of all mosses. Its growth habit produces many branches, and each year a new shoot rises from the middle of the old. The leaves are oval or elongated and pointed at the tip. The long setae are red. Antheridia are produced on the side branches, archegonia on the main stem.

The Cedar Mosses (of the genus *Hypnum*) are usually found growing in dense, thin mats on soil or rotten wood; or, less frequently, but not rarely, on stones or the trunks of trees. Some species are slender, others robust and woody. Often these mosses form stolons or grow prostrate, with occasionally ascending branches. The leaves are commonly thin and membranous, sometimes scaly and glossy and tend toward a horizontal position. The spore cases always contain two rows of teeth. The group includes hundreds of species, often with only minor differences. In Great Britain Cedar Mosses are so common that they may compose a quarter of the island's vegetation.

The Plume Moss or Knight's Plume (*Hypnum cristacastrensis;* Latin, "crest") has a plume-like appearance as a result of the turning of all its leaves to one side. Common in cool woodlands, where it grows on decayed logs and stumps, it is seen in its greatest beauty in deep forests, where entire fallen trees may be clothed in its richly textured robe of light yellow-green. The leaves are as regularly branched as a feather, and the spore cases are curved and pendant. This moss appears on the coat of arms of the royal House of Lancaster, descended from John of Gaunt.

The Feather Moss (*Hypnum imponens*), an abundant species, grows most commonly in lowland habitats, where it is found almost exclusively on decayed wood. It is similar to the Plume Moss, but grows prostrate, in much more densely clumped and interwoven mats, and is of a darker yellow-green. The stems are reddish, and the broad, triangular leaves end in a narrow point. The cylindrical spore cases, which grow erect, are crowned with opercula that are convex at the base and come to a long, gradually tapering point. The spores mature in winter. This species fruits much more freely than the Plume Moss.

The Common Cedar Moss (*Hypnum haldanianum*), one of the most abundant of mosses, is almost sure to be found in any moist, shady place where decaying wood is present, upholstering its surface with broad, bright green mats. Its leaves, unlike those of its near relatives, are straight and spread equally in all directions. The spore cases, which are produced in large numbers, are cylindrical and only slightly curbed. They mature in late fall or winter.

Schreber's Cedar Moss (*Calliergon cordifolium*) is easily recognized at a glance. It forms dense, brightly colored cushions along damp, shaded roadsides, in moist open woods, in boggy pastures and swamps and along the margins of ponds. It grows in loose mats or tufts, composed of stems that may be from four to six inches in length and grow nearly erect. The color ranges all the way from yellow-green to purple. The stems, when held up to the light, appear bright red. The semitransparent leaves are large and broad, with an oval shape and a midrib extending their entire length. The spore cases, which mature in autumn, are less abundant than the luxuriance of the plant might lead one to expect. In shape the capsule is an oblong cylinder, which is pendant and contracted under the mouth when dry.

The Creeping Cedar Moss (*Amblystegium serpens*) is very common in shady places, where it grows on soil and on moist, decaying wood, as well as around the bases and roots of trees, forming thin, densely interwoven mats. The many stems are creeping and irregularly branched, and bear tiny, dull green leaves. The disproportionately large spore case is curved and cylindrical, with a bluntly pointed tip—whence the name *Amblystegium,* from two Greek words meaning "blunt" and "cover." The specific name, *serpens,* is a Latin word referring to the snake-like growth habit of the plant. The best means of recognition is the thinness of the mat formed by the plants of this species.

The Shaggy Moss (*Hylocomium triquetrum*) forms large yellow-green mats, from four to eight inches deep, in decaying wood or rich humus. The Greek word hylocomium means literally "wood rEvelers," and this moss is sometimes known by that name. The Latin word *triquetrum,* literally "having three angles," refers to the plant's habit of branching in three directions, with leaves standing out horizontally to produce a characteristically ragged appearance. The leaves themselves are large and triangular, with a distinctive gloss. The oblong spore case, which is produced infrequently, is borne on a curved seta that causes it to incline, and matures in winter or early spring. The stiff, springy, elastic stems make this moss a useful packing for chinaware.

The Slender Cedar Moss (*Plagiothecium denticulatum*) grows in loose, shining, bright green tufts, partly prostrate with erect, irregular branches. The oval to lance-shaped leaves are thin and glossy, and lack a midrib; they grow in two spreading rows. The spore case—to which the generic name (from two Greek words meaning literally "oblique little chest") refers—is somewhat nodding and bell-shaped when dry. As with all Cedar Mosses, it contains two rows of teeth.

The Common Beaked Moss (*Eurhynchium strigosum*) is frequent on the ground, about the roots of trees, and on decaying wood, where it forms delicate, loose mats, often intermingling with other mosses. The leaves, which overlap like shingles on a roof, are spoon-shaped with the apex coming to a slender point. The oval, oblong, nodding spore case is notable for the beaked operculum (whence the Greek generic name, "true beak"), without which the species may be difficult to identify.

GROUP TWO

MOSSES CHARACTERISTICALLY FOUND IN FRESH WATER, EITHER PARTLY OR COMPLETELY SUBMERGED

The Fountain or Water Mosses are entirely aquatic, and grow submerged. Some attach themselves to stones and sticks in rapidly flowing streams. They are never found in stagnant water where dissolved oxygen is not so abundant. With their long, slender, floating stems and branches, they are particularly distinctive. In addition, it may be noted that every third leaf is placed directly over the first in a series, and that the leaves have no veins. The spore cases, which are oval or cylindrical with cone-shaped lids, are immersed in the leaves at the base, and are not commonly found. When they are, it may be observed that they contain two rows of sixteen teeth each.

The Giant Fountain Moss (*Fontinalis antipyretica*), common in cool streams, produces branches that are frequently a foot or more long, and that are attached only at the base. The flaccid stems range in color from golden through yellowish-green to brownish-green. The leaves are more or less imbricate and broadly oval in shape. Fruits are rarely produced. Linnaeus gave the name *antipyretica* (literally, "against fire") to the species because it was the custom of Swedish peasants to surround chimneys with it to prevent their houses from catching fire. It has also had the reputation of serving to reduce fever— apparently, however, for no more fundamental reason than that it grows in cold water.

The Torn Veil Mosses (*Rhacomitrium;* from the Greek words *rakos,* "shred," and *mitrion,* "veil") comprise a group of mosses for which waterfalls or wet rocks in mountain streams, or in cool, shaded situations high in the mountains, are the usual habitat. They grow in close, flat patches consisting of broad tufts, attached to stones. In color the plants are a dull, dark green above and black or brownish near the point of attachment. They reach a length of one to three inches. The leaves, which are broad and toothed at the apex, are crowded and imbricate when dry but erect and spreading when moist. The oblong, cylindrical spore case is borne erect on a seta which twists to the right. Four species have been identified by taxonomists, but the differences among them are minor. The name refers to the torn or shredded appearance of the veil at its base.

The Beard Mosses (of the genus *Grimmia*) are a family of exceedingly small, common, dingy-looking mosses whose distribution is world-wide, and most of which grow mainly on stones or the trunks of living trees. There are, however, a few varieties that grow in streams. The members of the family form conspicuous gray tufts, varying from dense cushions 1/3 inch high to large mats whose stems may be as much as 8 inches long. The dingily colored leaves, which are usually tipped with white hairs of varying length, are the best means of identification. The absence of chlorophyll from the apex of the leaves also contributes to the distinctive appearance of a growing colony. The spore cases are not easily found; when present, they are smooth and elliptical or cylindrical in shape. When the operculum is removed, sixteen red, lance-shaped teeth may be observed through a hand lens. Altogether, more than 240 species have been identified. The generic name honors a German botanist and physician, J. F. C. Grimm.

The Common Beard Moss (*Grimmia apocarpa*), the most common representative of the group, forms loose olive green or black tufts on rocks or stone walls—always in shady places— and it may also be found occasionally in streams. The leaves are imbricated when dry but erect and spreading in the presence of moisture. The specific name (from two Greek words—*apo,* "without," and *carpos,* "fruit") refers to the difficulty of finding the spore case, which grows well concealed among the leaves, and is the most characteristic feature of the plant. The capsule is egg-shaped, and its bright red cap is tipped with a sharp point. The water-loving representatives of this species are to be found on the upper surfaces of rocks in fast-moving mountain streams.

The Aquatic Apple Mosses (of the genus *Philonotis;* Latin, "moisture-loving") is commonly seen where water drips, runs slowly or flows over a shallow, rocky stream bed. It may also grow in wet soil, around springs, in swamps, or on lake shores. It looks somewhat like the Common Apple Moss (*Bartramia pomiformis*) but prefers much wetter places and its stems are longer and more slender.

Philonotis fontana, the only aquatic species in this group that is at all widespread, has dense, imbricated leaves that are bright green or pale yellow-green. The rarely seen spore cases are apple-shaped, whence the common name, and have a peculiar swelling on the underside that is entirely lacking in the Common Apple Moss.

The Water Mosses (of the widely distributed genus *Dichelyma*) are found wholly submerged in swamps, pools and slow streams. Frequently they are attached to the stems of bushes growing in swamps and along the shores of ponds—a habit that helps in identifying them. The most common one, *Dichelyma capillaceum,* is slender and delicate, with branching stems that are shorter than those of the Fountain Moss. The leaves are long and narrow, green to golden green near the tip, but black below. The four species are not easily differentiated. The generic name is derived from two Greek words, "to halve" and "a covering" and refers to the one-sided calyptra or veil.

The water-loving Plume Mosses (of the genus *Fissidens*) grow in mats on wet, shady banks and rocks, and occasionally on the trunks of trees; a few float freely in water. Their color is a lovely, metallic green, and their stems are simple or only slightly branched. The leaves grow in two rows on opposite sides of the stem, both rows lying in the same plane, so as to give a peculiar flattened appearance that suggests the Scale Mosses or Leafy Hepatics. The spore cases may be borne erect, or they may be horizontal or pendant. Within the spore case is a single row of teeth which are red at the base. The generic name (from the Latin words *fissus,* "split," and *dens,* "tooth") is a reference to their incurved appearance when dry. Nearly 600 species have been described. They occur throughout the tropical and temperate regions of the world. Mungo Park, the Scottish physician who explored the Niger River, was probably referring to one of this group in a poem appearing in his *Travels in the Interior of Africa,* which contains the following lines:

> *One tiny tuft of moss alone,*
> *Mantling with freshest green a stone . . .*
> *O! shall not He who keeps thee green,*
> *Here in the waste, unknown, unseen,*
> *Thy fellow exile save?*

Maiden Hair Moss (*Fissidens adiantoides*) grows in mats that range in color from bright to dark green, on moist, shady ground, on wet rocks and about the roots of trees. The specific name (from the Greek word *adiantos,* "maiden hair") is a reference to the ease with which its leaves shed water. The stems are from one to five inches long, with numerous branches growing from the apex, overlapping like shingles on a roof and appearing clasped about the stem at their base. The leaves taper to a sharp point at the tip, and have transparent and somewhat irregular margins. The oval spore case is red-brown in color, and the cone-shaped operculum ends in a long beak. The spores mature in winter.

Another species, *Fissidens julianus,* which grows on stones in swiftly flowing, calcareous water, suggests a very small Fountain Moss. The stiff, dark green plant measures one to five inches. There are several other aquatic species.

One of the water-loving Cedar Mosses *Hygroamblystegium irriguum* (the specific name means "water-loving"), is a small moss ranging from dark green to black in color, that clings to rocks in streams and becomes so conglomerated with mud and sand that it cannot be freed of them until after it has been thoroughly dried and shriveled. Even after being completely washed it remains harsh and gritty to the touch.

The Rivulet Cedar Moss (*Brachythecium rivulare*) is partial to wet, gravelly soil at the edges and in the beds of cool, swift-flowing streams. During the summer in the mountains, it may be found covering the gravelly bottom of a stream that is nearly dry. At high-water it may be submerged. In these circumstances the stems become tremendously elongated. In shallow water, or when it is only partly submerged, on the other hand, the stems may grow tall, stout, and shrub-like. The plant is only sparingly branched; the leaves range in color from dark green to yellow-green. The seta is red-brown and rough to the touch. It bears a spore case that is oval or oblong and characteristically inclined to the horizontal. There are several other species in this group.

Group Three

Mosses Growing on the Bark of Trees, Frequently Well Above the Ground

The Tree Apron Mosses (of the genus *Anomodon*) are commonly found growing about the bases of trees in cool, moist woods. The colonies are so extensive that trees may seem to wear an apron of dark green, extending from the roots to three or four feet above the ground and sometimes encircling a tree entirely. Usually such a colony is made up of one or more species of Tree Apron Mosses, frequently mixed with a Leafy Hepatic. A network of nearly leafless stems, growing close to the bark, sends out crowded branches, which make up the "pile" of the mat. These mosses tend toward a bluish cast on the surface, but are brownish below. The imbricated leaves are brittle, and are little changed by drying. The seta, which becomes twisted when dry, bears erect capsules. The generic name (from the Greek *anomos,* "irregular," and *odon,* "tooth") refers to the peculiar character of the peristome.

The Common Tree Apron Moss (*Anomodon attenuatus*) grows almost exclusively on trees, where it forms thin mats, loose tufts or scattered shoots. The simple, blunt, slender branches bear tongue-shaped leaves.

The Velvet Tree Apron Moss (*Anomodon rostratus*) is particularly common about the bases of trees in swamps, where it is sometimes found spreading from the tree onto the ground. The lance-shaped leaves are dense, and overlap like shingles.

The oval to oblong spore case is red-brown in color and is borne erect. The Latin name *rostratus,* "beaked," refers to the form of the cap. Perfect spore cases with typical beaks may be collected in October.

The Feather Mosses (of the genus *Neckera*), whose name is not to be confused with *Hypnum imponens,* grow in very extensive mats on tree trunks and occasionally on rocks. The primary stems are creeping over a horizontal surface; secondary stems are branching, feathery and pendulous, and occasionally have a whip-like appearance. The glossy, transparent leaves usually lie flat; most often they are green, but in some species they may tend toward a yellowish-brown. The spore cases, borne on short setae, seem to be buried in the leaves; they have tiny, cone-shaped lids. The genus is named in honor of a noted eighteenth-century botanist, Dr. J. N. Necker of Mannheim, Germany.

The Feathered Neckera (*Neckera pennata*) is found growing in extensive mats of pale green, usually high up on the trunks of trees, but less commonly on moist cliffs and ledges. The location is rarely near the base of the tree, and may extend to a height of twenty-five to fifty feet above the ground, according to the size of the trees and the density of the forest. The primary stems are creeping and rather large. Branches usually extend out from the tree trunk at an angle between 45°-75°. The oval or oblong spore cases, dirty yellowish in color, and with a beaked cone-shaped lid, are borne on setae shorter than themselves, and are produced—often in great numbers—on the older section of the plant. They mature in summer. The Latin word *pennata,* "feather," refers to the branching arrangement of the stems.

The Light Green Tree Mosses (of the genus *Pylaisia*) are at home on the bark of living trees, and are extremely common east of the Rocky Mountains. Old apple trees in dense orchards are a favored habitat. The light green color is a typical characteristic. Mosses of this group are pleurocarpous—that is, the spore case, seta and foot are borne laterally on the stem rather than at the apex. When dry, the branches are somewhat hooked at the tip.

The Common Pylaisia (*Pylaisia intricata*), the most widespread member of the group, may be seen in the open woods or on shade trees in any small town. It does not thrive near large cities. The plants grow so closely interwoven that their individual appearance is not evident unless they are disentangled. The erect, somewhat cylindrical spore cases mature in the fall. The moss was named for De La Pylaie, a well-known student of mosses.

The Hardy Leucodon Mosses (of the genus *Leucodon,* from the Greek *leukos,* "white" or "pallid," and *odontos,* "tooth") grow almost exclusively on the bark of deciduous trees, although they may occasionally be found on rocks. They almost never grow at the base of a tree, but rather at a height of five feet or more. They are capable of surviving without moisture for months or even years. The main stems are long, slender, and branching, with abundant rhizoids anchoring them to the bark. The generic name refers to the teeth of the capsule, which are difficult to see except under a very strong lens.

The Southern Leucodon (*Leucodon julaceus*) is easily recognized under a hand lens by its perfectly round stems and sharply pointed leaves, which lie closely overlapping like shingles against the stem. The secondary stems are shorter than the primary ones. The Latin *julaceus,* "worm-like," refers to the appearance of the branches when dry.

The Northern Leucodon (*Leucodon brachypus*) is rare south of New York, whereas the Southern species is rare beyond southern New England. Otherwise the two are difficult to tell apart, except that the branches of the Northern species tend to be longer.

The Glossy Entodon Mosses (of the genus *Entodon*) commonly grow on trees, but may also be found in dense mats on bark, earth or rocks. Their erect, symmetrical spore cases and the beautiful, glossy yellow-green of their leaves make identification easy. In most members of the group the leaves have the appearance of being pressed flat rather than arranged in a double row. The generic name (from two Greek words meaning "inside teeth") refers to the arrangement of the peristome.

The Round-Stemmed Entodon (*Entodon seductrix*), probably the most common member of the family, grows on rotten wood, soil or moist rocks, as well as on the bark of trees. It is often found in dry situations. The stems and branches are round and worm-like, with closely imbricated leaves.

The Flat-Stemmed Entodon (*Entodon cladorrhizans*) found on decayed wood or, rarely, on rich soil and humus, is readily differentiated from the preceding species by its strongly flattened stem and branches.

The Straight Hair Tree Mosses (of the genus *Orthotrichum*) resemble those of the genus *Grimmia* except that they nearly always grow on trees—or occasionally on rocks—where they form short tufts or cushions. The plants are small, rarely more than an inch high, and range in color from light green to yellowish-green on the outside and from blackish to brownish-green below. The leaves spread when moist. The veil is conspicuous and nearly always hairy—whence the generic name, from the Greek prefix *ortho-*, "upright." and *trichos,* "hair." The spore case contains sixteen short teeth. Members of this group may become so dry and brittle that they may be crumbled between the fingers, yet still remain capable of springing into renewed growth with the next rain.

The Drummond Moss (*Orthotrichum strangulatum*), one of the commonest of all species, is abundant on shade trees almost everywhere, and is named for an early collector. The long stems are closely attached to the bark, sending out short horizontal branches so thickly that the stems below become visible only when the plant is disengaged from the colony. The stems are very dark—almost black—and the leaves are long and narrow. The spore case, borne on a short seta, has a characteristic dark red-brown color, and an appearance of compression about the neck—whence the specific name *strangulatum.*

The Curled Leaf Moss (*Ulota phyllantha*) is another member of the Straight Hair Tree Moss group. Found mainly on the bark of trees, but now and then on rocks, it grows in small round cushions, which have a characteristic brownish-green or blackish-green color, and which are more noticeably rounded than those of the Drummond Mosses. The spore case, which is covered with a hairy veil, develops conspicuous longitudinal wrinkles when dry. The narrowly lance-shaped leaves are noticeably curled when dry—whence both the common and the scientific names (*Ulota* means "curled").

The Common Thelia (*Thelia hirtella*) likewise grows almost exclusively on the bark of stumps and the bases of trees, forming thin, closely adherent mats that are easily recognized by their whitish-green color. White oaks seem to be the most favored trees. The plants are slender, with worm-like branches. The symmetrical spore cases, borne erect on red setae, are whitish about the mouth.

The Fern Mosses (*Thuidium*), though they grow mainly on soil, among grass or along ledges, include a few small species for which trees are the preferred habitat. These have the same characteristics as those described earlier in this section, but are much smaller.

The Knothole Moss (*Anacamptodon splachnoides*), the sole species in its group, is most commonly found growing in knotholes in deciduous living trees—especially maple, apple and oak. Sugar maple trees that have split so that water collects in the cleft and gradually seeps down the trunk are an especially favorable location. The plant is small and delicate, and when dry the leaves are regularly and closely imbricated. The oval capsules are borne erect; when empty and dry, they are strongly contracted under the mouth.

GROUP FOUR

MOSSES GROWING ON BOULDERS, STONES, CLIFFS, CEMENT AND ABOUT THE BASES OF TREES

The Common Beard Mosses (of the genus *Grimmia*) are probably the most widespread of rock-growing species.

The Common Beard Moss (*Grimmia apocarpa*) usually grows in the shade, forming loose tufts of olive green or black on rocks or stone walls. Its stems are about 1/2 inch long, and the leaves are imbricated but erect, and spread when moist. The spore cases are well hidden among the leaves at the apex of the stem.

The Torn Veil Mosses (of the genus *Rhacomitrium*) are larger than the Grimmias, and grow on rocks in loosely tufted mats that range in color from yellow to blackish. One species, the Woolly Torn Veil Moss—so named for the woolly appearance that is caused by the transparent tips of the leaves—grows commonly on stone walls and on rocks in mountainous regions, where the thick, grayish-white tufts form extended patches.

Hedwig's Mosses (of the genus *Hedwigia*) are very commonly found growing in hoary, fragile patches on boulders, ledges and stone walls in dry, exposed places. They are remarkable for the transformation they undergo when moistened. The plants vary a good deal in size, but in general they have longer stems and branches than the Grimmias. The broad, oval leaves are without veins. The globular spore cases, borne on setae so short as to appear almost nonexistent, and showing no detectable mouth, appear immersed among the leaves. The genus is named in honor of J. D. Hedwig, a noted German botanist.

Hedwig's Fringe Leaf Moss (*Hedwigia ciliata*) grows on rocks in loosely tufted, hoary green patches that may be small or extensive. The Latin specific name (derived from *cilium,* "eyelash") refers to the fringed leaves which are spread outward when moist but are crowded and overlap like shingles when dry. They are grayish-green above—the effect of their colorless tips—and brown or black below the surface of the colony. The spore case, borne on a short seta, appears immersed in the leaves at the apex of the stem.

The Rock Mosses (of the genus *Andreaea*) are found growing small, fragile tufts or cushions of dark green, reddish-brown or black on granite or slate at high altitudes. They are among the first mosses to establish themselves on rock, and are very effective in preparing soil. The oval to lance-shaped leaves are very brittle and dense, with a thick outer layer that enables them to resist the severe storms occurring in the mountain areas where they are most abundant. In growth habit and in the structure of the leaves—of which only the very youngest show the presence of chlorophyll—they resemble the Grimmias. The spore case, however, is distinctive: It splits into four valves much in the manner of the Hepatics, but the valves remain attached to the apex. Rock Mosses of this genus such as *Andrea petrophila,* the Rock Moss, are common in the mountains of Georgia, North Carolina and New England, but are rare in the Rockies. They may be seen most abundantly growing over the face of the Old Man of the Mountain at Franconia Notch, New Hampshire. The generic name honors J. G. R. Andrea, a German naturalist and apothecary from Hannover, Germany.

The Apple Mosses (genus *Bartramia*) are a cosmopolitan group, found on earth or rock in moist, shaded places, where they form deep tufts or cushions that look like bright green wool. Inside of the tuft, the color varies from yellowish to bluish green. The generic name honors John Bartram of Pennsylvania, one of the earliest American botanists. The preferred habitat is on rocky cliffs, but Apple Mosses may also be found on wet, shady banks. The common name refers to the shape of the spore case. The leaves are long, narrow and yellowish-green. The plants, which live from year to year, consist of erect, two-forked stems felted with soft hairs toward the base.

The Long-Leaved or Common Apple Moss (*Bartramia pomiformis;* Latin *pomum,* "apple") grows in soft bright green or yellow-green tufts on shady banks and in clefts of rock. The long, narrow leaves appear somewhat twisted when moist, but are erect and crisp when dry. The cone-like veil is split up one side, and the spore case, borne on a seta about $1/2$ inch long, is spherical with shallow longitudinal grooves. This moss is unmistakable if the spore case is present.

The Short-Leaved Apple Moss (*Bartramia oederi*) differs from the preceding species only in length of its leaves and in being much less common.

The Rock-Loving Fountain Moss or Aquatic Apple Moss (*Philonotis fontana*) is common where water drips or runs in shallow streams over rock. The Fountain Mosses (*Fontinalis*) are found in much wetter places.

The Thread Mosses are represented by the Pear-Shaped Thread Moss (*Leptobryum pyriforme*), an almost cosmopolitan species. It is found growing in close, soft tufts that are light green or yellowish-green on moist, shaded cliffs and on rocks near trickling water. It has also been observed on damp cement walls, and has been found in Colorado at altitudes of 10,000 feet. The generic name, from the Greek words *leptos,* "slender," and *bryum,* "moss," applies both to the plant as a whole and to the narrow, tapering, glossy leaves, which turn in several directions. The lower leaves are relatively smaller than those above. The stems are about $1/2$ inch long. The spore cases, borne on setae that may be orange or brown, are long-necked and pear-shaped—whence the specific name, from the Latin word *pirus,* "pear." They have a thick coat and a double row of teeth. Plants of this species are easy to identify by the spore case and the almost hair-like slenderness of the leaves.

The Wood Reveler (*Hylocomium proliferum*) often carpets rocks in soil with deep mats of bright, glossy yellowish-green. Most members of the genus, however, prefer decaying wood and humus. They are large and robust, with irregular, feathery branches on which the leaves spread abruptly from the base or turn to one side. This species is at home in North American forests of spruce and fir, where it seems especially partial to rocky bluffs. The reddish-brown, egg-shaped spore case is borne on a long red seta.

The Rivulet Cedar Moss (*Brachythecium rivulare*) belongs to a widespread group that grow mainly near springs or brooks. This species may be in a rocky habitat, growing in dark green or yellow-green mats. The plants are woody and prostrate, easily recognized.

The Homalia Moss (*Homalia Jamesii*) frequents moist locations in the mountains, where it forms small, flat, shiny sheets in shaded places, particularly on the under sides of overhanging rocks in cool ravines. *Homalia,* from the Greek, means "flattened," referring to the very flattened appearance of this moss. Its single strands may hang downward, giving a very pretty effect. The single member of this group does not fruit freely, and spore cases are thus not easy to find. On first inspection it may suggest a Leafy Hepatic, but closer examination will show that the leaves have a well-developed midrib.

The Slender Cedar Moss (*Plagiothecium denticulatum*) belongs to a group that has been described in detail under Group One. This member of the family, however, may be seen in glossy green mats on stones where moisture is abundant.

The Little Beard Mosses (of the genus *Barbula*) are found growing on stone walls, rocks or newly exposed soil, where they form rusty-brown tufts or cushions. The lance-shaped leaves have a vein throughout their length and extending beyond the apex in a tiny bristle; when dry they are usually much curled and twisted. The egg-shaped or cylindrical spore cases are borne on long setae; the lids may be either long or short. Careful dissection will reveal that the teeth are long, slender forks, much twisted about one another. Plants of this group are notable for their capacity for holding dust on and between their leaves.

The Claw-Leaved Barbula (*Barbula unguiculata*), the most

common member of the group, is partial to stone walls, rocks and damp, hard earth, forming dirty-green tufts that are simple to identify. The plants measure from $1/4$ to $1/2$ inch in height. The leaves are erect and spreading in the presence of moisture, and spirally twisted when dry. The oblong or cylindrical spore case is borne on a reddish-brown seta, and contains long, slender, spirally twisted teeth.

The Twisted Mosses (of the genus *Tortula*) are a large family closely related to the Little Beard Mosses. Their preferred habitat is on walls or stones that contain lime, although they may very occasionally be found growing on trees; they form tufts of yellowish-green. The spatula-like leaves, with a vein extending their full length and extending from the apex in an exceptionally long bristle, make them easy to recognize. The generic name (Latin, "twisted") refers to the teeth or peristome.

The Common Twisted Moss (*Tortula princeps*) is the most widespread representative of this group, growing on rocks, walls, and (more rarely) the trunks of trees, in tall, loose, reddish-brown tufts. Its color, its interrupted stems, and the rusty color of its leaves make it easy to recognize. The brown, cylindrical spore case is arched like a bow.

The Extinguisher Mosses (*Encalypta*) form bright green cushions on rocks and, more particularly, in rocky crevices. They are common in the mountains of New England, in the Rockies and on the Pacific slope. The plants, which are from 1 to $1^1/_2$ inches tall, have branching stems and tongue-shaped leaves. The spore cases, borne on long, solid setae, are regular, erect and ribbed or twisted when dry. A large, cylindrical, bell-shaped veil that extends well below the spore case (and in some species is fringed at the base) accounts for the generic name (Greek, "covered with a veil"). The common name takes note of a fancied resemblance of the veil to an old-fashioned candle extinguisher.

Group Five

MOSSES GROWING ON SOIL OF ANY KIND

The Cushion Moss or White Moss (*Leucobryum glaucum*) is common in moist, shaded woods and on the borders of swamps, where it grows about the roots of trees in greenish-white or grayish-white tufts or cushions. Those produced by the larger members of the group may be three or four inches deep, the plants that compose them densely packed together. Those at the center are continually being elongated, while new plants develop around the edges. When moist, these cushions are soft and spongy and take on an intense, green hue. When dry they are grayish-white and are easily crumbled. The lance-shaped, somewhat fleshy leaves, which narrow gradually toward the apex in the form of a tube, are crowded closely together. Although spores are produced in abundance after a wet summer, it is a rare thing to find these mosses in fruit. The pale color is, except in moist conditions, the result of the arrangement of the relatively small chlorophyll-containing cells, which are surrounded by transparent cells many times larger—a contrivance for protecting the chlorophyll-bearing cells from the heat of the sun and also for providing a means of carrying water to all parts of the plant. The thin walls of the large colorless cells are punctured with small holes that permit communication with adjacent cells, and thus allow the cells to fill with water, so as to provide a reservoir for times of drought. There are several species, all very much alike, but easily identified as belonging to this group.

The Hairy Cap Mosses (of the genus, *Polytrichum*) comprise a large group and include the most common and widely distributed, as well as the most highly developed, of all mosses. The members vary greatly in size. They are found growing in conspicuous patches on roadside banks, in fields and open woodlands. The densely hairy, hood-like veils from which they derive their name also make them easy to recognize. Their cylindrical or angular spore cases are borne on long wiry setae, and have a mouth covered by a thin membrane and bordered by thirty-two or sixty-four blunt teeth.

When dry, a colony of these mosses appears brown, dead and unattractive; but with the arrival of moisture, it promptly becomes fresh and luxuriantly green, thanks to the ability of the leaf to roll and unroll its thin margin in response to the absence or presence of moisture. Awned Hairy Cap Moss, *Polytrichum piliferum,* has a long, sharply pointed lid and hairy cap. When the plant is well hydrated, the leaves are glistening, bright green and well spread. *Pogonatum brevicaule* retains its green protonema at the base of the plant, quite contrary to all other mosses.

The plants are frequently tall, ranging from one to eighteen inches in height, and they live from one year to the next. The male plants rise perpendicularly from the center of a "flower head," which each year forms a cluster, or rosette, of modified leaves (bracts). The regular leaves are long, slender and lance-shaped with a sharply pointed apex and a vein extending to the full length of the leaf. The scientific name (from the Greek prefix *poly-,* "many," and *trichos,* "hair") refers to the hairy veil that covers the spore case and its operculum. The spore cases themselves are erect or horizontal, with from four to six angles. The opercula are cone-shaped, with a point at the center. Sixty-four short, rigid teeth, united at the base, compose the peristome that surrounds the opening of the spore case. In general, male and female plants tend to be segregated in separate banks or beds.

The Common Hairy Cap Moss (*Polytrichum commune*) is the largest of the group, with stems that may be as much as a foot long; more commonly they measure three to six inches. One of the most widely distributed of plants throughout North America, the Common Hairy Cap Moss grows in beds that may be one hundred feet across.

The Juniper Hairy Cap Moss (*Polytrichum juniperinum*) is commonly found in exposed situations along damp, sandy roadsides or in boggy places. Named for its appearance, which suggests a miniature juniper tree, it is similar to the Common Hairy Cap Moss except for the very light, glaucous green of its open leaves, which is in striking contrast to the dark, rich green of that species. The difference is most evident when the two mosses grow intermingled in a moist environment. The Juniper Hairy Cap may be gray or brown. The position of the sharp four-angled spore case varies all the way from erect to horizontal. Members of the Hairy Cap group vary considerably in the shape of the spore case, the length of the veil and other features; however, there should be no problem in establishing their identity from the descriptions given here.

The Green Felt Mosses (of the genus *Pogonatum*) are so called because the protonema, which in most species disappears after the earliest stage of the life history, often persists as a felting of thread-like cells around the base of the mature plant. Again unlike most others, the plants are not crowded together but grow singly or in small, scattered groups. Apparently the protonema carries on an active part in the plant's nutrition, a function normally reserved for the leaves—which in mosses of this group are relatively few and short.

The Short Pogonatum (*Pogonatum brevicaule*), the most common member of the genus, grows on bare, moist banks of clay or loam where other plants have not yet obtained a foothold.

The Cord Mosses (of the genus *Funaria*) are among the commonest and most cosmopolitan of all. World-wide in distribution, they are especially abundant in waste places and on soil that has been recently burnt-over. The plant is short-stemmed and may be either simple or branching. The leaves are arranged in a bud-like cluster. The generic name (from the Latin word *funis,* "rope") refers to the habit of the setae of twisting one about the other when dry, and of untwisting when moist. The somewhat pear-shaped spore case is borne erect. Its peculiarly curved appearance at maturity, with the mouth drawn to one side, is an aid to identification.

The Water Measuring Cord Moss (*Funaria hygrometrica*), the most common member of the group, grows in large, loosely or closely tufted patches. Vacant lots, burnt-over woodlands and the ashes around picnic fireplaces are likely habitats. The common and specific names (*hygrometrica* means "water-measuring") both refer to the twisting and untwisting of the setae, which is a measure of the amount of moisture in the air. The pale green stems are erect and either simple or branching at the base. The leaves are small below and imbricated above into a bulb-like tuft. The plant is dioicous, the male parts occurring on the primary and the female on the secondary stems. The male receptacles are disc-like and spreading. The spore case is borne on a seta that may be straight or arched, and measures from 1 to $2^{1}/_{2}$ inches high. The capsule is covered by a cone-shaped, shining veil that is split up one side. When dry, the capsule is deeply grooved.

The Urn Moss (*Physcomitrium turbinatum*) is extremely abundant in gardens, lawns, pastures and open woods in the eastern United States. A close relative of the Cord Moss, it grows in loose, delicately textured tufts and is typically found in muddy places. It also commonly grows around flowerpots in greenhouses. The plants are small and sparingly branched, with spatula-shaped, taper-pointed leaves that are contorted when dry. The spore cases, borne erect on red setae, are pear-shaped when moist and fresh, and constricted when dry; after releasing the spores they persist as dark brown, urn-shaped capsules. Around the middle of May is the best time to look for fresh spore cases. The tiny veil, which reaches scarcely to the middle of the spore case, is an unmistakable means of identification. The generic name (from the Greek words *physcos,* "fat paunch," and *mitros,* "cone-shaped hat") refers to its shape, as does the Latin specific name, *turbinatum,* literally, "pointed like a top."

Mosses of the genus *Pottia,* seen growing in loose, bright green tufts in fields, gardens and lawns, are similar to the Urn Mosses except that they are much smaller—around 1/4 inch high. They are also less common. The generic name honors a German botanist, Professor D. F. Pott.

The Peat Mosses (of the genus *Sphagnum*) are exceedingly common throughout the northern United States, where they grow profusely about the many glacially formed lakes, forming dense floating patches that vary in color from whitish or yellowish through light green and purple. The soft, weak-stemmed plants vary in length from a few inches to several feet. Their habit of growing at the top while dying away below has been described in Chapter VI. Some botanists consider the plants of this group so distinctive as to warrant a separate classification. The structure of the leaves, for example, is very different from that of most other mosses. Translucent and without veins, they consist of a single layer made up of two kinds of cells, as in the Hairy Caps—some that are large, colorless and transparent, and others that are smaller and narrowly linear, and that contain chlorophyll. The latter form a network of hexagonal meshes around the former. Since fruiting specimens are difficult to find, the leaves are the most important means of identifying members of this family. The stem leaves are notably different from the branch leaves in being larger, and in their coloring, which ranges all the way from grayish- or yellowish-green through tints of pink to reddish-brown. In exposed places, the red pigments are more pronounced as a result of the formation of tannin. The spore cases, borne on short, stout setae, are chestnut-brown, with flattened opercula suggesting an inverted saucer. There are no teeth. The veil, rarely seen, is a ragged membrane at the base of the spore case.

The Reddish Peat Moss (*Sphagnum palustre*), a very cosmopolitan species, grows in large cushions or beds that may cover acres of bog, along the banks of quiet lakes or rivers and wet, wooded places. The living parts of the plant may be as high as a foot tall, supporting one another as they grow crowded together. The branching is variable; the color is usually reddish-brown.

The Spread-Leaved Peat Moss (*Sphagnum squarrosum*) is widely distributed in North America. The plant is bluish-green, and grows crowded together in colonies. The leaves are tongue-shaped, soft and spreading, or turned backward from the stem. The large, spherical spore cases are a shining dark brown, and are very numerous near the apex of the stem. The specific name *squarrosum*—a Latin word meaning "scurfy" or "scabby"—refers to the scale-like stem leaves.

The Boat-Leaved Peat Moss (*Sphagnum cymbifolium*) is common in bogs, where it grows densely crowded above the water. It does not float as other Sphagnum Mosses do. The stem leaves are large and spatula-like, turned back from the stem. The leaf at the apex is notched and rounded. The translucent branch leaves are a boat-like oval in shape, whence both the common and the specific name—from the Latin *cymba,* "small boat," and *folium,* "leaf"—and grow densely overlapped. The dark brown, spherical spore case has a plate-like lid. There are many Sphagnum Mosses, but the common characteristics described here should make recognition easy.

The Catherinea Mosses (of the genus *Atrichum*) are closely related to the Hairy Caps, with the notable distinction that the veil is generally hairless—whence the generic name *Atrichum,* "without hair," as opposed to *Polytrichum,*"many hairs." They are conspicuous in their habit of forming extensive patches on the soil of partly shaded locations. The leafy part of the plant grows erect and is large enough to form soft, luxuriant beds of green. The effect is particularly lovely when the slender, pale immature spore cases are to be seen interspersed among the brownish, richly colored mature capsules. The bright green, strap-shaped or oblong leaves are wavy when fresh, and twist or curl in various directions when dry. The spore cases are oval, cylindrical and nodding. The old name of the genus, *Catherinea,* dates to a time when many botanists worked under the patronage of royal families: It was assigned by Dr. Friedrich Ehrhart in honor of Catherine II, Empress of Russia.

The Wavy Catherinea (*Atrichum undulata*) is one of the most common of mosses, occurring in almost every part of northern North America. Its usual habitat is along the moist, shady banks of brooks. The plant is soft and undulating when moist, but strong and wiry when dry. The setae are reddish; several may grow on a single plant. The long, slender, slightly curved spore cases are the best means of identification. There are several other species in this genus, but this one is typical.

The Tree Mosses (of the genus *Climacium*) grow in wet or swampy woods, in moist, grassy places, and about the bases of tree stumps along mountain streams. Large, handsome plants suggesting miniature evergreen trees, they are sometimes confused with ground pine, which is classified botanically with the ferns. The robust, erect, tree-like shoots grow from stolons—root-like processes that run partly or entirely underground—producing new shoots each year. Thus the primary stem is creeping, and only the branches are lance-shaped. The spore cases, borne in clusters on long, erect setae, are symmetrical cylinders with beaked lids. The generic name (from the Greek word *climax,* "staircase") refers to the ladder-like arrangement of processes in the inner row of the peristome.

The Common Tree Moss (*Climacium dendroides*) is a bright green species found growing on wet soil, in swamps, on rotten logs and in similar situations. The stem leaves are broad and

194 Forests of Lilliput

clasping; the branch leaves are narrower and are often folded lengthwise. All are loosely imbricated and spreading when moist. The seta, which grows to a height of an inch or more and is a striking deep red color, twists to the right when dry. It bears an erect, cylindrical, red-brown spore case. Although this is a very common moss, fruiting specimens are difficult to find.

The Collar Mosses (of the genus *Splachnum*) are by no means common, but when found, they are unmistakable. They invariably occur on decaying animal matter, such as dung or logs soaked with urine of Husky dogs in the far North. The plant is a perennial, with soft, slender branches and lance-shaped leaves. The distinctive feature is a bell-shaped collar or swelling of the seta below the small spore case, capable of producing a foul-smelling solution that is attractive to flies, which serve to carry the spores to the refuse heaps that are the plant's favored habitat. The Greek name is one assigned by the botanist Dioscorides to lichens and nonflowering plants generally.

The Red Collar Moss (*Splachnum rubrum*) is the commonest member of the group, and the one most likely to be seen. It has large, open leaves that narrow toward the base. The small, oval spore case, which is thin, membranous and dirty-yellow in color, ends abruptly at the top, as though cut off; there is a small, cone-shaped, slightly slit veil. The very long red seta is enlarged just below the capsule to form the characteristic bell-shaped collar, whose color in this species is purplish. The specific name *rubrum*—Latin for "red"—refers to the conspicuous hue of the seta.

The Pygmy Mosses (of the genus *Pleuridium*) form dense, silky cushions of green among the grass of dry, sandy fields in early spring. In May—the best time to look for them—these cushions glisten with countless tiny, emerald green spheres, which are actually the spore cases nestling among the leaves. The beauty of these mosses, wet with spring snow or rain, must be seen to be appreciated.

The Common Pygmy Moss (*Pleuridium subulatum*) is the most likely of the group to be found, though its small size means that one must look closely for it. Individual plants may be no more than $1/10$ to $2/10$ inch high. They grow in loose, bright green, silky tufts on earth and clay in woods, along banks and in moist, grassy places. The specific name—from the Latin word *subular,* "awl"—refers to the shape of the upper leaves.

Two other Pygmy Mosses may be found growing with *Pleuridium. Astomum Sullivantii* forms loose clusters on bare ground, clay or clods interspersed with grass, and is especially at home under old willows and along brooks and garden paths. The leaves are lance-shaped and crowded together to form small heads or clusters, and are spirally twisted when dry, a very distinguishing characteristic. The spore cases borne on short, erect setae, are spherical or egg-shaped, with a short point or blunt beak often concealed by the leaves when dry. A second Pygmy Moss, *Bruchia Sullivantii*—named for a nineteenth-century biologist—may be recognized by its extremely small size and by the peculiar shape of its spore case.

The Long-Necked Mosses (of the genus *Trematodon*) are unmistakable in appearance. Found in moist clay or sandy soil, where the grass is thin, a plant of this genus is short and sparingly branched and grows in tufts of pale green or dusky brown. The long neck of the spore case, and the bright yellow seta, make identification easy. The generic name (from the Greek words *trematos,* "perforation," and *odon,* "tooth") refers to the lengthwise cleft or perforation that characterizes the teeth around the rim of the spore case. One species, *Trematodon longicollis* ("long neck"), has a neck twice the length of the rest of the capsule.

The Purple Horn-Toothed Moss (*Ceratodon purpureus*), one of the commonest mosses, is at home wherever the soil is barren and compact, and may be seen growing on lawns and in the cracks of sidewalks. The lance-like young sporophytes appear early in the spring, as soon as the snow melts. The plants are short and grow close together to form dense, thin mats of dark green, tinged with red—or purplish when in fruit. The red spore cases are long, egg-shaped and slightly arched, with short necks. They are borne on wine-red or yellow setae. The generic name (from the Greek words *ceratos,* "horn," and *odon,* "tooth") refers to the cleft teeth and to the grooving of the spore case.

The Spoon-Leaved Moss (*Cirriphyllum boscii*), one of a group known as the Beaked Mosses, is found growing among the grass of open fields and in the shade of woods, where it sometimes forms sods twenty feet across. The leaves closely overlap like shingles, and the leaf-bearing section of the stem itself is glossy, green and rope-like.

The Toothless Twisted Mosses (of the genus *Gymnostomum*) are found growing on the ground in matted tufts, and appear to prefer areas where lime is present, in the form of stone walls or wet cliffs. The leaves low on the stem are small, becoming larger and more tufted toward the apex. The spore case, borne erect on a long seta, has a long beaked lid. There are no teeth—whence the generic name, from the Greek *gymnos,* "naked," and *stomum,* "mouth." The members of the group differ in size, but the description fits them all.

The Glossy Entodon Mosses (of the genus *Entodon*) have been described among those found growing on trees or rocks, but may occasionally also grow on soil. Their beautiful, glossy yellow-green makes them easily recognizable. A majority of the family have the appearance of being pressed flat. The most common species, however, is an exception. (See *Entodon seductrix*).

The Cedar Mosses (of the genus *Hypnum*) are partial to decaying wood but may occasionally be found growing on the soil. Among the most common and easily recognized are the Plume Mosses.

The Little Beard Mosses (of the genus *Barbula*), mainly associated with rock and stone walls, may also be found occasionally growing on soil.

The Apple Mosses (of the genus *Bartramia*) likewise prefer rock and harder surfaces, but may occasionally form extensive tufts on soil.

Although they flourish chiefly on decaying wood or peaty humus, the Broom and Little Broom or Fork Mosses (of the genera *Dicranum* and *Dicranella*) may occasionally form extensive patches on the soil in wooded areas.

Reading List
BOOKS

Ahmadjian, Vernon, *The Lichen Symbiosis,* Blaisdell Publishing Co., Waltham, Mass., 1967.

Bodenberg, E. T., *Mosses, A New Approach to the Identification of Common Species.* The Burgess Publishing Co., Minneapolis, Minn., 1954.

Conrad, H. S., *How to Know the Mosses.* Wm. C. Brown Co., Dubuque, Iowa, 1944.

Dunham, E. M., *How to Know the Mosses.* The Mosher Press, 81 Washington St., Boston, Mass., 1951.

Fink, B., *The Lichen Flora of the United States.* University of Michigan Press, Ann Arbor, Mich., 1961.

Grout, A. J., *Mosses with a Hand Lens and Microscope,* published by the author, now deceased. Obtainable at the Book Shop, Chicago Natural History Museum, Roosevelt Road and Lake Shore Drive, Chicago, Ill., 1903–1910, (in five parts).

Grout, A. J., and others. *Moss Flora of North America.* Published by the author, now deceased. Obtainable at the Book Shop, Chicago Natural History Museum, Roosevelt Road and Lake Shore Drive, Chicago, Ill. 1928–1934.

Hale, M. E., *Lichen Handbook.* Smithsonian Inst., Washington D. C., 1961.

Marshall, N. L. *Mosses and Lichens, A Popular Guide to the Identification and Study of Our Commoner Mosses and Lichens, Their Uses and Methods of Preservation.* Doubleday, Page & Co., New York, 1907.

Nearing, G. G., *The Lichen Book, Handbook of the Lichens of the Northeastern United States.* G. G. Nearing, Ridgewood, N. J., 1947.

Schneider, A., *A Guide to the Study of Lichens.* Knight & Millet, 2nd ed., Boston, 1904.

Schneider, A., *A Textbook of General Lichenology.* Willard N. Clute & Co., Binghampton, N. Y., 1897.

Smith, A. L., *Lichens.* Cambridge University Press, p. 405, 1921.

Smith, Annie L., *British Lichens.* Wm. Clowes and Sons, Ltd., Duke St., London, 1963.

Welch, Winona H., *Mosses of Indiana,* Indiana Department of Conservation, Indianapolis, Ind., 1957.

PUBLISHED PAPERS

Algard, Göran, "Lapland's Reindeer Round-up." *National Geographic Magazine,* 96:109–116, July, 1949.

Arnold, C. A., *An Introduction to Paleobotany.* McGraw-Hill Publishing Co., pp. 43–45, 1947.

Barry, Vincent, "Anti-Tubercular Compounds." *Nature,* 158:863–865, 1946.

Barry, Vincent and McNally, P. H., "Inhibitory Action of Dialkyl Succinic Acid Derivatives on the Growth in Vitro of Acid Fast Bacteria." *Nature,* 156:48–49, 1945.

Berggin, S., "Musci et Hepaticae Spetsbergenses." Kongl Svenska Vetens-Akod. *Haudl,* 13:1–103, July, 1875.

Beschel, R. E., "Lichenometrical Studies in West Greenland." *Arctic II*, 254–268, 1958.

Beschel, R. E., "Dating Rock Surfaces by Lichen Growth and Its Application to Glaciology and Physiography. Repr. in Proceedings lst International Symposium Geology of the Arctic, 11:1044–1062, Jan., 1961.

Beschel, R. E., "A Project to Use Lichens as Indicators of Climate and Time." *Arctic*, 10:60, 1957.

Bourne, G. and Allen, R., "Vitamin C in Lower Organisms." *Nature*, 136:185–186, 1935.

Britton, E. G., "Climacium Dendroideum for Millinery." *Biologist*, 5:98–102, 1902.

Church, A. H., "The Lichen As a Transmigrant." *Journal of Botany*, 59:7–13, 40–46, 1921.

Church, A. H., "The Lichen Symbiosis." *Journal of Botany*, 59:7–13, 1920.

Conrad, H. S., "Mosses and Soil Erosion." *Iowa State College Journal of Science*, 9:347–351, 1935.

Dachnowski-Stokes, A. P., "Moss Peat, Its Distribution and Uses in the U.S." U. S. Dept. of Agriculture Circular 167, 1931.

Dachnowski-Stokes, A. P., "Sphagnum Moss for Use in Surgical Dressings." *Scientific Monthly*, 55:291–292, 1942.

Darbishire, O. V., "Some Aspects of Lichenology." *British Mycological Society Transactions*, 10:10–28, 1924.

Darbishire, O. V., "The Structure of Peltigera with Especial Reference to P. Praetextata." *Annals of Botany Journal*, 40:727–758, 1926.

Daubeumire, R. F., "Tufa Deposits at Clifty Falls State Park." Proceedings Indiana Academy of Science, 38:123–125, 1929.

Davis, C. A., "The Preparation and Use of Peat as Fuel." *Mineral Resources of Alaska*, U. S. Geological Survey, Bulletin 442, pp. 101–132, 1910.

Densmore, F., "Uses of Plants by the Chippewa Indians." Bureau of American Ethnology, 44th Annual Report, pp. 275–397, 1928.

Emig, W. H., "Mosses as Rock Builders." *Bryologist*, 21:25–27, 1919.

Flowers, S., "On Fossil Mosses." *Bryologist*, 36:26–27, 1933.

Fry, E. J., "A Suggested Explanation of the Mechanical Action of Lithophytic Lichens on Rocks (shale)." *Annals of Botany*, 38:175–196, 1924.

Fry, E. J., "The Mechanical Action of Corticolous Lichens." *Annals of Botany*, 40:397–417, 1926.

Glob, P. V., "Lifelike Man Preserved 2000 Years in Peat." *National Geographic Magazine*, 105:419–430, 1954.

Haines, M. P., "Mosses and Their Uses." Transactions Indiana Horticultural Society, 16:68–72, 1877.

Hantzsch, B., "Contributions to the Knowledge of Extreme Northeastern Labrador." *Canadian Field Naturalist*, 45:169–174, 1931.

Harwood, A. R., "Lichen Dyeing Today: Revival of an Ancient Industry." *Scientific Progress*, 23:279–283, 1928.

Hodson, J. W., "Sphagnum As A Surgical Dressing." *Science*, 48:203–208, 1918.

Hrdlicka, A., "Anthropological Survey in Alaska." Bureau of American Ethnology, 46th Annual Report, 19–374, 1930.

Jackson, A. B., "Climacium Americanum in Decoration." *Biologist*, 10:54, 1907.

Kursanov, A. L., and D'Yachkov, N. N., "Lichens and Their Practical Utilization." Acad. Sci. U.S.S.R., Archives Botany Gardening & Institute Biochemistry, 1945.

Lamb, I. M., "Lichens." *Scientific American*, 210:144–156, 1959.

Leach, W., "On the Importance of Some Mosses as Pioneers on Unstable Soil." *Journal of Ecology*, 19:98–102, 1931.

Lindsay, W. L., "Commercial Lichens." *Edinburgh New Philosophical Journal*, p. 40, 1854.

Lindsay, W. L., "Dye Lichens as Exports and Imports." *Edinburgh New Philosophical Journal*, p. 26, 1855.

Llano, G. A., "Lichens, Their Biological and Economic Significance." *The Botanical Review*, Vol. 10, 1944.

Llano, G. A., "Economic Uses of Lichens." Annual Report of Smithsonian Institution, 1950.

Llano, G. A., "Utilization of Lichens in the Arctic and Subarctic." *Economic Botany*, 10/4:367–392, 1956.

Macfayden, W. A., "On the Deposition of Calcareous Tufa in a Mountain Stream at Bin Canton Valais, Switzerland." *Geology*, 65, 1–5, 1928.

Munro, R., "Notice of the Excavation of a Crannog at Lochlee, Tarbolton, Ayrshire." Proceedings Society Antiquity of Scotland, 1:175–252, 1879.

Nichols, G. E., "Sphagnum Moss: War Substitute for Cotton in Absorbent Surgical Dressings." Smithsonian Inst. Annals Report, pp. 221–234, 1920.

Porter, J. B., "Sphagnum Surgical Dressings." *International Journal of Surgery*, 1:129–135, 1917.

Read, B. E. "Famine Foods," Henry Lester Inst. of Medical Research, 1946.

Rymill, J., "Southern Lights, Official Account of British Graham Land Expedition, 1934–37," Chatto & Windus, London, 1938.

Shiu-Ying, H., "Medicinal Plants of Cheng Tu Herb Shops." *Journal West China Border Research Society*, B15:95–176, 1944.

Sinton, W., "Further Evidence of Vegetation on Mars." *Science*, 130:1234–1237, 1959.

Slipher, E. C., "New Light on the Changing Face of Mars." *National Geographic Magazine*, 108/3:427–436, 1955.

Smith, A. L., Presidential Address. "The Relation of Fungi to other Organisms." *Transactions British Mycological Society*, 6:17–31, 1918.

Smith, A. L., "Recent Lichen Literature." *Transactions British Mycological Society*, 15:193–235, 1931.

Taylor, A., "Mosses as Formers of Tufa and of Floating Islands." *Bryologist*, 22:38–39, 1919.

Vartia, K. O., "On the Antibiotic Effects of Lichens and Lichen Substances." *Annals Medical Experimental Biology*, 28:1–82, 1950.

Glossary

Acrocarpous: With the spore case or fruit at the tip of the stem or branch.

Antheridia: The male reproductive organs containing the germ cells or sperm.

Apothecia: A spore-bearing structure of lichens, open or disc-shaped fruit.

Archegonia: The female reproductive organs, more or less flask-shaped, enclosing the egg cell.

Areolae: A small round space on the surface of the lichen thallus.

Ascogonium: Female reproductive organ in lichens, microscopic in size, made up of a coil in the medulla and a trichogyne that protrudes through the cortex.

Ascus: A cavity in which the spores are developed.

Bract: The leaves surrounding the reproductive organs; those surrounding the antheridium (male) are called perigonial bracts; those surrounding the archegonia and the base of the seta are called perichaetial bracts.

Calyptra: The thin veil or cap covering the capsule (spore case) of mosses.

Capsule: The spore case or fruit of the moss, the enlarged terminal end of the sporophyte containing the spores.

Cephalodia: Abnormal, irregular outgrowths on or within the lichen thallus.

Corticolous: Living on the bark of trees.

Crustose: Crust-like, closely adherent to the substrate, one of the three classes of lichens.

Cyphellae: Tiny, cup-like depressions on the bottom side of the lichen thallus.

Dioicous: Having the male and female organs on separate plants, (archegonia and antheridia borne on separate plants.)

Foliose: Lichens leafy in form and stratified in structure, one of the three classes of lichens.

Foot: The basal portion of the sporophyte, penetrating the gametophyte.

Fruit: Often applied to the spore case of mosses.

Fruticose: Upright or pendulous lichen thallus with radiating structure.

Gametophyte: In plants that have alternation of generations, the phase or generation that bears the gametes or sexual cells. It begins with a filamentous protonema, resembling green algae, eventually giving rise to leafy stems which finally bear the sex organs (archegonia and antheridia). When fertilization of the egg in the archegonia occurs, the sporophyte is produced.

Gemmae: Small, more or less bud-like bodies, able to reproduce the moss plant.

Gonidia: Green algal cells, a normal constituent of the lichen thallus.

Heteromerous: The fungal and algal lichen components arranged in definite strata in the thallus.

Homoiomerous: The fungal and algal cells randomly mixed in the thallus.

Hygroscopic: Capable of absorbing water with consequent change in form or direction (referring to mosses or lichens).

Hyphae: Fungal filaments.

Hypothallus: Growth of hyphae persisting at the margin of the lichen thallus.

Hypothecium: In lichens, the layer below the asci and paraphyses (spore bearing structures).

Isidia: An outgrowth on the lichen thallus, capable of propagating the lichen when broken off, resembling coral.

Medulla: The loose hyphal layer in the interior of the thallus.

Microconidia or spermatia: Asexual spores produced in pycnidia (spermagonia) in lichen thalli.

Monoicous: Having the male and female organs separate but on the same plant (antheridia and archegonia on the same plant).

Mycelium: A tangle of fungal hyphae.

Nitrophilic: Preference for growth on nitrogenous substrate.

Omnicolous: Growing successfully almost anywhere.

Operculum: Lid of the spore case (capsule) of the moss, covering the peristome and coming off at spore maturity.

Paraphyses: Slender, rarely branched, sterile fungal filaments among and along side the spore sacs.

Perichaetial leaves: The whorl of bracts around the female organ, i.e., around the base of the seta or the sessile spore case.

Peristome: The fringe of teeth surrounding the mouth of the spore case, visible on removing the lid. It may be a single row or double row. It aids in closing the mouth of the spore case.

Perithecia: Round lichen fruit containing ascospores.

Pleurocarpous: Having the spore case lateral on a short special branch. Pleurocarpous mosses are easily recognized by their creeping growth habit while acrocarpous mosses are commonly erect.

Podetium: Stalk-like secondary thallus of Cladonia.

Protonema: Green filamentous phase of the gametophyte, derived directly from the spore's germination; sometimes the protonema persists, more often disappearing. This green branched alga-like thread is the beginning of the gametophyte generation.

Pseudocyphellae: Very small pores in cortex of lichens, both upper and lower, usually white in color and may extrude soredia.

Pycnidia: Flask-shaped structure in medulla of lichen, opening through a pore in the cortical surface, containing microconidia (spermatia).

Receptacle: Base of the apothecium; tissue surrounding it.

Rhizoids: Root-like structures of lower plants, particularly mosses or lichens, lacking the circulatory function of true roots, serving only as holdfasts. Also rhizines.

Saprophyte: A plant living on dead or decaying matter.

Saxicolous: Growing preferentially on rock.

Seta: The stalk or stem of the spore case (capsule) in a moss sporophyte.

Silicophile: Growing on silica by preference.

Sod-flakes: Thin, laminar flakes of lichen thallus, e.g., growing about the base of cladonia.

Soralia: Few algal cells in a weft or tangle of fungal filament, erupting through the lichen cortex in dusty clumps, a method of reproduction.

Soredia: A small spherical body of algae in a hyphal network, capable of developing into a new lichen. Synonymous with soralia.

Spermatia: See microconidia.

Spore case: A closed, sac-like structure in mosses in which the spores are formed; borne in the seta: synonymous with capsule.

Sporophyte: The spore-bearing generation of the moss, arising from the fertilization of the egg in the archegonium.

Stomata: Breathing pores or openings in the outside layer of a plant.

Terricolous: Growing on the ground.

Thallus: The vegetative and assimilative part of the lichen, bearing apothecia and soredia.

Trichogyne: A female reproductive structure in lichens, microscopic in size, extending from the ascogonium through the cortex.

Veil: The hairy covering of the spore case and cap in mosses.

Zygote: The fertilized egg cell.

Index

Ahmadjian, Vernon, 36
Alectoria, 102
Algae, 11-17
  chlorophyll in, 11, 14-15
  environmental range of, 11
  form of, 11
  in lichens, 12-17, 21, 25
    advantages of, 13
    crustose types of, 21
    in foliose and fructicose types of, 21, 25
    fungal parasitism of, 15-16
    gonidial zone, 21
    nutrition of, 13, 15
  as pioneer species, 11
  reproduction in, 11, 47
  water absorption by, 27
Alsia, 81, 105
Amblystegium serpens (Creeping Cedar Moss), 174
Anacamptodon splachnoides (Knothole Moss), 183
Anaptychia speciosa (Plume Lichen), 19, 158-159
Andrea, J. G. R., 184
Andreaea (Rock Mosses), 41, 68, 184
Andreaeobrya, 42
Anomodon (Tree Apron Mosses), 179-180
Anomodon attenuatus (Common Tree Apron Moss), 179
Anomodon rostratus (Velvet Tree Apron Moss), 179-180
Anthoceros, 86-87
Anthoceros leavis, 87
Anthocerotae, *see* Horned Liverworts
Antitricha californica, 81
Anthocyanin, 68
Apple Mosses (Bartramia), 184-185, 196
Aquatic Apple Moss *(Philonotis fontana)*, 177, 185
Archidium alternifolium, 5
Ascomycetes (sac fungi), 16, 29
Astomum Sullivantii, 194-195
Atrichum (Catherinea Mosses), 192-193
Atrichum undulata (Wavy Catherinea), 193
Aulacomium turgidum, 99
Awned Hairy Cap Moss *(Polytrichum piliferum)*, 188

Bachman, E., 59
Bacillus subtilis, 117
Bacteria, 8-9, 11
Bacteriochlorophyll, 8
Baeomyces roseus (Rosy Crust Lichen), 17-18, 62, 134
Bancroft, George, 125
Barbula (Little Beard Mosses), 69, 186-187, 196
Barbula unguiculata (Claw-Leaved Barbula), 186-187

Barry, C. V., 118
Bartram, John, 185
Bartramia (Apple Mosses), 184-185, 196
Bartramia oederi (Short-Leaved Apple Moss), 185
Bartramia pomifermis (Long-Leaved or Common Apple Moss), 185
Basidiomycetes (bracket fungi), 29
Bazzania trilobata, 86
Beaked Mosses *(Cirriphyllum)*, 195
Beard Lichen *(Usnea florida)*, 21, 106, 162-163
Beard Mosses *(Grimmia)*, 45, 60, 68, 176-177, 183
Beschel, Roland, 73-74
Biatora, 14
Blister Lichens *(Physcia)*, 4, 158-159
Blistered Rock Tripe *(Umbilicaria papulosa)*, 155
Blood Lichens, 150
Boat-Leaved Peat Moss *(Sphagnum cymbifolium)*, 192
Bonkei (dish gardening), 131, 133-137
Bonnier, Gaston, 35-36
Bonsai, 130
Boulder Lichen *(Parmelia conspersa)*, 5, 151-152
Boulder Lichen *(Parmelia saxatilis)*, 92, 109
Brachythecium rivulare (Rivulet Cedar Moss), 178-179, 186
Bracket Fungi (Basidiomycetes), 29
British Soldier Lichen *(Cladonia cristatella)*, 21, 36, 63, 90, 132, 140, 143, 160
Broom Moss *(Dicranum scoparium)*, 121, 168, 196
Brotero, De Avellar (quoted), 124
Brown-Fruited Cup Cladonia *(Cladonia fimbriata, v. amplex)*, 159-160
Bruchia Sullivantii, 195
Bryophytes, 10, 40-41, 67
Bryum (Bryum Mosses), 90-91, 107, 169-171
Bryum argenteum (Silver or Common Weed Moss), 62, 136-137, 170
Bryum caespiticium (Matted Bryum), 171
Bryum Mosses *(Bryum)*, 90-91, 107, 169-171
Bryum pendulum, 91
Bryum roseum (Giant Bryum), 132, 170
Buddle, Adam, 110
Bugs on a Stick *(Buxbaumia aphylla)*, 52, 169
Bustinza, Florencio, 117
Buxbaum, J. C., 169
Buxbaumia (Humpbacked Elves), 169
Buxbaumia aphylla (Bugs on a Stick), 52, 169

Calcareous soil
  lichens and, 59, 62
  mosses and, 62, 76-77
Calliergon cardifolium (Schreber's Cedar Moss), 173-174
Catherinea Mosses *(Atrichum)*, 192-193

Cedar Moss *(Hydroamblystegium irriguum)*, 77, 178
Cedar Mosses *(Hypnum)*, 88, 105-106, 137, 172-173, 196
Ceratodon purpureus (Purple Horn-Toothed Moss), 195
Cetraria (Spanish Shield Lichens), 32, 153-154
    glucose from, 102
    identification of, 153-154
    in outdoor gardens, 138
    wind resistance of, 70
Cetraria islandica (Iceland Moss)
    appearance of, 153-154
    color of, 66, 154
    as food, 93-95, 97
    identification of, 153-154
    recipes for, 94-95
    spermagonia in, 32
    sunlight and, 66
    uses for, 101-102, 112, 121
Cetraria juniperina, 19
Cetraria richardsonii, 105
Cetraria tuckermanii (Pitted Cetraria or Lettuce Lichen), 153
Chlorophyll, 8, 11, 14-15
Chlorophytes, 34
Church, A. H., 16-17
Cirriphyllum (Beaked Mosses), 195
Cirriphyllum boscii (Spoon-Leaved Moss), 195
Cladonia, 5, 14, 28-33, 70, 159-162
    cosmetic use of, 119
    as decoration, 121
    glucose from, 102
    growth pattern of, 73
    identification of, 159-162
    perithecia in, 29
    reproduction in, 29, 33
    siliceous soil and, 62
    soredia in, 33
    spermagonia in, 32
    structure of, 21
Cladonia chlorophaea (Mealy Goblet Lichen), 161
Cladonia cornucopioides (Cornucopia Cladonia or Red-Fruited Cup Cladonia), 160
Cladonia cristatella (British Soldiers or Scarlet-Crested Cladonia), 21, 90
    identification of, 160
    in outdoor gardens, 140
    synthesis of, 36
    in terraria, 132
Cladonia degenerans (Frayed Lichen), 161
Cladonia fimbriata, v. amplex (Brown-Fruited Cup Cladonia), 159-160
Cladonia gracilis (Spoon Lichen), 161, 162
Cladonia physiata (Goblet Lichen), 109
Cladonia rangiferina (Reindeer Lichen), 21, 38, 105
    in alcohol manufacture, 101-102
    appearance of, 160
    bread from, 93
    as food, 91, 93, 100
    harvesting of, 100-101
    identification of, 160
    medicinal uses of, 118
    in perfume, 120
    as reindeer forage, 98-100
    as tonic, 117
    usnic acid from, 118
    water and, 27-28, 75
Cladonia verticillata (Ladder Lichen), 21, 161
Cladophora, 4
Claw-Leaved Barbula *(Barbula unguiculata)*, 186-187

Climacium (Tree Mosses), 122, 138, 193
Climacium dendroides (Common Tree Moss), 122, 193
Club-mosses (Pteridophytes), 39
Coin Lichen *(Crocynia zonata)*, 58-59, 149
Collar Mosses *(Splachnum)*, 62, 193-194
Collema, 27
Common Apple Moss *(Bartramia pomiformis)*, 185
Common Beaked Moss *(Eurhynchium strigosum)*, 175
Common Beard Moss *(Grimmia apocarpa)*, 176-177, 183
Common Cedar Moss *(Hypnum haldanianum)*, 173
Common Fern Moss *(Thuidium delicatulum)*, 172
Common Hairy Cap Moss *(Polytrichum commune)*, 108, 113, 189
Common Pygmy Moss *(Pleuridium subulatum)*, 194
Common Pylaisia *(Pylaisia intricata)*, 180-181
Common Thelia *(Thelia hirtella)*, 182-183
Common Tree Apron Moss *(Anomodon attenuatus)*, 179
Common Tree Moss *(Climacium dendroides)*, 122, 193
Common Twig Lichen *(Ramalina calicaris)*, 112
Common Twisted Moss *(Tortula princeps)*, 187
Common Weed Moss *(Bryum argenteum)*, 62, 136-137, 170
Common Yolk Lichen, 149-150
Conocephalum conicum, 84
Cook, O. F., 117
Cord Mosses *(Funaria)*, 62, 190
Cornucopia Cladonia *(Cladonia cornucopioides)*, 160
Creeping Cedar Moss *(Amblystegium serpens)*, 174
Crocynia zonata (Coin or Zone Lichen), 58-59, 149
Crombie, J. M. (quoted), 115
Crustose Lichens, 17-18, 148-150
    appearance of, 148-149
    areolae of, 18
    bark-growing, 63-64
    collection of, 143
    competition and, 71-72
    dyes from, 123
    form of, 17
    hypothallus of, 18
    identification of, 148-150
    as primary pioneer species, 56
    water absorption by, 27
    wind damage to, 69-70
Culpepper, Nicolas (quoted), 107-108
Cup Moss *(Cladonia chlorophaea)*, 161
Curd Lichen *(Lecanora subfusca)*, 92
Curled Leaf Moss *(Ulota phyllantha)*, 182
Cushion Moss *(Leucobryum glaucum)*, 187-188
Cyanophytes, 35
"Cyprus Powder," 119
Cystococcus, 34

Darbishire, O. V., 17
DeBary, Anton, 114
Dichelyma (Water Mosses), 177
Dichelyma capillaceum, 177
Dicranella (Little Fork Mosses), 168-169, 196
Dicranella heteromallo (Green Hair Moss), 168-169
Dicranum (Broom, Little Broom or Fork Mosses), 132, 138, 167-168, 196
Dicranum bonjeani, 115
Dicranum elongatum, 105
Dicranum flagellare (Wavy Broom Moss), 168
Dicranum scoparium (Broom Moss), 121, 168, 196
Dillenius, Johanan Jakob, 110, 124
Dioscorides, Pedanios, 106, 107, 170, 194

Diphyscium foliosum (Powder Gun Moss), 52, 169
Ditrichum moss, 50
Doctrine of Signatures, 87, 107-110
Dog Tooth Lichen *(Peltigera canina)*, 16, 19, 35
  appearance of, 156
  identification of, 156
  as rabies cure, 110-112
Doody, Samuel, 110
Dorstenius, 107
Drummond Moss *(Orthotrichum strangulatum)*, 182
Dundonald, Lord, 121
D'Yachkov, D., 99, 102

Earth Bread lichens, 92
Easter Lichen *(Stereocaulon paschale)*, 162
Ehrhart, Friedrich, 193
Eichenmoos, 120
Emerson, Ralph Waldo (quoted), 65
Encalypta (Extinguisher Mosses), 187
Entodon (Glossy Entodon Mosses), 181-182, 196
Entodon cladorrhizans (Flat-Stemmed Entodon), 182
Entodon seductrix (Round-Stemmed Entodon), 181, 196
Eubrya, 42
Eurhynchium strigosum (Common Beaked Moss), 175
Evernia (Oak Moss or Flabby Lichen), 14, 120-121
  in embalming, 106
  form of, 21
  identification of, 164
  in outdoor gardens, 138
  in perfume, 120, 164
  in soap, 121
  as wolf poison, 113-114
Evernia furfuracea (Oak Moss), 106, 120-121, 164
Evernia prunastri (Flabby Lichen), 113-114, 120, 164
Extinguisher Mosses *(Encalypla)*, 187

Fairy-cup lichens *(Cladonia)*, 133
Feather Moss *(Hypnum imponens)*, 173
Feather Mosses *(Neckera)*, 180
Feathered Neckera *(Nechera pennata)*, 180
Fern Mosses *(Thuidium)*, 137, 171-172, 183
Fink, F., 147
Fissidens (Plume Mosses), 177-178
Fissidens adiantiodes (Maiden Hair Moss), 178
Fissidens julianus, 178
Flabby Lichen *(Evernia prunastri)*, 113-114, 120, 164
Flat-Stemmed Entodon *(Entodon cladorrhizans)*, 182
Fleecy Rock Tripe *(Umbilicaria vellea)*, 19, 155
Foliose Lichens, 17-19, 150-159
  appearance of, 150
  colors of, 151
  cortex of, 27
  dehydration of, 27
  form of, 18-19
  growth forms of, 151
  identification of, 150-159
  rock erosion by, 59
  as secondary pioneer species, 56
  structure of, 150-151
  water retention by, 27
Fontinalis (Fountain or Water Mosses), 141, 175, 185
Fontinalis antipyretica (Giant Fountain Moss), 113, 175
Fork Mosses, 50, 167-168, 196

Fountain Mosses *(Fontinalis)*, 45, 175, 185
Franklin, John, 96
Frayed Lichen *(Cladonia degenerans)*, 161
Fringed Cup Moss *(Cladonia chlorophaea)*, 161
Fructicose Lichens, 17, 19, 21, 159-164
  form of, 19
  growth of, 21, 72-73
  identification of, 159-164
  reproduction of, 21
  scyphi of, 21
  specimen storage of, 143
  structure of, 21
  wind damage to, 70
  See also Lichens *and specific genus and species*
Frullania eboracensis, 85-86
Fry, E. J., 60
Funaria (Cord Mosses), 62, 190
Funaria hygrometrica (Water Measuring Cord Moss), 190
Fungi, 11-17, 21, 25, 29-32
  age of, 12
  in lichens, 12-17, 21, 25
    cortex, 13, 21
    growth, 13
    haustoria of, 15
    medulla (pith layer), 13, 21, 25
    organic acid synthesis of, 59
    parasitic nature of, 15
    rhizines, 12, 15, 25
    skeletal function, 16
    thallus, 14
    water storage by, 14-15, 27
  parasitic or saprophitic nature of, 12
  reproduction of, 29-32
    apothecia, 29, 30, 31, 33
    asci, 29, 31
    hypothecium, 30-31, 32
    perithecia, 29, 32
    paraphyses, 31
    spores, 29, 31-32
    thecia, 29, 32

Garnet, 59
Gerard, John, 109
Giant Bryum *(Rhodobryum ontariense)*, 132, 170
Giant Fountain Moss *(Fontinalis antipyretica)*, 113, 175
Giant Kelp, 10
Gloeocapsa, 35
Glossary, 200-202
Glossy Entodon Mosses *(Entodon)*, 181-182, 196
Goblet Lichen *(Cladonia physiata)*, 109
Gordon, Cuthbert, 126
Granite, 58-59, 149
Great Golden Hair Moss *(Polytrichum commune)*, 108, 113, 189
Green Felt Mosses *(Pogonatum)*, 53, 189-190
Green Hair Moss *(Dicranella heteromalla)*, 168-169
Grete Herball (Treveris), 109
Grimm, J. F. C., 176
Grimmia (Beard Moss), 45, 60, 68, 176-177, 183
Grimmia apocarpa (Common Beard Moss), 176-177, 183
Grout, A. J., 91, 169
Gymnostomum (Toothless Twisted Mosses), 195

Hairy Cap Moss *(Polytrichum)*, 6, 42-46, 138, 188-189
  as food, 88, 90-91, 99
  leaves of, 43-45
  phototropism of, 45-46, 68
  reproductive structures of, 48, 50

Hairy Cap Moss *(continued)*
size of, 104
spores of, 50-52
uses of, 104-105, 112, 113
water absorption by, 45
Hardy Leucodon Mosses *(Leucodon)*, 181
Harris Tweed, 126-127
Hayes, Isaac, 112
Hedwig, J. D., 184
Hedwigia (Hedwig's Mosses), 184
Hedwigia ciliata (Hedwig's Fringe Leaf Moss), 184
Hedwig's Fringe Leaf Moss *(Hedwigia ciliata)*, 184
Hedwig's Mosses *(Hedwigia)*, 184
Hepaticae, *see* Liverworts
Herball (Gerard), 109
Hill, John, 108
Hippocrates, 106
Historia Muscorum (Dillenius), 110
History of Plants (Theophrastus), 106
Holiday, F. W., 76
Homalia Jamesii (Homalia Moss), 186
Homalia Moss *(Homalia Jamesii)*, 186
Horned Liverworts, 57, 81, 86-87
Hornchurch, Friedrich, 114
Hornworts, *see* Horned Liverworts
Hortus Samitatis (Treveris), 109
Horwood, A. R., 126
Houston, Charles, 3-4
Humpbacked Elves *(Buxbaumia)*, 169
Hydroamblystegium irriguum (Cedar Moss), 77, 178
Hydrothyria venosa (North American Lichen), 76
Hylocomium alaskanum, 99
Hylocomium proliferum (Wood Reveler), 122, 186
Hylocomium splendens (Mountain Fern Moss), 121, 172
Hylocomium triquetrum (Shaggy Moss), 174
Hypnum (Cedar Mosses), 88, 105-106, 137, 172-173, 196
Hypnum cristacostrensis (Plume or Knight's Plume Moss), 173
Hypnum haldanianum (Common Cedar Moss), 173
Hypnum imponens (Feather Moss), 173, 180
Hypnum tamariscinum, 81

Iceland Moss *(Cetraria islandica)*
appearance of, 153-154
color of, 66, 154
as food, 93-95, 97
identification of, 153-154
recipes for, 94-95
spermagonia in, 32
sunlight and, 66
uses for, 101-102, 112, 121
Iceland Scurvy, 94
International Code of Botanical Nomenclature, 142, 143
"Irish Moss," 38-39

Juniper Hairy Cap Moss *(Polytrichum juniperinum)*, 189
Jussef, General, 97

Knight's Plume *(Hypnum cristacastrensis)*, 173
Knothole Moss *(Anacamptodon splachnoides)*, 183
Kursanov, A., 99, 102

Ladder Lichen *(Cladonia verticillata)*, 21, 161
Ladybird Cup Moss *(Cladonia chlorophaea)*, 161
Lamb, I. MacKenzie, 37
Lapps, 91, 97-101
Leafy Liverworts, 81, 85-86, 179, 186
reproduction in, 85
types of, 85-86

Lecanora, 61, 62
Lecanora esculenta (Manna Lichen), 18, 96-97, 118
Lecanora subfusca (Curd Lichen), 92
Lecidea, 25, 73
Leptobryum (Thread Mosses), 62, 185
Leptobryum pyriforme (Pear-Shaped Thread Moss), 185
Lettuce Lichen *(Cetraria tuckermanii)*, 153
Leucobryum, 132, 138
Leucobryum glaucum (Cushion or White Moss), 187-188
Leucodon (Hardy Leucodon Mosses), 181
Leucodon brachypus (Northern Leucodon), 181
Leucodon julaceus (Southern Leucodon), 181
Lichen Flora of the United States (Fink), 147
Lichens
age of, 4
air pollution and, 62-63
algae in, 12-17, 21, 25
advantages of, 13
crustose types of, 21
in foliose and fructicose types of, 21, 25
fungal parasitism of, 15-16
gonidial zone, 21
nutrition of, 13, 15
antibiotic properties of, 117-118
aromatic substances in, 119
chlorophyll in, 14-15
classification of, 142-143
collection of, 143-147
dissection of, 145-147
mounting, 147
tools for, 143
colors of, 14, 35
competition among, 71-72
composite nature of, 142
as decoration, 121-122
dehydration of, 26-27
dyes from, 106, 122-128
discovery of, 122
fastness of, 126, 127
lichen acids in, 123
mothproofing by, 127
world trade in, 123, 124, 125
erosion prevention by, 75, 77
evolution of, 16-17
fire and, 62
as food, 88-103
as animal feed, 97-101
glucose from, 102-103
for humans, 91-97
lichenin in, 91, 92, 97
as liquor, 101-102
nutritive value of, 91
potential of, 103
starch in, 91, 92, 94, 96
fungi in, 12-17, 21, 25
cortex, 13, 21
growth, 13
haustoria of, 15
medulla (pith layer), 13, 21, 25
organic acid synthesis of, 59
parasitic nature of, 15
rhizines, 12, 15, 25
skeletal function, 16
thallus, 14
water storage by, 14-15, 27
gardens of, 129-138
bonkei, 131, 133-137
in outdoor, 137-140
in terraria, 131-133
gas exchange in, 27-29

Lichens *(continued)*
  glues from, 121
  identification of, 147-164
    crustose, 148-150
    by environment, 60
    foliose, 150-159
    fructicose, 159-164
  immortality of, 4
  as insulation, 122
  medicinal uses of, 106-118
  metabolism of, 28-29
  minerals and, 68-69
  organic acid synthesis by, 59-60, 117-118
  oxygen production by, 3
  as pioneer species, 7, 55-62
    dominance of, 58, 61
    humus creation by, 56, 59, 76
    in plant succession, 56-58, 76
  reproduction in, 29-34
    fragmentation, 33
    fungal, 29-33
    isidia, 33-34
    soralia, 33
    soredia, 33
    spermagonia, 32-33
    spermatia, 32-33
    spores in, 29, 31-33
    trichogyne, 32-33
  respiration in, 27
  rock corrosion by, 59-60
  size of, 14
  smoke and, 62
  snow cover measurement by, 65-66
  structures of, 27, 34-35
    cephalodia, 35
    cyphellae, 27
    medulla, 34
    pseudocyphallae, 27
    thallus, 12, 14, 34
  sunlight and, 66-67
  synthesis of, 35-37
  temperature range of, 3-4
  tree damage by, 66
  types of, 59-70
    aquatic, 76
    arboreal, 63, 70
    corticolous, 63-65
    dead wood, 63
    maritime, 60
    omnicolous, 61
    saxicolous, 58-59
    terricolous, 62
  water and, 27, 75-76
  wind damage to, 69-71
    moisture and, 70-71
    soredia dissemination in, 70
    spore dissemination, 71
    thallus dissemination, 70
  See also Crustose Lichens; Foliose Lichens;
    Fructicose Lichens *and specific genus and
    species of lichens*
Lichens (Smith), 17
Light Green Tree Mosses *(Pylaisia)*, 180-181
Lindsay, Lander (quoted), 115, 123, 125
Linneaus (quoted), 56, 105, 112
Little Beard Mosses *(Barbula)*, 69, 186-187, 196
Little Broom Mosses *(Dicranum)*, 196
Little Fork Mosses *(Dicranella)*, 168-169, 196
Liverworts, 39-41, 81-87
  appearance of, 39-40
  evolution of, 40-41
  gemmae of, 54
  as greenhouse weeds, 117

Liverworts *(continued)*
  nitrophilic, 62
  rhizoids of, 39
  sexual reproduction of, 40, 46-47
  succession of, 116-117
  uses for, 87
  See also Horned Liverworts; Leafy Liverworts;
    Thallose Liverworts *and specific genus and
    species of liverworts*
Llano, George A., 89, 117
Lobaria (Speckled Lichens), 157-158
Lobaria pulmonaria (Lung Lichen), 107
  appearance of, 157-158
  in beer manufacture, 101
  dye from, 126
  as food, 93
  identification of, 157-158
  medicinal uses for, 112
    for lung diseases, 107-108
    tuberculosis bacteria inhibition, 117
Lobaria quercizans (Spreading Leather Lichen), 157
Long-Leaved Apple Moss *(Bartramia pomiformis)*,
    185
Long-Necked Mosses *(Trematodon)*, 195
Lowell, Percival, 2
Lung Lichen *(Lobaria pulmonaria)*, 107
  appearance of, 157-158
  in beer manufacture, 101
  dye from, 126
  as food, 93
  identification of, 157-158
  medicinal uses for, 112
    for lung diseases, 107-108
    tuberculosis bacteria inhibition, 117
Lungwort, *see* Lung Lichen
Lynge, B., 94

Maiden Hair Moss *(Fissidens adiantoides)*, 178
Manna Lichen *(Lecanora esculenta)*, 18, 96-97, 118
Many-Fruited Dog Tooth Lichen *(Peltigera poly-
    dactyla)*, 156
Marchantia polymorpha, see Thallose Liverworts
Materia Medica (Dioscorides), 106
Matted Bryum *(Bryum caespiticium)*, 171
Mead, Richard (quoted), 111-112
Mealy Goblet Lichen *(Cladonia chlorophaea)*, 161
Minford, R. W., 121
Mnium (Mnium Mosses), 171
Mnium cuspidatum (Pointed Mnium), 171
Mnium Mosses *(Mnium)*, 171
Morison, Robert, 110
Mosses
  collection of, 165-167
  competition among, 71-72
    as decoration, 168
  environmental change and, 67
  erosion prevention by, 77-81
  evolution of, 40-41
  as food, 88-91
  fossils of, 41
  gardens of, 129-141
    in bonkei, 131, 133-137, 141
    in outdoors, 137-140
    in terraria, 131, 133
  growth habits of, 42
  hydrotropism of, 45
  identification of, 39, 51, 165-196
    colony appearance in, 166
    in decaying organic matter, 167-175
    in fresh water, 175-179
    on soil, 187-196
    on stone, 183-187
    on tree bark, 179-183

Mosses *(continued)*
  medicinal uses of, 106-118
  minerals and, 68-69
  number of species of, 41-42
  as pioneer species, 6-17, 55-62
    burnt-over areas, 62
    humus creation by, 56, 60
    in plant succession, 57-58
    rock corrosion by, 60
  reproduction of, 46-54
    asexual, 54
    fragmentation, 54
    gametophyte generation in, 47-49
    gemmae in, 54
    protonema, 52-53
    sexual, 46-55
    spore mother cells, 50
    spores in, 46-47, 50
    sporophyte generation in, 47, 49-51
    water and, 40-41, 47-49
    zygospore development, 49-50
  size of, 39
  structure of, 39-51
    antheridia, 48
    archegonia, 48, 50-51
    bracts, 47, 48
    calyptra, 50
    foot, 47, 49
    gametophyte, 47-49
    leaves, 43-44
    operculum, 51
    perichaetal leaves, 47, 48
    peristome, 51
    rhizoids, 43, 47
    seta, 39, 42, 47, 50, 52
    spore capsule, 39, 47, 50
    sporophyte, 47, 49-51
    stomata, 49
  sunlight and, 67-68
  temperature range of, 5-6
  types, 42-48
    acrocarpous, 42, 47-48
    aquatic, 45
    bark-growing, 64
    calciophiles, 62
    dioicous, 48, 54
    mixed, 45
    monoicous, 48
    nitrophiles, 62
    pleurocarpous, 42, 48
    polygamous, 54
    polyoicous, 53, 54
    silicophiles, 62
    terrestrial, 45
  water and, 40-41, 45-49, 76
  wind damage to, 69-71
Mountain Fern Moss *(Hylocomium splendens),* 121, 172
Musci, *see* Mosses

Natural History of Selborne (White), 113
Necker, J. N., 180
Neckera (Feather Mosses), 180
Neckera menziesii, 81
Neckera pennata (Feathered Neckera), 180
Nodding Moss *(Pohlia nutans),* 171
North American Lichen *(Hydrothyria venosa),* 76
Northern Leucodon *(Leucodon brachypus),* 181
Nylander, W., (quoted), 115

Oak Moss *(Evernia),* 106, 120-121, 164
Old Man's Beard Lichens *(Usnea),* 21, 90, 106
  cosmetic use of, 119

Old Man's Beard Lichens *(continued)*
  glucose from, 102
  medicinal uses of, 113
    tonic, 106
    uterine ailments, 106
  in perfume, 119
Oribatidae, 90
Orthotrichum (Glossy Hair Tree Mosses), 6, 182
Orthotrichum strangulatum (Drummond Moss), 182

Parmelia (Shield Lichens), 14, 19, 65, 93, 119, 151-153
Parmelia caperata (Wrinkled Shield Lichen), 152-153
Parmelia conspersa (Boulder Lichen), 5, 151-152
Parmelia perlata, 19
Parmelia physodes (Puffed Shield Lichen), 152
Parmelia saxatilis (Boulder Lichen), 92, 109
Pear-Shaped Thread Moss *(Leptobryum pyriforme),* 185
Peat bogs, 77-81
Peat Mosses *(Sphagnum),* 21, 191-192
  in bonkei (dish gardens), 135
  color of, 68, 191
  as food, 91
  as fuel, 79, 81
  growth pattern of, 78-79
  leaf structure of, 191
  medicinal uses of, 115-116
  in outdoor gardens, 138
  sunlight and, 68
  water and, 75, 115-116, 141
Peltigera (Toothed Lichens), 138, 155-156
Peltigera canina (Dog Tooth Lichen), 16, 19, 110-112, 156
Peltigera polydactyla (Many-Fruited Dog Tooth Lichen), 156
Philonotis fontana (Rock-Loving Fountain or Aquatic Apple Moss), 177, 185
Phycos Thalassion (Pliny the Elder), 107
Physcia (Blister Lichen), 4, 158-159
Physcomitrium turbinatum (Urn Moss), 190-191
Pitted Cetraria *(Cetraria tuckermanii),* 153
Plagiothecium denticulatum (Slender Cedar Moss), 174, 186
Pleuridium (Pygmy Mosses), 194
Pleuridium subulatum (Common Pygmy Moss), 194
Pliny the Elder (Gaius Plinius), 107, 170
Plume Lichen *(Anaptychia speciosa),* 19, 158-159
Plume Moss *(Hypnum cristacastrensis),* 173
Plume Mosses *(Fissidens),* 177-178
Pogonatum (Green Felt Mosses), 53, 189-190
Pogonatum brevicaule (Short Pogonatum), 188-190
Pohlia nutans (Nodding Moss), 171
Pointed Mnium *(Mnium cuspidatum),* 171
Polytrichum, see Hairy Cap Moss
Polytrichum commune (Common or Great Golden Hairy Cap Moss), 108, 113, 189
Polytrichum juniperinum (Juniper Hairy Cap Moss), 189
Polytrichum piliferum (Awned Hairy Cap Moss), 188
Porella platyphylla, 86
Pott, D. F., 191
Pottia, 191
Powder Gun Moss *(Diphyscium foliosum* or *Webera sessilis),* 52, 169
Puffed Shield Lichen *(Parmelia physodes),* 152
Purple Horn-Toothed Moss *(Ceratodon purpurens),* 195
Pygmy Mosses *(Pleuridium),* 194
Pylaisia (Light Green Tree Mosses), 180-181

Pylaisia intricata (Common pylaisia), 180-181

Quaking bogs, 79, 116
Quartz, 59
Quartzite, 59

Radula complanata, 86
Ramalina (Twig Lichens), 70, 138, 163
Ramalina calicaris (Common Twig Lichen), 112
Ramalina reticulata, 70
Red Collar Moss *(Splachnum rubrum),* 194
Red-Fruited Cup Cladonia *(Cladonia cornuco-pioides),* 160
Reddish Peat Moss *(Sphagnum palustre),* 192
Reindeer, 98-101
Reindeer Lichen *(Cladonia rangiferina),* 21, 38, 105
    in alcohol manufacture, 101-102
    appearance of, 160
    bread from, 93
    as food, 91, 93, 100
    harvesting of, 100-101
    identification of, 160
    medicinal uses of, 118
    in perfume, 120
    as reindeer forage, 98-100
    as tonic, 117
    usnic acid from, 118
    water and, 27-28, 75
Reinke, J., 115
Rhacomitrium (Torn Veil Mosses), 175-176, 183
Rhacomitrium lanuginosum, 105
Rhodobryum ontariense (Giant Bryum), 132, 170
Riccia, 81, 84
Riccia fluitans, 84-85
Riccia frostii, 41, 84
Ricciocarpus natans, 53
Rivulet Cedar Moss *(Brachythecium rivulare),* 178-179, 186
Roccella, 107, 117, 122-123
Roccella tinctoria, 106, 107, 124
Rock-Loving Fountain Moss *(Philonotis fontana),* 177, 185
Rock Mosses *(Andreaea),* 41, 68, 184
Rock Tripe *(Umbilicaria vellea),* 19
Rock Tripes *(Umbilicaria),* 14, 19, 154-155
    appearance of, 154
    as food, 93, 95-96
    growth pattern of, 65
    hydrotropism of, 28
    identification of, 154-155
Rosy Crust Lichen *(Baeomyces roseus),* 17-18, 62, 134
Round-Stemmed Entodon *(Entodon seductrix),* 181, 196
Rucellai, Federigo, 122

Sac fungi (Ascomycetes), 29
Scale mosses, *see* Leafy Liverworts
Scarlet-Crested Cladonia Coral Fungus *(Cladonia cristatella),* 21, 36, 63, 90, 132, 140, 160
Schiaparelli, Giovanni V., 2
Schistostega osmundacea, 67
Schneider, Albert, 113
Schreber's Cedar Moss *(Calliergon cardifolium),* 173-174
Schwendener, Simon, 34, 114-115
Seton, Ernest Thompson (quoted), 93
Shaggy Moss *(Hylocomium triquetrum),* 174
Sherard, William, 110
Shield Lichens *(Parmelia),* 14, 19, 65, 93, 119, 151-153

Shore Lichens *(Xanthoria),* 14, 158
Short-Leaved Apple Moss *(Bartramia oederi),* 185
Short Pogonatum *(Pogonatum brevicaule),* 188-190
Shrublet Lichens, *see* Cladonia
Silica soils, 62
Silver Moss *(Bryum argenteum),* 62, 136-137, 170
Slender Cedar Moss *(Plagiothecium denticulatum),* 174, 186
Slipher, E. C., 2-3
Smith, Annie L., 16-17, 89, 90
Smooth Rock Tripe *(Umbilicaria mammulata),* 154-155
Southern Leucodon *(Leucodon julaceus),* 181
Spanish Shield Lichens *(Cetraria),* 32, 153-154
Speckled Lichens *(Lobaria),* 157-158
Spermatophyta, 10
Sphagnobrya, 42
Sphagnum (Peat Mosses), 21, 191-192
    in bonkei (dish gardens), 135
    color of, 68, 191
    as food, 91
    as fuel, 79, 81
    growth pattern of, 78-79
    leaf structure of, 191
    medicinal uses of, 115-116
    in outdoor gardens, 138
    sunlight and, 68
    water and, 75, 115-116, 141
Sphagnum cymbilfolium (Boat-Leaved Peat Moss), 192
Sphagnum palustre (Reddish Peat Moss), 192
Sphagnum squarrosum (Spread-Leaved Peat Moss), 192
Splachneceae, 62
Splachnum (Collar Mosses), 62, 193-194
Splachnum rubrum (Red Collar Moss), 194
Spoon-Leaved Moss *(Cirriphyllum boscii),* 195
Spoon Lichen *(Cladonia gracilis),* 161, 162
Spread-Leaved Peat Moss *(Sphagnum squarrosum),* 192
Spreading Leather Lichen *(Lobaria quercizans),* 157
Stenberg, S., 102
Stereocaulon, 162-163
Stereocaulon paschale (Easter Lichen), 162
Stick Cup Moss *(Cladonia chlorophaea),* 161
Sticta, 138, 157
Stigonema, 35
Straight Hair Tree Mosses *(Orthotrichum),* 182

Tacitus (quoted), 81
Taylorias, 62
Terraria, 131-133
Tetradontium brownianum, 67
Thallose Liverworts, 41, 81-85
    alteration of generations in, 84
    appearance of, 81, 82
    Doctrine of Signatures and, 108-109
    fragmentation reproduction in, 84
    gemmae reproduction in, 84
    sexual reproduction in, 82-84
    structures of, 82-84
Thelia hirtella (Common Thelia), 182-183
Thread Mosses *(Leptobryum),* 62, 185
Thuidium (Fern Mosses), 137, 171-172, 183
Thuidium abietinum (Wiry Fern Moss), 172
Thuidium delicatulum (Common Fern Moss), 172
Toothed Lichens *(Peltigera),* 138, 155-156
Toothless Twisted Mosses *(Gymnostomun),* 195
Torn Veil Mosses *(Rhacomitrium),* 175-176, 183
Tortula (Twisted Mosses), 187
Tortula princeps (Common Twisted Moss), 187

Tree Apron Mosses *(Anomodon)*, 179-180
"Tree Moss" *(Usnea barbata)*, 90, 109
Tree Mosses *(Climacium)*, 122, 138, 193
Trematodon (Long-Necked Mosses), 195
Trematodon longicollis, 195
Treveris, Peter, 109
Tuberculosis bacteria, 117-118
Tuckerman, Edward, 93
Twig Lichens *(Ramalina)*, 70, 138, 163
Twisted Mosses *(Tortula)*, 187

Ulota phyllantha (Curled Leaf Moss), 182
Umbilicaria (Rock Tripes), 14, 19, 154-155
  appearance of, 154
  as food, 93, 95-96
  growth pattern of, 65
  hydrotropism of, 28
  identification of, 154-155
Umbilicaria mammulata (Smooth Rock Tripe),
  154-155
Umbilicaria papulosa (Blistered Rock Tripe), 155
Umbilicaria vellea (Fleecy Rock Tripe), 19, 155
Urn Moss *(Physcomitrium turbinatum)*, 190-191
Usnea (Old Man's Beard Lichens), 21, 90, 106
  cosmetic use of, 119
  glucose from, 102
  medical uses of, 106, 113
  in perfume, 119
Usnea barbata ("Tree Moss"), 90, 109
Usnea florida (Old Man's Beard Lichen), 21, 106,
  162-163
Usnea trichodea, 21
Usnic acid, 118

Velvet Tree Apron Moss *(Anamodon rostratus)*,
  179-180

Von Esenbeck, Nees, 114

Water Measuring Cord Moss *(Funaria hygrometri-
ca)*, 190
Water Mosses *(Dichelyma* or *Fontinalis)*, 141, 175,
  177
Wavy Broom Moss *(Dicranum flagellare)*, 168
Wavy Catherinea *(Atrichum undulata)*, 193
Webera sessilis (Powder Gun Moss), 52, 169
Whip Fork Moss *(Dicranum flagellare)*, 168
White Moss *(Leucobryum glaucum)*, 187-188
Wiry Fern Moss *(Thuidium abietinum)*, 172
Wood Reveler *(Hylocomium proliferum)*, 122,
  186
Wrinkled Shield Lichen *(Parmelia caperata)*, 152-
  153

Xanthoria (Shore Lichens), 14, 158
Xanthoria parietina (Yellow Wall Lichen), 14, 61,
  158
  appearance of, 158
  beryllium in, 92
  hoary marmot and, 69
  identification of, 158
  in outdoor gardens, 128

Yellow Wall Lichen *(Xanthoria parietina)*, 14, 61,
  158
  appearance of, 158
  beryllium in, 92
  hoary marmot and, 69
  identification of, 158
  in outdoor gardens, 128

Zoned Lichen *(Crocynia zonata)*, 58-59, 149, *see
also* Coin Lichen